CHILD
HEALTH

America's Future

George A. Silver, M.D.

ASPEN SYSTEMS CORPORATION
GERMANTOWN, MARYLAND
1978

Library of Congress Cataloging in Publication Data

Silver, George A.
Child health: America's future.

Includes index.
1. Child health services— United States.
2. Child health services— Europe.
I. Title. [DNLM: 1. Child health services—
Standards— United States. WA320 S587c]
RJ102.854   362.7'8'0973   78-14217
ISBN: 0-89443-043-2

Library of Congress Catalog Card Number: 78-14217
ISBN: 0-89443-043-2

Printed in the United States of America

1 2 3 4 5

*This book is dedicated to
the mothers and children of America,
with tender regard, and hope*

Table of Contents

Foreword

On December 9, 1970, Vice-President (then Senator) Walter F. Mondale, delivered a long and impassioned address to the Senate on the subject "Justice for Children." Among other points he made was this appeal for recognition of the fearful damage we are inflicting upon succeeding generations and how desperately we need advocacy for the cause of the children:

"For we are failing our children. Erick Erickson has said, 'The most deadly of all possible sins is the mutilation of a child's spirit.'

"This sin is being committed every day, all over America. Our national myth is that we love children. Yet we are starving thousands. Other thousands die because decent medical care is unavailable to them. The lives of still other thousands are stifled by poor schools and some never have the chance to go to school at all. Millions live in substandard and unfair housing in neighborhoods which mangle the human spirit. Many suffer all of these mutilations simultaneously.

"In every society some people are consigned to the scrap heap—the irretrievably handicapped, the incurably ill, the incorrigibly criminal, the hopelessly ineducable.

"But, in America we have needlessly allowed the scrap heap to pile up and up.

"The most obvious victims of course are the 10 million children living in poverty and the untold millions maimed by racism.

"But the scrap heap is not outsized merely because of poverty and racism.

"Have we reduced the victims of physical handicaps to the irreducible minimum? Not when 45 percent of the children born in U.S. hospitals do not receive the prenatal care which could prevent some of the handicaps in the first place. Not when there are 3.7 million handicapped children who are not receiving the special education services they require.

"Have we reduced the victims of mental illness to the irreducible minimum? Not when there are 1.3 million children who need mental health services but are not getting them.

"Have we reduced the victims of mental retardation to the irreducible minimum? Not when there are 1 million educable mentally retarded children who will never get the help they need to reach their full potential.

"The victims are most emphatically not just the poor and the minorities.

"Consider the victims of bad health care. It is not surprising, perhaps, that the infant mortality rate in Coahama County, Mississippi, which is nearly two-thirds poor, is over twice the national average. But it may give pause to realize that the infant mortality rate in Westchester County, New York—one of the wealthiest counties in America—is just about equal to the national average, a national average which is higher than at least a dozen other countries. No, the victims of bad health care are not just the poor.

"Consider the victims of the tremendous shortage of preschool child development programs. Research shows that approximately 50 percent of a person's intellectual development takes place before he is 5 years old. Headstart and day care reach out to only one child in 10 among the poor, and the figures for children in other income groups are not much different. It is not just the poor who are missing out on crucial stimulation during the preschool years.

"Consider the victims of drug abuse. Millions of children—not just the poor—are having their lives twisted by the pandemic spread of drug abuse. It is not just the poor who are the victims of drug abuse.

"The children whom we are daily consigning to the scrap heap come from every income group, every racial group, every geographical area in our Nation. And every child consigned to the scrap heap is a useful life lost to the country, and indeed, a lifetime of costs to the taxpayers in welfare, prison or other expense.

"Fifty-five percent of Americans live in families with incomes of less than $10,000 a year. Whether the problem is schools or health care or preschool programs or what happens when a child is physically handicapped or mentally disturbed, all Americans share the same problems. And the sooner we can come to the shared realization that this is in fact the case, the sooner we shall create in America the atmosphere that our children need and deserve in which to grow up.

"What I have been saying today comes down to a few simple sentences. We have to place a higher priority on our childern and their families than we do on expensive military gadgetry or expensive space extravaganzas. And we desperately need to instill some understanding, humaneness and sensitivity into the existing institutions, which are supposed to serve our children. We need to instill an attitude of respect for a child's heritage, for his family, for his language, and for his individuality, and his potential. We need to involve children themselves and their parents in a significant decision-making role in these institutions. We need to recognize that we can and must provide far greater life chances for our children than we do now. Our children are our chance for change. They are our bridge to a better world. They are our only hope. Let us begin to act like we understand this."

Preface

In the past few years, there has been a growing sense of dissatisfaction with the lack of comprehensive, equitable child health services in the United States. True, the many recent books and critical articles are evidence more of professional than general dissatisfaction. The American people's frequently noted apathy toward child care hardly seems to be affected. Nevertheless, discontent does appear to be growing, if slowly. During the 1976 presidential election, the winning candidate, Jimmy Carter, drew national attention to the need for improved child health care, a problem which he promised to attack vigorously. The newly appointed secretary of Health, Education, and Welfare, Joseph Califano, then did the same, announcing that improvement in child health services would be a high priority in his program planning. Almost immediately, he sent up for congressional consideration a bill that would strengthen, if only marginally, existing federal program operations in child health serivces. He promised to follow up later with more far-reaching legislative proposals.

My own concern about child health services came about through academic research in health policy development, which in turn had been stimulated by my own administrative and political experiences outside the academic setting. None of these experiences had been extensively child health experiences, but in my public health career as an HEW official I had worked in well-baby and prenatal clinics and had had some responsibility for developing increased midwifery services for the poor, black, and deprived populations of the Mississippi delta and other impoverished areas of the United States.

But it was only when I undertook my studies at Yale and began to grapple with child health policy as a national issue that the full extent of the problem became apparent to me. My studies very early began to drift away from the narrower concerns of public health programs to social policy questions; for example, why consider *child* health, why not *family* health? or *community* health? As the information on attitudes, barriers, and performance began to accumulate, it became increasingly clear that it was the *child* that was central to the social policy concerns.

The future of social policy is embedded in child health.

True, the family needs help to survive the onslaughts of bureaucratic "megastructures" in the phrase of Berger and Neuhaus; needs protection from the centrifugal forces of industrial technological demands and hostile social philosophy. It needs stronger social support from government: family-centered programs of financial support for working parents and especially for parents not able to work, or unable to find work, so that children do not suffer the consequences of fragmentation because of employment practices or unemployment. The family needs family-centered housing, not "projects" or "income-related facilities." Most of all, the family needs to be seen as needed and valued.

Such family support from society will help the children. And it is important to plead that social action for the family and for the child. But the child needs help independent of that, an emphasis and focus on the *child*. In the matter of health services, for example, action for improvement of community health services will raise the level of health services to everyone, including the children, and so improved community health services are needed and should be stressed. But children need special attention besides that, an emphasis on preventive care, on family guidance that does not come naturally with our customary "health" (really medical) care. Medical services in our country tend to be repair services and children need preventive attention more than they need repair, in order that they shouldn't need repair.

A healthy family, stable and supportive, is important for child health, but it is insufficient of itself to guarantee child health.

But for two disparate reasons, an effective child health service can benefit the family and the community, even if society doesn't take all the necessary social steps to improve the stability of the family. First, illness and the fear of illness are destabilizing forces in a family. This is not only an emotional but an economic reaction. Provision of an effective child health service, focused on the child, will not only help the child to grow strong, healthy, capable and responsible, but in this way will strengthen and help stabilize the family structure. And this in turn will strengthen forces within the family that themselves will improve child health.

It is also ground for consideration that the nature of a child health service focused on the child rather than on the medical care system will offer a model for an effective adult health system as well. Community health services today concern themselves principally with economics, not health. Paying for medical care services, cost-containment, conflict over the payment of doctors, nurses, all preoccupy the planners and legislators, not health services. Design and successful operation of a child health program, with health as the centerpiece, may powerfully influence the eventual design and operation of health services for adults as well.

Helping the child is to assist the forces that aim to strengthen health services in the community.

I learned, too, that medical care systems are not good or bad in themselves, nor is their quality measurable solely by their cost. They are valuable insofar as they effectively serve their social purpose. Simple or pluralistic, rigid or flexible, private or public, complex or hierarchic—whatever the nature of the system, only the degree to which the social purpose is served is important.

For these reasons, this book is addressed to the need for a properly structured, family-involved child health service, national in scope, predominantly preventive in concept, and private as well as public and official in character—one that will guarantee quality health services for America's children.

GEORGE A. SILVER, M.D.
August 1978

Acknowledgments

In the six years this book has been gestating, I have had a great deal of support and counsel from good friends, colleagues, and coworkers. Much of the work was supported by grants from the National Center for Health Services Research, and the European explorations by a fellowship from the Fogarty Center of the National Institutes of Health. The Commonwealth Fund supplied a generous grant for editorial services, and the Ford Foundation a grant for European travel. Phil Lee read and reread many drafts and treatments of specific bits and pieces of this book. His unfailing enthusiasm, incisive comments, and generous praise were extraordinarily helpful. My colleagues in the U.S. Study—Christa Altenstetter, Jim Bjorkman, Milton Chen, and Anne-Marie Foltz—provided me with data, counsel, and thoughtful insights along with useful criticism and encouragement. Estelle Siker in the Connecticut State Health Department and Tony Robbins in Vermont were very helpful in providing entry to data and people, reviewing material and commenting, all of which made the research task possible and infinitely easier. Jim Fesler at Yale and Herb Kaufman at Brookings offered sound criticism, useful advice, and good counsel.

In Europe, Sir John Brotherston, then chief medical officer of the Scottish Home and Health Department, Ada Watt, his secretary, and John Grant, his maternal and child health executive, were all extraordinarily kind, thoughtful, and helpful. Leo Kaprio, director of the European office of WHO, provided access to data and material otherwise unavailable. Drs. Siderius and Phaff of the Netherlands

Department of Health and the Environment introduced me to the work setting there and made it possible to obtain so much of the information and observations on the child health services in Holland. Dr. le Nobel in Amsterdam was kind enough to give his time not only to discussion but to translation of an important document on organization of child health care in that city. My special thanks must go also to the Centre International de l'Enfance in Paris, whose library played a key and crucial part in finding the information and data required to flesh out the description and analysis of European child health systems used in this book. Dr. Manciaux, Dr. Sam Barenberg, and Genevieve Morel were incredibly efficient and helpful.

So many others helped in many ways, I would be remiss not at least to mention their names: Thanks to Brian Abel Smith, Margaret and Arthur Wynn, and John Warder in London; Vera Carstairs in Edinburgh; Dr. Hazemann in Paris; Mme. Peerts-Niçoise in Brussels; Marsden Wagner in Copenhagen; and to Odin Anderson in Chicago for the opportunity to prepare the preliminary form of this material in the Michael M. Davis lecture. And finally, I need to show my appreciation to the typists (and interpreters): Valerie Webb, Nell Short, Lil Merriam, and Jean Conklin.

I had much help. I hope I used it well.

Part I

Introduction, Synopsis, Summary, Recommendations, and Epilogue

For nearly six years I have been pursuing a course of study in the contradictions of a particular, significant aspect of American social program—child health services. Like many other students, I have had to observe and read more than I had originally intended; the subject turned out to be so much more complicated than I had imagined it would be. At different times I thought I had reached a satisfactory answer to what had puzzled me at the outset, and each time the answer was different. There were two such occasions when I was so sure I had resolved the baffling paradox, that I very nearly terminated the study. However, nagging questions from colleagues who pointed out still unanswered portions of the argument compelled further study and further analysis.

Let me describe for you the contradictions as I saw them, the puzzling discordance between America's thoughts, expressions, and capabilities in regard to children and children's health, on the one hand, and America's performance in providing child health and medical care services, as reflected in the statistics concerning illness, neglect, and death of America's children.*

The United States should be at the very top in health matters, certainly as they relate to children. With our wealth, technological capabilities, scientific knowledge, medical manpower resources, and industrial pharmaceutical capacity certainly the greatest of any

---

* For this approach to analysis and the outline of attack and explanation, I am grateful to Herbert Kaufman, senior fellow, the Brookings Institution.

single nation, attaining and retaining the highest possible health level for our children should be a simple matter. It is true that the aggressive, fast-paced, achievement-oriented, competitive character mold said to be typical of American adults might very well be the source of increased morbidity and even early mortality among adults. Also, poor eating habits and the various addictions to which Americans are prone (e.g., heavy smoking and alcoholism) may play a part in the comparatively disadvantaged situation of American adults revealed by the statistics of some other countries. So too, the profit-dominated, laissez-faire economy permits pollution of air, water, food, and the workplace that is far more scandalous than that found in most other countries. This also contributes to the United States' morbidity and mortality rates—high when compared with, for example, Sweden's. Although some of these factors may be affecting the children as well, this does not explain the difference between child health in this country, with its capabilities, and child health in less wealthy, even poor countries.

Children's health is much more a matter of protection and prevention than adult health is. Adults inherit a body machinery conditioned in childhood, and the breakdowns in it—the illnesses—require treatment because prevention wasn't practiced, or if it was, failed. But children, properly nourished, immunized against the bulk of the crippling or lethal epidemic diseases, need little treatment. Those with congenital or acquired handicaps, when found, can be treated and repaired so that they are able to face adult life on a reasonably fair footing with others. A broader area of prevention—psychological and social protection—is not so simply dealt with. But here, too, what is needed is an early warning system, and linked to it, a treatment device, a system for repair.

None of these are strangely new or uncomfortably foreign concepts. This is essentially the sort of child health program we believe we now have. Over the years, in the name of prevention and child care, we have tried to teach families about feeding their children properly and have established national nutrition programs for poor children. Health departments are responsible for well-baby clinics and immunization programs. Prenatal clinics have been set up to look after pregnant women and try to prevent the kinds of illness, handicaps, and defects sometimes associated with uncared-for childbirth. Child guidance clinics and mental health centers have been set up to try to aid the psychologically injured child and family. Educational departments are charged with caring for the child in schools, assessing health, and recommending treatment where needed. Recently, we added a special program to find, examine and treat the handicaps of poor children.

Looking at the problems of child health in this way is at once reassuring and discomforting. We know we have done these things, but clearly not enough of them, or not properly. The evidence is too clear that, in child health, the United States is shamefully behind nearly every other economically and industrially advanced country in the world. That is the paradox. If we "have done what we ought" and "not done that which we ought not," why is there "no health in us?"

More important, since the health of children is the eventual health of adults, and the health of children is therefore the health of the nation, why aren't we more concerned about it? Why aren't we doing more?

We have many problems as a nation, and we can't solve all of them at once, not even the ones that are entirely within our capacity to solve. So we "establish priorities," in the current managerial lingo, and "allocate resources," as the economists' jargon has it. In simple terms, it means that we do the things we consider important, "exercise choice" and pay whatever price we consider worthwhile for those important things. Conversely, we don't do, or spend the money for, those things we consider of lesser importance. If we are such poor international models of child health services, child health services can't be a high priority.

Odd.

In addition to immense wealth and technological capabilities, Americans are noted for their almost obsessive devotion to children! Throughout the world, the United States is pictured as uncritically indulgent to its children, spoiling them with lavish gifts and unwilling to check their willful demands. We, too, see ourselves as a child-centered society, endlessly examining and reexamining child-rearing practices, for example. Millions of books on child care are sold. Youth preempts the television and movie screens; clothing and literature are youth focused. To be young and American is paradise.

The theme of this book is the examination of these contradictions: capability versus performance; attitudes versus performance; programs versus performance; intention versus results. Not everyone, perhaps not even every seriously interested reader, will want to examine the progress of the study from its inception, in all the details of evidence and proof, to the recommendations. For that reason, I have elected to provide a condensed version of my findings and observations in this preliminary section (hence the outlandish title) along with a summary of the recommendations based on these findings and analysis. For those who are reasonably sympathetic, that may be quite enough. The tiresome details can be left to opponents and graduate students who will seek out the errors of fact and printing (and thinking) to come up with their triumphant counter-analyses and counter-conclusions.

The book, and Part I, will be divided into sections dealing with the following significant elements of description, analysis, and conclusions:

1. evidence that United States' child health services should be, but aren't, at peak performance
2. some reasons for this failure
3. other countries' approaches to child health services
4. lessons from experiences abroad and their adaptation
5. long-term benefits of a meaningful child health program

Chapter 1

The State of Child Health in the United States

In the later amplification of this same topic (Part II), detailed references will be given for the statements made and figures quoted here. The purpose of this section is to provide a logical sequence. It may be taken for granted that we are among the wealthiest of the world's nations, that we have held this leading position for generations and so have acquired the medical resources for the foundation of a formidable medical establishment, richly staffed, liberally supported financially, and with an abundance of research, educational, and medical service institutions. With the provisos noted below, we are not only highly literate, but well supplied with information about health and disease, modern medicine, and prevention and treatment of illness. Facts about health and human disease are taught in the schools and are increasingly being presented in realistic or dramatic form by the media. Voluntary health agencies, specifically devoted to numerous diseases, collect huge sums of money as voluntary contributions from the populace, spending it (what is left after reimbursing the fund raisers) on education, research, and publicizing the importance of each particular disease. And the federal government is not niggardly in its largesse, either, devoting in FY 1976 almost $40 billion to health and medical care, with state and local governments adding their share—$20 billion. A total of $140 billion was spent for health care in that year, including $80 billion from the private purse.

This picture must be qualified in a number of ways. In the first place, because of the entrepreneurial nature of the medical care system and the heavy emphasis in traditional American economics on protecting and securing profit, the benefits from these substantial resources may not be as great as they would be if they were assigned in more orderly, nonprofit ways.

Second, the competition within the system for the use of the funds is not always in the best interest of the public.   Health insurance companies, basically insuring against hospital costs, guarding an empire worth $30 billion, resist rationalization of the system. Although less hospitalization, for example, would be less costly to the system, the alternatives are not so easily controlled and are riskier to the companies. Emphasis on hospital insurance also skews the system costs in other ways; it increases the development and use of expensive technology, multiplies the demand for trained and high-salaried technicians, and so on.

Other, less readily visible expenses benefit the system managers rather than the public, the ostensible beneficiary. Heavy investment in medical research is certainly warranted, but the union of medical education and medical research distorts the objective, draining off large sums for research that pays no research dividends and is essentially no more than jockeying for place on the academic ladder. This in turn magnifies the cost of medical education and other manpower resource development by adding to the salary base and personnel needed to maintain the status, rather than the educational functions, of the institutions.

Public health education, while widespread, is often so distorted and emphasized in line with profit motives that the effect is possibly worse than if no information were provided at all. Further, in the schools, there has not been sufficient quality teaching to overcome the power of misinformation that is supplied to the public. As a consequence, despite wealth and an abundance of nutritious food, many people ignore the known and taught virtues of proper eating, drinking, and playing and pursue instead dangerous, unwholesome, and even lethal, lifestyles. The voluntary agencies have done little to change this, despite the outpouring of public contributions that support them, in part because the narrow emphasis on specific diseases prevents appropriate attention to the needs of living as a whole person. Also, the boards and administrators of these agencies are too concerned with the profits of their sponsors and with their own professional status and advancement.

But the greatest obstacle to maximum effectiveness of our rich and heavily endowed health and medical care system is the lack of a clearly defined objective or goal. Everyone appreciates that the function of a health and medical care system is to promote health, prevent disease, treat illness, and rehabilitate the maimed and handicapped. What is not clear is that in order to accomplish this, the various elements of the system have to be integrated and orchestrated. The American medical care system is *not* integrated. Each individual element is capable of making and demands the right to make, an independent decision on what it does, and to whom. This is in the American tradition of free enterprise, but this tradition forbids subordination of parts to the purpose of the whole. And because no one person or group orchestrates this vast and complex machinery comprising almost 5 million people and 30,000 institutions scattered over the 53 territorial jurisdictions of this nation of 215 million souls, the system fails inevitably to provide its public with quality service. Maldistribution of resources, a significant defect of the U.S. medical system, is a result both of its entrepreneurial character and its lack of orchestration or leadership.

Children, like the rest of the population, benefit—and suffer—from the wealth and disorder of the health and medical care system. The ineffectiveness of the system will affect children to the extent that certain elements of the system are appropriately devoted to them or needed by them. Children are most in need of preventive services; deficiencies there will hurt children more than adults. Children are less in need of physicians and hospital services and so will be less harmed by deficiencies in those areas.

It must be repeated: the United States has an enormously wealthy, well-staffed medical care system. Despite the hazards of living in a competitive, industrialized society, there should be a reasonably good quality of health among the people, especially the children. If not the best, it should certainly be quite near the top. In fact, by any standard, U.S. children are in worse state than the children of most other countries with similar standards of living. Infant mortality—the numbers of children who die in the first year of life per every 1,000 live births—is higher in the United States than in 15 other countries. Deaths of children under five are proportionately higher here; so are suicides among young people. Certainly we do not reach all children with our health services; epidemics of wholly preventable diseases, like diphtheria, occur, and we find at least 25 percent of school children unimmunized. Many school children with visual defects do not receive corrective glasses when recommended; not all deaf children receive needed hearing aids. It is not surprising, then, when surveys show that as many as 5 million children have no regular source of medical care and that 40 million children under 17 (more than half the population in that age range) have not been examined by a doctor within the last two years.

Poverty and minority status impose a special disadvantage. Poor children and minority children—40 percent of whom are not immunized—are at the greatest disadvantage since epidemics occur with greater frequency and larger impact among them. Poor children do not grow as tall and suffer more from anemia. There are more parasitic infestations among them. Lead poisoning is common among poor children. And among minority children, nutritional deficiency is three times as common as among children generally.

Infant mortality is twice as high among minority children as among the others and this may be, in part, because poor and minority children get fewer medical services. Also, poor and minority pregnant women are 50 percent less likely to obtain prenatal care than upper-income, white women. These women are also four times as likely to die in childbirth as their upper-income, white sisters.

Despite this emphasis on poverty and minority status as lethal factors, it should not be overlooked that the system fails the rest of the population as well, if not to the same degree. The lowest infant mortality rates in the United States, among white, upper-income women, does not yet approach the average for countries such as Sweden and Holland.

But something else, something besides poverty, race, and skin color, must be at work depriving American children of the benefits of modern health services. What is the root of our failure?

Chapter 2

The Sources of Failure in Children's Health Care

The entrepreneurial nature of our health care system, its lack of leadership and unity of purpose, and the undermining influence of the profit motive are overriding concerns that would be formidable barriers to the functioning of *any* medical care system, no matter how well-functioning the individual elements. If these are our main problems, then recommendations can be few and simple: eliminate the profit motive and appoint a czar. Neither of these recommendations would get very far, but even if they were adopted, what would be the shape of a system that could meet our objectives in child health care—equity, universality, quality, and security? Are the existing elements of the health and medical care system sufficient, reliable, and useful enough that they could be integrated into an effective system? Do they suffer from individual defects that must be corrected?

Let us examine children's needs and how they are now met within the framework of the existing health care system. In the first place, a good many of children's needs can be met neither by the medical care system nor, possibly, by any one agency.

Children are poisoned physically by environmental factors in the air, food and water. They are injured psychologically by the violence of the media, especially television and the comic books that surround them inescapably. Doctors, preventive services, good intentions can have but little impact on these powerful influences.

Lest it be thought that no consideration has been given such crucially important *global* causes of disease and death among children (and adults as well, of course) as war and environment, I will note here that these matters are of paramount importance, but of no possible usefulness for discussion here. If one takes the position that disease and death are socially conditioned by the political nature of society, that jobs, foreign policy, and the profitability of pollution are the basic determinants, then dealing with structures and content of health and medical care systems would be pointless. However, even if one accepts the primary etiological character of politics, *all* social systems will be plagued with some kind of health and medical care needs. Then, structure and content, while modifiable depending on circumstance, still maintain their importance. For this reason, even though the psychological effects of joblessness on the family, the anxiety provoked by dangerous and threatening foreign policies, and the cancer induced by uncontrolled pollution of air and water and food and the workplace all contribute to the *need* for efficient and effective health and medical care services, their total elimination would still leave a residue of disease and disability to be dealt with. So while the concerns expressed in the following chapters may seem narrow to some, they are deliberately restricted and do not result from a lack of understanding of the larger causative, sociopolitical factors.

NEGLECTED SOCIAL NEEDS OF CHILDREN

Children need to be fed, housed, clothed, protected from violence, and sheltered by law from abuse and neglect. Helpless and at the mercy of the adult world, their protection and growth requires organized and orderly attention. Except for the very poor—welfare clients essentially—the United States has shown itself very reluctant to exercise authority in these areas. We do have a federal program for aid to families with dependent children, but as with most welfare programs, effectiveness and equity are problematic. Welfare theory in the United States emphasizes the need to avoid paying nonworking people out of tax funds at rates that begin to equal what working people earn. The theory is that people will not work if they find they can be granted an identical income without working. Since many people work for incomes well below what is needed to feed, clothe, and house themselves and their children decently, welfare clients receive even less. In the effort to protect the taxpayer's dollar and eliminate altogether the possibility of shirkers, welfare budgets are adjusted rigidly and often according to outdated price schedules for food and clothing. Welfare families are therefore legally deprived of the basic support needed for their children.

The working poor, whether a couple, parents with several children, or a large family, need aid to obtain adequate housing. Yet general housing subsidies, like general support, are simply not available—they are not in keeping with the American tradition.

Even nutritional programs for children (school lunches, for example) are means tested, for fear the spirit of independence might be corrupted if *children* were eligible, rather than just specifically designated *poor children*. As in the case of food subsidies and food stamp privileges, also means tested, many families with children abstain from the stigma of announcing poverty and reject the food support for their children. All of these food programs began originally as *agricultural* support programs, to help farmers dispose of their products and to maintain farm prices. While the poor are now the beneficiaries, the limitations of the programs derive from their earlier purpose. They were not intended to assure a healthy diet for children; that was incidental. The congressional dickering over support now derives in no small part from the lack of a specific commitment to feeding children.

In short, there is no national commitment to providing adequate food and shelter, basic requirements for the healthy growth of children. Since there is no minimum wage tied to minimum living costs, as many as 40 million people may be living below the minimal standard necessary to purchase sufficient food and shelter. At least 10 million children live in such families. Another 10 million live under welfare budgets, which, as explained, are even harsher and less likely to provide needed food and shelter.

Even before family income support or children's allowances, there is the need to guarantee a safe and healthy pregnancy. Some of this is a professional responsibility, but there is also a social responsibility to protect and support the mother during pregnancy. The United States does not have a national maternity leave nor a national maternity allowance program. Women can be compelled to work, in order to retain their jobs or their seniority, up to and including the time of delivery. Time off with pay for a period before and after delivery is not guaranteed. Special grants to cover the extra costs of delivery, child care, and housekeeping are not part of the national welfare policy. Again, it is the poor who suffer the most, especially the working poor. Antiabortion forces would do well to consider a maternity income policy as a dramatic alternative in their propaganda programs: maternity leave without loss of pay or seniority for working women as well as postpartum maternity allowance and home help service for working mothers.

As far as legal protection of children is concerned, the situation is no less ominous. By and large, the police force and the courts are concerned with crimes and punishment. The responsibility of protection of children is more vaguely spelled out. So processes and institutions are geared to capture, try, sentence, and punish lawbreakers. To a very considerable degree, this derives from the strong American tradition of family responsibility. Like the American tradition of independence and self-reliance, family responsibility comes from good and important historic sources. And like those other traditions, it has failed to adapt to a monumentally changed social situation. In today's world, the family needs official (state) support to cope with the complexities and frustrations of a changed world. However, the state is considered intrusive in family relations and is barred from intervening preventively.

It is almost impossible to obtain court protection to prevent a child from being injured; the state will intervene only if an injury has already taken place. No matter how much neighbors and friends may know of the explosive violence implicit in a family situation, official intervention is difficult and sociologists, psychologists, or nurses cannot intervene unless the family *asks* for help. Even after disruption, when the child or parent is in court, the judge, following a strong precedent, will try to maintain the family structure, even at the expense of the child. The child's welfare is a secondary consideration. Social workers in welfare departments are so busy protecting the system from cheats that they rarely have the time (or often the skill) to make assessments of family needs and to try to provide the psychological or educational counseling necessary to improve either family relations or child care.

Ezekiel points out that "the fathers have eaten of the sour grapes and the children's teeth are set on edge." Vulnerable families are generationally linked. Failure to lift the level of coping of a family condemns some or all of the children to head up or become part of vulnerable families of their own. Social support to help a family improve the setting in which children are raised and to help provide food, shelter, and guidance may not do much for the parents, but it may save the children. But there is no national commitment to the social and emotional protection of children.

INSUFFICIENT PREVENTIVE SERVICES: PRESERVING THE HEALTH OF CHILDREN

While many health support measures are outside the specifically medical orbit, there are some that could be considered a medical, that is a doctor's, responsibility. And while some of these measures are customarily within the realm of the physician, they could be supplied by someone other than a physician. Except in rare instances, physicians cannot prescribe food or shelter. Illness can result from inadequate or insufficient diet, but if the problem is finances, doctors usually do not prescribe money. So it is with housing. In the area of legal protection, the main responsibility lies with psychologists, social workers, and perhaps public health nurses working with courts and social agencies.

However, in the major areas of prevention—prevention of illness and epidemic disease as well as prevention of psychological illnesses deriving from the family setting, up to and including the physical, sexual, and mental abuse of children—physicians are commonly involved and very often assigned the major responsibility for undertaking the preventive measures. At the same time, other professionals are routinely involved. Nurses particularly—in doctors' offices, health department clinics, neighborhood health centers, and group practices—provide preventive services. They provide prenatal care and family planning services, immunize children, offer emotional guidance, and work in school health settings. They even visit homes to seek out problems that require attention even before they reach crisis stage and come to medical or legal notice. Social workers in similar settings, while not involved in prenatal care, immunization, or school examination programs, are often involved in outreach and guidance.

As pointed out earlier, pregnancy and childbirth are social policy as well as health matters. The health matters are undergoing revised consideration worldwide. The tendency of the professions—science and medicine particularly—to broaden their reach is being "combatted" by the public. "Medicalization," in a pejorative tone, is heard more and more often. The public is reacting against physicians, especially psychiatrists, who have intruded into politics and law by analyzing leaders and criminals (although for different reasons). This tendency is now increasingly being resisted. Overactive school children, or even those with whom some teachers could not cope, have been "treated," i.e., drugged. The whole tendency to deal with social and interpersonal problems and difficulties by drug therapy and medical intervention is declining in power. Childbirth is still an arena of controversy in this regard. Slowly, the notion of pregnancy as a medically defined condition is being reconsidered. More and more, pregnancy is being seen as a normal human event, with medical supervision and hospital care in childbirth reserved for those cases in which a clear medical indication of illness or prospective danger exists. Pregnancy and childbirth, then, belong to the category of health supervision with or without a physician.

For all the reasons given earlier—unwillingness to involve government in what is considered family responsibilities; strong traditional wishes to maintain independence and self-reliance; the defiant American attachment to the entrepreneurial, profit-making way, even in the arena of child health care—there is no uniform approach to providing this "other" kind of health care, preventive medical services. Consequently, there are several orders of effort. Families who can afford it buy private preventive services for their children from a doctor. Sometimes the doctor or medical group uses nurses and/or social workers in the service. One may estimate, but not prove, that perhaps 70 percent of American children obtain some, albeit uneven, health care.

Another 10 to 15 percent will receive similar attention from federally supported clinics of one kind or another. But the remainder, without funds to buy private services, without access to the government-supported clinics, or without the education or the language ability to avail themselves of what existing federally supported clinics do offer, go without. And since it is catch-as-catch-can, there are even well-to-do families, unwilling or uneducated, that do not buy their children the needed preventive services.

The lack of leadership and the lack of a unifying philosophy prevail. School health services—or the absence of them—is very much to the point. Here is a place where more than half the population of children 19 and under can be found—a captive population! If younger siblings, not yet in school, could be included in the program, nearly 75 percent of that age group's population could be touched by preventive services. But school health services are minimally attended to. Health education, where it exists, tends to be old-fashioned; family life education and sex education are generally nonexistent. True, most states have laws requiring that schools have part-time or full-time doctors and nurses, but the preventive aspects are slighted. Children are examined casually, hurriedly, and superficially, if at all. If defects are found, follow-up is desultory. Immunizations are sometimes given, sometimes not. The attempt to share (retaining services for the poor in the schools and for the well-to-do in the private physician's office) falls between the two stools since there is no overall supervision. Connecticut assigns school health services —undefined—to the state department of education, which has had no person in charge for years. A clerk in the department of health, paid by the department of education, collects data and writes memoranda to the school nurses. The lack of a comprehensive school health program in the United States is probably one of the key elements in the poor record of untreated handicaps among American adults.

It should be pointed out here that the medical profession has not as boldly staked out its claim to this area as it has to the area of curative medicine. To many people, it appears as if doctors don't believe in or care nearly as deeply about prevention as cure. And it may not be altogether a financal decision, since doctors can be paid and are paid for preventive services. Medical education arms the modern doctor to care for the sickest patient, to diagnose the most complex and arcane illness. This education stimulates a competitive spirit of diagnosis and treatment that puts wellness, prevention, and health promotion in the shade. Status, awards, and the dignity of office in the professional ranks awaits the curative practitioner. There is no preventive practitioner. Prevention is a byline, perhaps even a bit of a nuisance that takes one away from important things like saving lives and easing pain. Doctors, then, are little interested in prevention, and if it is their responsibility, it will be, as it now is, a responsibility not very closely attended to.

INADEQUATE CURATIVE SERVICES: CARING FOR SICK CHILDREN

The medical care system, true to its name and in the purpose of its design, works best when it is working cures. This is not to say it works well, since it fails to reach promptly, adequately, safely, appropriately, and satisfactorily all those who need curative services. One might ask, since no system can be perfect in this imperfect world, why should we expect any medical care system to be perfect? But the limited extent to which the U. S. medical care system meets these obligations adds to the burden of failure in child health services. Social support, prevention, and health promotion failures cannot be charged against physicians since physicians are not essential to effectiveness in these areas. Failure of the medical care—the curative—system is, however, unquestionably a failure of the medical profession.

The health professions have ignored consideration of appropriate responses to children's medical care needs except as they fit the arbitrary design of convenient medical practice. This is true of both physical and psychiatric services. Institutional care is known to be completely unsuited to children's needs. Yet alternatives do not flourish. Out-of-hospital surgery for children with all but the most complicated conditions should be a sine qua non, yet it does not flourish. Cottage settings, family-type settings for the care of mentally retarded or mentally ill children is vitally necessary if civilized care of the hopelessly disabled and cure of the more hopefully diseased is to become an actuality. Not only the children, but social good sense demands it. Yet this is not the mode of medical care today.

Handicapped children, unfound and untreated; children of the poor and minority groups dying for lack of appropriate medical attention; morbidity unchecked for lack of care or medications—these are the marks of failure of a medical care system. Rising costs, uncontrolled, diminish the capacity of an entrepreneurial system to deal with the needs of the "medically indigent" as well as the penniless. Just as the federal government has powerful weapons with which to control economic disturbances and financial imbalance, agricultural dislocations, foreign trade balances, and the like, so a remedy for the dislocations and imbalances of medical care services is needed.

According to the rules of the U. S. medical care system, the individual patient must adjust to the professional design. The patient must seek out medical service. Hospitals and medical practitioners arrange themselves for their own convenience and provide services at their own convenience. Doctors decide on medication, hospitalization, and diagnostic and therapeutic procedures. No one but doctors can order most of these things. And the patient pays. The distance between order and payment insulates the doctor from the effects of cost.

Whether because of the professional mystique and the protection it provides, or the economics of medical service, or both, patients are not encouraged to learn too much about the nature of illness and the possibility, under some conditions, of caring for one's self. Under these circumstances, in serious illness, the doctor is of critical importance. And the ignorant patient is never sure of what may be serious. If physicians and other medical resources are not available because of maldistribution and economic barriers, it can create fear and resentment among the poor and among others with limited access. It may also induce a kind of hopelessness that forces them to adopt a fatalistic attitude and refuse to follow physicians' orders even when care is available. In the end, they may even refuse to avail themselves of medical care services.

It is difficult and perhaps unnecessary to assign a proportionate weight to each of the forces that deprive American children of health and, sometimes life. There is a *social* need to provide support for growth, nutrition, and housing. There is a *preventive* need to provide prenatal care and family planning, health protection, immunization, health education, and family support in child rearing. There is a *curative* need to provide treatment of sick children, to eliminate, as far as possible, the handicapping conditions that deprive a child of the chance to become a healthy adult. All of these are needed to assure American children a fair chance at life. Handicapped children will grow up to be handicapped adults. To worry about children's health is to worry about the nation's health.

ADMINISTRATIVE IMPEDIMENTS

During a four-year period, a group of us at Yale (The Health Policy Project) studied the federal/state relationship in child health services in Connecticut and Vermont. We undertook this because of the overwhelming evidence of malfunction in the child health care system. We selected the federal/state relationship as the point of attack for a specific reason. It seemed reasonable to assume that the private sector workings, as good or bad as they were, would one day become part of a national health program (optimism in this matter was at its peak in those years), and the federal/state relationship, as a system model, deserved examination. Further, the state and local governments, by federal law, bore direct responsibility and received large amounts of funds to provide protective and promotional health services and curative medical services for designated children. The clear failure of the health and medical care system to fulfill these obligations suggested a breakdown in communication or effectiveness in the federal/state relationship. The two states were chosen not because they were typical, but because it was convenient and was less expensive to mount a study there. As it turned out, they differed sharply from one another in many ways, and these differences were helpful in sorting out what might be termed general obstacles to effective performance from those that were idiosyncratic.

The administrative deterrents to effective performance are not strictly child health service problems, but are largely natural concomitants of a bureaucratic system in which instructions are ambiguous, supervision is slight, and the antagonisms within the system (what we often refer to when we use the term "bureaucratic") are large. It may be that similar programs for the old or the poor or the mentally ill suffer as much. However, two striking differences set off the children's health programs, with its failures, from other programs: one is that there is no powerful national advocacy group supporting child health; the other is the almost total lack of interest among legislators—federal or state—in the workings of the programs.

Two major pieces of federal legislation touch on children's health: Title V of the Social Security Act ("to improve the health of mothers and children") and Title XIX of the Social Security Act ("Medicaid," providing payment for specified medical care services for eligible poor people, including children). Both authorize very large sums of tax money to be used by the states on behalf of child health, and they compel equally large ("matching") financial investment by the states. Both laws also require state intervention in, if not operation of, child health programs. Title V was part of the original Social Security Act and went into operation in 1936; Title XIX was part of the later package that included Medicare and went into effect in 1966.

The unraveling of the tangled skein of federal/state relations is dealt with in detail in Part II. Here, let me just outline the findings that illustrate the bureaucratic contradictions impeding the provision of child health services.

From the start, historical records show national legislators' wariness to undertake support of child health services. The intrusion of the government into family affairs and the potential for weakening traditional family authority that such health legislation represented was strongly resisted. Nevertheless, in a compromise maneuver to gain a Social Security Law, the Congress, while yielding on universal health insurance, agreed to a limited child health section to the Social Security Act.

Title V then had two important sections—one to assist states in providing health services to pregnant women and infants, the other to treat handicapped children. Since 1963, a number of other sections have been added, allowing federal contributions to support a limited number of special clinic services (Maternity and Infancy Centers and Children and Youth Centers) as well as state support for family planning, dental care, and intensive care for high-risk infants.

The language of the law was deliberately ambiguous to allow states to do as much or as little as they chose; states were required to file a plan of action and to have it approved. The regulations were equally ambiguous in order to allow states to go on doing what they were doing and to define for themselves much of what they did. What is a child? How old? What diseases will be looked after? What is a handicapping condition? Over time, as state plans came in—and although some states took 20 years to file, no money was ever held up for that reason—these definitions were shaped into federal regulations. But it was left up to the state to take the initiative.

Despite the fact that the law intended that the states should use federal money *in addition* to state funds, the looseness of the regulations and the federal government's superficial review of budgets made it possible for states, by a variety of stratagems, to use the federal funds *instead* of additional state appropriations. Furthermore, while federal funds and state funds did increase, if not proportionately, inflation kept a step ahead of investment. Moreover, Congress, under the pressures of professional groups, essentially "devalued" the dollars it appropriated, by legislating increasing regulation of the system: "In addition to other duties," and therefore at the expense of services, child health offices in state health departments were required to inspect, certify, consult and to carry out a variety of administrative duties not directly related to providing services to children. Staff qualifications were also pushed higher and higher. Raising qualifications automatically raised salaries, created increasing numbers of petty fiefdoms (A Ph.D. can't do what a B.A. does, so the Ph.D. has to hire a B.A. to do it.), soaked up more money, and further reduced services. "Indirect" replaced "direct" services to children.

Much of this was calculated. The virtuous child health leadership seized this opportunity to build the health department structure, since the eventual distribution of services depended on effective structures, most of which did not exist before 1936. The policy was to build the structure and the services would follow. But, as in the case of the Sorcerer's Apprentice, the structure continued to grow, and the services languished.

If we actually intended to provide health and medical care services for children, our diversion from that intention might have been caught long ago. But this would have required full reporting by health departments and attention to reports and data as well as administrative oversight by either Congress or the executive branch. Data were and are, however, sadly deficient. For most states, and certainly for the states studied, there was no information on who was served, the extent of the demand, how many children met the eligibility requirements, what proportion of need this population represented, and so forth. There was no real knowledge of the extent of the problem or of the degree to which the problem was being met. Nor was there a plan for meeting immediate or long-term objectives. Reports tended to be records on system operation, unrelated to the clients. And, as if that weren't enough, inter- and intra-agency rivalries intensified the dysfunction.

Since Connecticut had a state hospital for care of crippled children, over and above the clinics and services paid for out of mingled federal funds, it was hard to know how much of this problem was met. After Medicaid went into effect it became impossible. As in many states, the Connecticut Medicaid reporting system itself became such a morass of internal confusion, no effective information could be retrieved.

The General Accounting Office, with its limited staff, could dip into states for an audit of expenditure and activity only on rare occasions. GAO reports are usually highly critical and condemnatory, but Congress rarely called upon such data in its consideration of child health programs and never made demands for the specifics of who needed service and who got service. Appropriations seem to have been made, in closed committee sessions, according to whim. Annually for six years, the Indian Health Service reported cases of kwashiorkor (a nutritional deprivation disease rarely seen in the United States, but common in impoverished developing countries) in an Indian reservation hospital, yet it never came up in hearings or review, which makes one question whether the committee members ever read the reports.

The Department of Health, Education, and Welfare long ago set up regional offices for decentralized supervision and liaison with state health and welfare agencies. Interviews and record review show that these offices become advocates for the states in Washington rather than Washington's representatives to the states, explaining, excusing, justifying, and allowing state actions that fit the states' own interests rather than the national norms.

It also should be pointed out that the *size* of the official bureaucratic structure itself is a very large obstacle standing in the way of accomplishing the objective—better health care for children. Large social institutions almost invariably lose sight of the true objective, service to people, and in many cases become self-serving instruments, acting in such a way as to keep themselves going, even at the expense of their ostensible services.

Many people believe that the problem is size, and size alone—not "bureaucracy," which is so often blamed. Consequently, future proposals, to be successful, must be small enough to avoid this trap. Frankly, I don't know how small a social institution has to be to succeed, but size is a problem of paramount concern that should be addressed in future trial efforts. Simply because an operational unit is small does not mean that it is divorced from the overall objectives or supervision of the national program. It means only that it must have a clear operational identity of its own.

Finally, lest all the blame fall on the federal legislative or executive branches, it must be pointed out that the state legislatures were equally remiss. In a 35-year period, fewer than three percent of state legislative actions concerned child health. State legislative hearings did not concern themselves with performance or need in child health programs. Nor was there a children's lobby to pressure the state legislatures into taking necessary action. Professional groups were preoccupied with legislation concerning work rules, fees, and other selfish economic considerations. Voluntary health groups pressed for appropriations for research or services for their particular diseases. But no one sought to explore or improve health services for children.

The same is true nationally, of course. No national advocacy body for children exists. Every ten years, since 1909, a White House Conference on Children has been held. Huge clusters of professionals and citizens "representing" children gather and discuss and issue declarations and programs. Yet no one actually expects any action between conferences since no permanent body exists to see to it that the declarations and programs are carried out.

In short, nothing in the administrative structure is organized to work effectively for a child health service, and nothing outside the administrative structure is organized to help that structure work. One might almost believe that no one really cares about child health and that the child health laws are merely something of a ritual, like

Fourth of July addresses. A more charitable view would be that no one really knows what else to do, that because the professionals do not come up with any better or more appealing model, Congress and the states, in desperation, simply appropriate money and hope. Traditional attitudes toward government intervention, welfare, the family, and official administrative organization all militate against effective child health services. The people want better, but given the limitation of their prejudices and despite their affection for children, cannot do better.

FINANCIAL IMPEDIMENTS

The obstacles enumerated—social attitudes, bureaucratic impediments, and the lack of direction—could all be sufficient to explain the inadequacies and the comparatively low statistical rating of child health services in the United States. But there has always been among us a strong belief in the remedial character of money, and many people have thought, and continue to think, that a shortage of funds is the problem. With more money, their argument runs, the system could be stimulated to improved performance, the staff could be enlarged, and more people could be served. It is my contention that this line of argument is illusory. While more money may be necessary in some future changed system of child care, simply adding money to the present system will not make it work. Proportionately and per capita, America is now spending as much, if not more, for health and medical care services as most of the other countries who surpass us in caring for the health of children. True, the Swedes and the Canadians are spending as high a percentage of their gross national product on health and medical care as we are, yet the Swedes show better results. Social expenditures in the United States are much lower per capita, and if it is money alone that is the determinant in success or failure of child health programs, Sweden and the United States and Canada should be on the same footing. They are not. Finland, a relatively poor country, spends relatively more of its gross national product on social and health activities, although the sums per capita are less than what the United States spends, and has a splendid record in child health. We know that investment in less expensive alternatives to the hospital, for example, can drastically reduce the overall cost of medical care.

It appears that money is important only insofar as it is spent economically and efficiently; more money doesn't guarantee needed services. It is easy to point out that the United States spends far more tax dollars on the old than on the young—perhaps five times as much per capita. This may indicate greater concern for the old than for the young, but I doubt it. Old people need more medical care, which is expensive, and more institutional care, which is even more expensive. From the stories one hears and the evidence of scandalous mistreatment in nursing homes and mental hospitals, I suspect that there is not any greater benefit from the money spent for the old than there is from that spent for the young. Perhaps, again, it is not the money, but what it is spent on, that counts. An analysis of social and medical care needs and of administrative malfunction and rivalries would probably reveal that the aged are, as the children, in poor circumstances.

In short, what is needed is a revelation, in a sense, of a workable system for child care—one that satisfies the criteria of need described earlier and yet fits into the American pattern of service and traditional attitudes. We need to cost out that child health system and to assess the specific elements of it to determine whether all, or some, or any are of such basic necessity as to be indispensable. With the pieces so laid out, a pattern of child health services for Americans can be designed.

We are not doing as well as we should in child health care, considering our wealth, technical sophistication and national dedication to children. The reasons for this are inherent in the system, and because of the many flaws in its operation, the system needs either repair or replacement of parts—not simply infusions of money.

Chapter 3

Other Countries Do Better

The fact that U. S. health services for children are poorly planned and organized and insufficiently staffed and directed, despite America's preeminent wealth and resources, leads to two questions. The first we have examined in the preceding pages: Why is the children's health service so inadequate? A lack of feeling for children, snarled programs, bureaucratic ineptitude, insufficient funding? Or all of these? It appears that all of these play a part, but lack of a clear program and program leadership is most to blame.

Which leads us to the next question: Can it be done better, and is it being done better elsewhere? If the answer is yes to both, then the corollary question that immediately arises is: Can we learn from the successful programs what we ought to do to design and carry out as a better program here? We must, however, be very cautious about jumping to conclusions based on the experiences of foreign countries. Lessons drawn from foreign experiences must be adjustable to native traditions and social concepts or they are useless. History creates forms of social behavior and institutional structures that continue to be accepted because they are familiar. Yet, although traditional attitudes are hard to change, demonstrated failure on the one hand and demonstrated success on the other can be a powerful lever. In the past, national crises, perceived or real, have operated in the same fashion. The patriotic fervor ignited by war suppresses traditional attitudes toward liberty and independence of character, on the one hand, and overcomes deep-seated prejudices toward job opportunities for minorities and women, on the other. Sputnik, taken as evidence of Communist educational superiority, was a catalyst for change in traditional U. S. educational methods and materials, not only because any Communist superiority seemed a threat to our security—however naive that thought might be—but also because it challenged our pride and concomitant confidence in the American way. Our educational system had failed us; revolutionary change could be considered.

It is this type of shock to tradition that could be useful in examining other countries' approaches to child health care. If we accept, and fully believe, that handicapped children become handicapped adults; that vulnerable families are headed by parents who came from vulnerable families; that worrying about children's health, therefore, is worrying about the nation's health; then knowledge about our failure and evidence of others' success may stimulate genuine change, despite the rigidities imposed by tradition and convention.

If an examination of foreign child health programs is to produce truly useful results, it must be conducted in a systematic way—along the axes prepared for examination of the U. S. system. Data that exactly parallel the American approach or experience will obviously not be available. Nevertheless, reasonably similar information can be obtained for some economically advanced countries and compared with each other. Particular lessons can then be drawn from the individual experiences.

During the 1976-1977 academic year, I had the opportunity to visit and to study in some depth the child health systems of Scotland and Holland. At the same time, through the kind offices of the European office of WHO in Copenhagen and the Centre International de l'Enfance in Paris, I was able to glean a good deal of data on Belgium, France, Denmark, Sweden, and Finland. From these data, interviews, observations, and conversations I drew together common patterns that offer interesting and feasible alternatives and additions to American child health program design.

At first blush, the problem of comparability is nearly insoluble. For instance, all European countries under discussion have some national financial support programs for families—family allowances, separate child allowances, maternity allowances, and rent subsidies. The size of the allowances varies from country to country; one country may have differential allowances, to avoid subsidizing the well-to-do, while another may treat all children the same. As a rule, rent subsidies are means tested; that is, only low-income families with children are eligible, and the amount of subsidy depends not only on the number of children, but on the family income as well.

Nonetheless, the success of child health service measures is uneven. Among countries that provide fair substantial financial support, there is no direct relation between the level of the national support and the level of child health as measured by usual standards. France spends the most, on allowances of various kinds. A median-income family with four children obtains 28 percent of its total income from such allowances. Yet, while France does well by its children, several other countries do better. What can be said is that there is a difference between countries that do a great deal (Finland, Holland, Sweden) and those that do very little (Scotland, Belgium). So, in general, we might say, financial support to the family is a necessary condition of child health, but how important is difficult to determine.

Another ticklish problem has to do with the role of national health programs. Every European country has a national health program, with almost universal entitlement to medical care. Scotland, as part of the United Kingdom and with a national health *service*, has 100 percent entitlement. The other countries reviewed, boasting national health *insurance*, provide coverage, in one way or another, for better than 80 percent of the population under mandatory regulations and allow for insurance coverage for the rest on a voluntary basis. It is fair to say that only the well-to-do are not legislatively mandated medical care coverage by the national health insurance programs reviewed. If this is the case, isn't further analysis really unnecessary? Universal entitlement would cover children wholly and absolutely, explain the relatively better level of child health in European countries and give us a fairly simple answer to America's dilemma in child health: what we need is a national health program, either insurance or service.

But that doesn't quite fit either. Scotland, as part of the United Kingdom, has a national health service, yet is not at the same high level as Holland or Finland, with insurance programs. Furthermore, the countries vary considerably in how, and how much, preventive services are performed for children.

In short, the review of European programs should enable us to say without much doubt, 1) whether universal entitlement to medical care services is sufficient to guarantee children all the health services they need, or 2) whether a separate preventive service for children may be necessary. The answers to these questions plus a transfer of experience may suggest a possible American approach to a national child health program.

SCOTLAND

In 1976, Scotland, like the United Kingdom as a whole, was undergoing serious reappraisal of its child health services, while at the same time carrying out several momentous, powerfully disturbing administrative reforms of the health service, social services, educational system, and local political organization. It is hardly fair to be critical of the situation so long before any effective change is identifiable. Nevertheless, it is possible to describe the elements of the operation and what reforms are in process and to make some guesses, based on the earlier experiences, about the possible results.

It is not necessary to describe in detail the workings of the British National Health Service (Scottish health services differ minimally). What must be said is that the 1974 reorganization of the national health service shook up long-standing administrative patterns and created new ones that still must take some getting used to. But in that health service, every child is entitled to a group of preventive services, specifically outlined by regulations, and to medical care, as needed, in home, doctor's office, or hospital, all without any payment at time of service.

Social Benefits

The social support provided by law includes a children's allowance, after the first child, with a "clawback," which taxes the allowance away in higher income brackets; modified maternity leave (no guarantee of reemployment at same job); means-tested rent subsidy for families with children; free school lunches for poor children; and subsidized meals for all children.

Preventive Services

Prevention includes prenatal care by a midwife or the family doctor; midwifery or delivery by the family doctor, at home or in a hospital; or obstetrical specialist delivery in a hospital. For infants and preschool children there are regularly scheduled screening examinations, and in most areas there are specialized "assessment centers" for in-depth study of children referred from these screenings. School children have three regularly scheduled examinations during schooling. Immunizations as well as the screening examinations may be performed in child health clinics or in the family doctor's office. Home visitation is provided by specially trained health visitors, who were formerly assigned to public health clinics, but are now generally assigned to work in teams with family doctors.

Curative Services

Every child is entitled by law to care without charge, by a physician in home, office and hospital. The general practitioner is the gatekeeper of this service and the family must request that service in order to obtain whatever additional services—hospitalization, out-patient diagnostic care, or specialist ("consultant") services. The general practitioner must certify need for special diet, housing, excuse from school, justify supplemental benefits in case of illness, special attendance grants for home help for a handicapped child, and even private agency grants in particular instances where such need exists.

There is no charge for hospitalization, drugs or applicances for children.

Administrative Considerations

Administrative problems are many and complex. Some are the effects of the new reorganization. Area Health Authorities, appointed by the Scottish Health Planning Council and mostly congruent with local political authorities, receive budgets and establish their own priorities. Within this Administrative Area, there are Community Medicine Specialists, a new title for health officers who are supposed to relate to both professional and administrative concerns. These people more frequently deal with elements of the public health administration rather than with specific community needs: environment, child health, planning, among others.

The Community Medicine Specialist, who is supposed to concern himself with child health, is in many instances a shadowy figure who has not yet established himself in the administrative hierarchy. This relates to the former condition of those public health officials, who worked in the child health field, and who had not the dignity or status of specialists. Called "child health specialists," they are not seen as specialists, and are not given either the recognition of consultants as other Community Medicine Specialists are, nor that of pediatricians, who are classically consultants with the status of specialist. This is a serious problem.

Problem number two is the traditional reliance on the general practitioners for preventive services, particularly children's preventive services. English (and Scottish) general practitioners are very busy, untrained in pediatrics, and impatient with the role of prevention. They cannot be depended upon to provide appropriate prenatal, infant, preschool, or school health services. Yet, more and more, this responsibility is being forced upon them and the role drilled into them. However, declining immunization rates, the continued discovery of handicapping conditions, and the persistence of a relatively high infant mortality rate are evidence of the futility of this approach.

The intention to increase and emphasize the reliance on the general practitioners—family doctors—is a good one. It derives from the established principle of "the union of preventive and curative medicine," a goal long dreamed of, but rarely attained, in public health ideology. In this case it is reinforced by another presumably sound principle: if you give intelligent, trained people responsibilities for which they are not exactly suited, they will "grow into it." So far, not yet.

Furthermore, the health visitor, splendidly trained to be a child health and family preventive service nurse, has been withdrawn from this arena and placed in the doctor's office. The purpose derives from another virtuous ideological concept, the doctor-nurse team concept, but its effect is pernicious. Since family doctors are very busy and have little interest in prevention or children, they would like the nurses to help relieve them of what they are most occupied with—chronically ill old people with lots of complaints. So the health visitor has gradually been withdrawn from visiting preschool children at home to visiting sick old people. Of course, the old people do need care, but the substitution, rather than supplementation, deprives children of needed preventive services.

A third problem—also found in the U.S.—is the lack of an effective national advocacy group for children. This is complicated in the United Kingdom by the parliamentary form of government and the intimate relationship of trade unions (a potential advocacy group) with a major political party. The health service reorganization did establish community advisory boards (local health councils) as channels of communication among professionals, administrators, and the public. But no measurable activity as community representatives for health, and certainly not for child health, is observable. There are two private bodies, the Poverty Action Group and the National Children's Bureau, which do speak for children's needs, but, as a rule, they reserve their communication for social services and income needs.

Financial Considerations

How little, and yet how much, money itself is a vital factor in the establishment of good child health services is vividly illustrated in the Scottish picture. For a number of reasons (chiefly Aneurin Bevan's surrender to professional and political pressures in 1948), Scotland receives more health service funding per capita than England. Scotland is also better supplied than England with other resources for dealing with health needs, having proportionately more doctors, nurses, and health visitors. Yet Scotland suffers from a lower level of child health than England. There is ample excuse for this in the sadly decayed Glasgow area (containing approximately half the population of Scotland) with its high unemployment, poverty, poor housing, and "multiproblem" families. Even though better-supplied than England, Scotland still has a shortage of health visitors, who make 50 percent more visits to old people in Scotland than health visitors do in England. More funds would enable employment of more health visitors and better services to the vulnerable "multiproblem" families. However, improving income or welfare grants or providing more housing depends on *national* policy, not Scottish policy alone. All of the United Kingdom is bound by the incomes policy. And poor housing is no worse in the Glasgow area than in many parts of England, where the child health situation is better.

Overview

Briefly then, Scotland offers a pattern of a highly centralized, universal-entitlement, national health service, in which the family doctor is heavily relied upon for preventive services and in which the specialized child health nurse plays a diminishing role. Yet with no private sector involvement, little advocacy, and arguably marginal financial support for social and medical services for children, the level of child health is no better than in the United States.

HOLLAND

Although the population of the Netherlands is almost three times that of Scotland, most of us are tempted to think of Holland as smaller than Scotland. In area it is, in fact, tiny, but it is the most densely populated country in the world. In policy and political philosophy, strangely enough, Holland is closer to the United States in a great many ways than the English-speaking Scots are. Their national medical system is on an insurance base and for 40 percent of the population is voluntary rather than mandatory. However, nearly 90 percent of the population is insured against the costs of medical care. Specialists are paid fee-for-service, family physicians dealing with insured patients receive capitation—a fixed sum per client per year—and hospitals are under voluntary organizational control. There are many private health organizations, and those offering preventive services and home nursing flourish. Over three-quarters of the population belongs to one or another of these voluntary health service groups known as Cross organizations. (There are three national cross organizations: Green, White-Yellow and Orange-Green, for different religious groups.)

What most sharply sets off the Dutch from Americans in social philosophy is the Dutch adherence to the principle of "separate and equal," which they call *verzuiling* (columnization). Briefly, because of religious divisions at the time of liberation from Spanish domination in the 16th century, the country might have broken into warring factions much as we see in Ireland, Belgium, Israel, and dozens of smaller areas of irreconcilable conflict throughout the world. The wealthy bourgeois families, being of different religions, were reluctant to destroy their splendid economic base and developed accommodations whereby each religion had full and complete access to all the social advantages the country provided. This separate, denominational equality extends throughout all areas of the society, each denomination having equal access to doctors, midwives, hospitals, Cross organizations, and welfare organizations; kindergartens, grammar schools, and colleges; newspapers, radio, and television; and political parties.

The major denominational groupings are Roman Catholic, Protestant, Strict Reformed, and secular. Some splinters represent minorities, which the Dutch, in their meticulous and methodical way, not only allow, but encourage. These minorities include, for example, several hundred thousand Indonesians, an inheritance of former colonial times, who have their own health organizations and a somewhat lesser number of Surinamese, from another more recently liberated colony, who have their own health organization.

One wonders what might have been accomplished in the United States if, in 1865, the victorious legislators had attempted this approach to resolving the inequities of slavery.

Social Benefits

The Dutch system of social benefits for families and children is the second most extensive in Europe. It provides a maternity allowance and leave arrangement, children's allowances, means-tested rent subsidies, and school lunches.

The Dutch also have an elaborate legal protection system for children, including an ombudsman ("referee") for children whom it is *suspected* are ill treated. Social agencies, a family court, and the family doctor are involved to make sure the child is not abused or neglected. A social worker can be appointed by the court as the child's "health guardian" if it is thought necessary.

Preventive Services

Preventive services are a complex patchwork, but coverage reaches every pregnant woman, every child, and every family. Midwives are fined for not reporting births immediately (Fifty percent of births are at home.), and the child's allowance begins immediately upon reporting. Prenatal care, infant and preschool examination, discovery of handicap, and immunizations can be taken care of in a doctor's office or in a public clinic. However, if she elects a family doctor for her pregnancy, a pregnant woman must register with a midwife as well. Very few childbirths are in the hands of family doctors, a somewhat larger number in the hands of specialists in hospitals. Midwives deliver in hospitals as well as at home.

Families that belong to the private Cross organizations can obtain preventive services there. In communities where the Cross organizations are small, and in large cities like Amsterdam, the city health department runs amalgamated clinic services utilizing the various Cross nurses. No child is unregistered, and nurses are assigned follow-up to be sure no child fails to obtain immunization, examination, treatment of any handicapping conditions, and glasses or hearing aids, if needed. About 2,500 children live on barges or among gypsies. Those nomadic children are kept track of by the office of the director general of health services, who periodically reviews their records and assigns district nurses for follow-up. Child health nurses are specially trained to deal with family problems and are expected to visit and discover family and social problems before they come to the attention of the police or health authorities.

School health services include a completely staffed system of physicians and nurses who are responsible for fixed periodic examinations and reports, follow-up on family difficulties brought out in school, referral for handicapping conditions, and the health education of school children.

Curative Services

As mentioned, curative services are paid for through an insurance system. For ordinary illness, this implies individual (or worker) contributions plus employer contributions. For serious and chronic illnesses, there is a separate fund paid for by employers and the government to which everyone is entitled. All children are covered. No one pays at the time of service.

Administrative Considerations

The Dutch system is so complex as to be almost chaotic. However, certain principles operate to keep it on a relatively even keel.

- There is strong central supervision. The Dutch National Health Service is responsible for (among other health matters) the operation of the preventive health services for children.

- This central supervision is delegated to district directors.

- There is a separate national inspector's office, responsible to the ministry, which also delegates authority for evaluating and supervising *all* health and medical care services to the district inspectors.

- There is a strong private sector health service operation.

- There is a separate social insurance agency for collecting information and paying for medical care.

- There is a strong link between health and social agencies and the courts.

The system's most visible weakness is the lack of data on operations in the medical care system, and the consequent lack of effective controls on costs. The fee-for-service and voluntary hospital operations also contribute to weakened cost controls. Excess medical care cost inflation over general inflationary trends parallels the U.S. experience. And cost sensitivity is an important administrative matter. Even as I write this, the government of the Netherlands, a special working party of the European Organization for Economic Cooperation and Development, and consultants from the World Health Organization are preparing modifications and recommendations for change in this loosely knit, seemingly inefficient, but *effective* health and medical care system.

Financial Considerations

While weak cost controls and the rate of inflation of medical care costs are comparable to those of the United States', the cost of the preventive service is separate from that of the medical care costs and much less subject to inflationary pressures. As a matter of fact, it appears that the cost of preventive services, because it is separate —delivered largely by salaried nurses and supervised and controlled at the local rather than at the national level—is quite low and not unduly inflated. (Inflation inevitably accompanies national rates.)

Preventive services are paid for by budgetary appropriations. These appropriations support public clinic services and top off the private Cross organizations' expenditures on behalf of preventive services. Since the regimen for preventive services is scrupulously described and nationally prescribed, and since nurses' salaries and physician salary/session rates are set by national negotiations, Cross agency budgets are easily decided upon. Then *all* the public treasuries—national, state, and local—contribute a share of meeting the cost. A small part of the Cross agency administration and operation is met from "dues" paid by the membership. This operational financing is uniquely Dutch and a fascinating exercise in public/private, federal/state/local relations and cooperation.

Overview

The Netherlands represents a comprehensive, integrated, combined but separate, preventive and medical care system in which all children are entitled to, sought out for, and provided with preventive services and in which a combined voluntary/compulsory medical care insurance system offers curative services to all children. Child health is officially advocated by the legal system and actively worked toward by the private Cross organizations. Social services are well financed and include special legal protection for children. Nurses are relied upon for preventive services, and midwives for maternity care. Decentralized operations allow the private sector and separate denominational units to play an important role. Finally, there is a separate official organization whose sole purpose is to supervise the child health care system.

OTHER EUROPEAN CHILD HEALTH SERVICE MODELS

The child health care systems of Scotland and Holland have been described in some detail because they offer such interestingly different approaches to child health. In many ways, their attempts to fulfill this social responsibility should serve to prod the American conscience.

What emerges from this comparative examination of systems is the suggestion that certain key elements are essential to successful program performance. Before reviewing some other national models, it may help first to enumerate the different effects of the following on the Scotch and Dutch programs.

- location of policy development
- location of program control
- role of family doctor
- role of public health nurse
- separateness of preventive service
- influence of private sector

For the most part, policy development seems to be the same, the primary difference being the varying degree of input from different sectors. Both Scotland and Holland are parliamentary democracies. Interest groups other than professionals seem to have little concern for program and make little contribution to policy. Social policies are similar, but in fuller blossom in Holland, a wealthier country than Scotland. Program control, although decentralized in both countries, is more heavily supervised in Holland. Legal and social rights of children are more broadly interpreted in Holland, and the family less dominant in the court's eyes.

More important is the wide difference in responsibility for preventive services. In Holland these services are fully separated, and there is less emphasis on the family doctor and more on the nurse. Also, the private sector is prominent in Holland, almost invisible in Scotland. Child health advocacy is more developed in Holland.

What about some other countries, those whose child health care records are better than Scotland's or worse than Holland's?

Social Benefits

The public health services of all of the countries studied (Scotland, Holland, Belgium, Denmark, Sweden, and France) provide maternity leave and maternity allowances, family and children's allowances, rent subsidies, and school lunches. In Scandinavia, the benefits for the pregnant woman are most generous; in all countries the children's allowance is paid to the mother rather than to the father to ensure that unwed, abandoned, or divorced mothers are not discriminated against and their children deprived. In Scandinavia, special benefits are paid working mothers to permit hiring sitters for small children.

The courts in Finland can arrange prepayment, whereby court-ordered child support payments from a divorced spouse will be paid by the government which in turn will collect it from the spouse. This prevents the unhappy situation of a parent and children made destitute by the negligence or malice of the other parent. Courts and social agencies in Scandinavia are assisted by local youth committees (generally part of the local councils), which can officially intervene in cases of child neglect or abuse.

Preventive Services

There is a much greater variation in range, administration, and responsibility among preventive services than among social services. All of the systems offer prenatal and childbirth coverage. In Denmark, the family doctor is primarily responsible for maternity care, and the patient is expected to register both with him and with a midwifery service. In France the nurse has become increasingly the responsible person. In Belgium, the ONE (Oeuvre Nationale de l'Enfance) a quasi-governmental private agency supported by tax funds, provides prenatal care, but a woman can elect to obtain this service from her family doctor and the medical care insurance system will pay. In Sweden, county clinics are under medical supervision, but the nurses carry out the activities.

In most counties, registration for infancy and preschool care will trigger allowance payments to the family, which serves as an incentive to registration. France has elaborated this system into a series of levels whereby payments will be continued only if each level of examination and screening for handicaps is completed. All countries provide for assessment centers—either separate or as part of teaching hospital pediatric departments— to follow up on referrals from the screening examinations. Except in Belgium, where physicians staff the ONE units for such screening examinations, nurses will do most of the screening. In France, a physician's screening examination is mandated at specific ages in infancy, but if the child is not brought to the clinic, a nurse can visit the home and do the screening. Home visitation is mandatory in all countries if a child misses the official examination schedule or immunization. In most countries, home visitation is not simply a routine outreach measure. Handicapped children, "vulnerable families," and those who have missed appointments are priority entries on a nurse's visitation list. However, it appears that only in Holland is a family's failure to have a child immunized considered sufficient cause for legal action.

School health services, on the other hand, tend to be of uniform design. Primary responsibility lies with the national education departments. Local school districts employ physicians and nurses to carry out nationally mandated examinations and then to follow up to ensure compliance with prescribed care. Health departments are often charged with cooperative service (supplying school doctors or nurses) and invariably with supervision and evaluation of the services. (In Holland, the Cross nurses may supply school health services.)

Curative Services

In Belgium, all the costs of childbirth are paid for out of social security funds, but in other countries only the hospital care is charged to social security, unless a specialist (i.e., obstetrician) is involved. Except for Holland, nearly all births are in hospitals, which are almost exclusively government operated. And again except for Holland, the daily cost includes physician services and, since most midwives do deliveries in hospitals, midwife services.

Social security and health insurance funds pay for all other medical services. In Belgium, the patient pays and is reimbursed by the insurance fund according to a fee schedule. In Sweden, the patient need not pay at the time of service, but if he does he is reimbursed in toto. In Finland, as in Scotland and Holland, no money changes hands at the time of service. In all countries, medical care insurance covers all children of working parents, those eligible for social security, and the upper income groups who subscribe to the insurance scheme.

Administrative Considerations

Basically, the countries divide into two categories: those whose preventive and medical (curative) services are linked, and those whose are not. Belgium is the weakest in preventive services, weak in its linkages, more limited in social benefits, and the victim of powerfully divisive cultural and racial forces. France, too, maintains a significant separateness between preventive and curative services, although the two services are part of the same ministry. The Scandinavian countries retain some control of the liaison by requiring health department supervision of medical care services; however, this supervision is more theoretical than real. Social security, the health insurance system, maintains a strongly independent character. The strength of the Scandinavian nursing service, with its extensive outreach program, does, however, create a strong bond between medical and preventive services.

Another distinction is in the nature of local control. In Sweden, the county, adhering to national standards, is the operational unit. The funds for preventive services are collected at the county level and supplemented by national funds. The same is true in Holland, where municipal and district tax funds are a greater share of the preventive health service expenditure than is the national tax support. Denmark and Finland also operate largely on local funding for these services. But Belgium, Scotland, and France operate on national tax funds. Local control is less likely to be present and, where attempted, less successful, because there is less local political concern. Many people question the uniformity and effectiveness of France's departmental organization because the arrangement is so strongly hierarchical and, from a political standpoint, disabling to local responsibility.

Official intervention on behalf of children is the mode (youth committees), and private agencies either do not exist or play a very minor role. ONE in Belgium considers itself a private agency on behalf of children, but its total budget is from the government.

Financial Considerations

Holland is the only country in which private payments for preventive services are encouraged, through the Cross organizations. Belgium is the only country in which significant payment for medical care may come from the private purse. In Scotland, the patient does not pay for anything—preventive or curative; in Sweden, Denmark, France, and Finland, some small part of the cost may be borne by the patient.

In all, returning to the observations made at the beginning of this section, the countries that have the best records—Holland, Sweden, and Finland—share a system design. All have:

- separate preventive services, reasonably well linked to the curative;

- nurses playing an important role in the preventive services and in the linkage of the preventive and curative;

- national standards with local control;

- powerful national health department supervision.

The child health systems in the other countries lack one or more of these elements and do not measure up to the standards set by Holland, Sweden and Finland.

Also characteristic of good service is strong evidence of social concern: generous benefits to pregnant women and families with children; a legal system that considers the child's welfare as important as, or even more important than, the welfare of the family (i.e., parents). An ombudsman program, as in Holland, or equivalent youth committees, as in Scandinavia, are critically needed to protect children from abuse and neglect, including neglect of health needs.

How can this be transplanted in the American soil? Social philosophy antithetical to American tradition will not be accepted; sweeping social or health system change is unlikely in view of traditional congressional caution; foreign strains of health care are unlikely to take root here. If we really do want a good health service for our children, we must discover in this analysis native elements that are usable, adoptable and adaptable, and build an American child health service.

Chapter 4

Some Native Elements: What We Can Learn From Europe

Even when reasonable people are presented with the incontrovertible fact that the American child health care system is not working, they face up to the necessity for change and the accompanying inconvenience and dislocation only very reluctantly. Shibboleths are plucked at random to delay action: Other systems also have defects! You won't reach everybody! True, but the other systems are working better, more children are reached than here. Even the children of migrant families are reached. (One European worker in seven is now a migrant worker, and probably a third have children with them.) European countries are aware of and moving to remedy the deficiencies in their systems. The French and Dutch are aiming at unification of disparate elements, and the Dutch, Belgians, and Danes are moving to simplify the chaotic multiplication of sources of care.

Or else the European models are dismissed as inappropriate: population size for example, makes systems noncomparable. But Holland has three times the population of Scotland and manages better. The size of the country may be used as an argument against comparability—that small densely populated countries can handle care more easily. But Sweden and Finland are geographically quite large, with many sparsely settled communities, yet seem to manage equitable distribution of services. Amsterdam and Glasgow have similar urban density, yet Amsterdam offers a higher-quality, more easily accessible comprehensive system of care for children than

Glasgow. The Dutch and Belgian systems are very complex and coordinated with great difficulty yet seem to work very effectively. The answer may not be structural simplicity or complexity but focus—the definition of function.

As an academic exercise, reviewing other nations' programs for health and medical care services for their children is a stimulating and rewarding experience. We can see the successes, and the degree of success related to the amount and kind of effort, and can admire the success, without approving of the methods. But unless we can approve, identify our own traditional response to social problems, and compare them with their responses we cannot use the information. Perhaps if we rearrange the findings into an orderly listing so that the relationship of the European action may be viewed against the American tradition and action along the same axis, a more realistic perspective on what is possible may be obtained.

SOCIAL BENEFITS

In the area of *social* support, where European nations provide children's allowances, maternity allowances, and housing rent subsidies, the United States is in the throes of legislative proposals, social demands, and tentative actions already. We are far behind Europe, but social pressures are building for a family support system, whether based on the model of allowances or of minimum income policy. Court action for job security and social payments in pregnancy for working women has already been undertaken. Rent subsidies and urban housing rehabilitation support for poor families is already beyond the pilot stage. In a word, there is nothing startling in the European model, nothing that U. S. legislators and public interest groups are not aware of and agitating for. At the moment, conflicting economic theories seem to be keeping the political process from following this pattern. But a concerted national advocacy effort and the economic example of the European experience could move us toward a broad social program of financial support for families and children.

The prospects of increased legal intervention and support of the child as a person, with rights equal to those of parents, is less promising. The strength of judicial tradition and the lack of strong social agency support for change stand in the way of building a child-oriented legal protection system. Social workers tend to be immobilized by two forces. The most obdurate barrier is their immersion in eligibility decisions that devour their time and energies, especially since most welfare services are focused on detecting and eliminating "cheats" and "shirkers." Then, conflict among the competing psychological theories upon which social work efforts are based impedes collaboration and a unified advocacy effort among these professional guardians of children.

Nutrition services, on the other hand, are very close to a national program for children and pregnant women. There is still an unwholesome emphasis on means testing, on keeping out as many as possible, instead of including as many as need it; but large sums of money are now being devoted to school lunches, for example. With a broad-scale legislative push aimed at improving children's health, an effective nutrition program for pregnant women and all children could be built on what already exists.

There is an important area of social philosophy that needs to be touched on here.

It has to do with the almost religious attachment we have to means testing for social programs. Whether it derives from early conditioning against idleness, coupled with capitalist fear of a labor shortage, or from an ethical scruple against "freeloading," our social programs invariably include designs for keeping some groups out. The groups to be kept out are those expected to provide for themselves whatever the social program provides. The Medicare program, for example, allows every person over 65 to become a participant and to enjoy the support of federal financial contributions. But even here, the older person is expected to make a contribution, and those too poor to contribute receive added financial support from another federal pocket. Maybe the only way to overcome the rigidity of this attitude in regard to children is to undertake a contributory system of a similar kind for the nutrition and prevention programs.

PREVENTIVE PROGRAMS

Preventive programs in Europe are separate from curative programs, some to a greater degree than others. The separation is not so much in the administration as in the funding, which makes it possible to maintain a powerful independent preventive service for children. We do have local public health services in the United States, but as analyzed earlier, they are weak, disorganized, and not very effective. We have no national health service with a leadership and supervisory role to give shape and direction to a national preventive program.

We do, however, have the seeds of such programs. With funding and positive direction, local public health departments can become stronger and fulfill their potentialities. Congress can remove the legal barriers to U.S. Public Health Service intervention in state and local operations, authorize more inspection and supervision, and appropriate more funds for preventive services.

We already have well-prepared nurses, midwives, pediatric nurse practitioners, physician associates and pediatric associates, and training programs in place ready to train many thousands more. It is job opportunities and program structures that are lacking, not trained people. Childbirth centers, diverting the bulk of normal deliveries from the unnatural and even dangerous world of hospital delivery, have been tried successfully and are increasingly in demand.

School health programs are too weak, too leaderless to instill any optimism. But with a broad scale program in other areas, they, too, could be taken under the wing of a comprehensive preventive program. If the education departments continue to reduce health concerns to insignificant parts of their activities, these programs should then be placed under health agency control.

CURATIVE PROGRAMS

At the curative level, America's flirtation with a national health program, either insurance or service, is hard to take seriously. Seventy years of discussion—in and out of Congress—arguments and polemics, earnest academic publications along economic lines, political science dissertations, and health professional diatribes have so muddied the waters that the public and the legislators are helpless. The media, upon which we depend (perhaps too much) for popular education, are no more helpful in their analyses and presentations. Every recommendation is soundly supported by statistical and (social) scientific evidence, and equally soundly refuted by similarly collected evidence. One is tempted to believe that, in the words of Thomas McKeown, a distinguished elder statesman of social medicine, "political contraception is being practiced, in which no matter how suggestive the preliminary movements, there will be no embarrassing legislative consequences."

Yet it is clear that no program of child health can be successful without a program of paid-for medical care. It is clear as well that a program of universal entitlement to medical care is not enough to guarantee every child health services, but without it, the totality of health service needs cannot even begin to be carried out.

ADMINISTRATIVE CONSIDERATIONS

The administrative lessons to be learned from Europe are extremely important. Clear and strong national standards, supervised and enforced by a national health agency, are an administrative necessity. An almost paradoxical corollary is the need for local control of operations, which includes local budgetary control and participation.

What America possesses in abundance is a history and tradition of pluralism and of private participation in public and social enterprises. This emphasis on public participation of the private sector, seemingly best developed in the Dutch health care system, may serve as a strong foundation on which to build the public/private model of an American child health system.

It should be mentioned, even emphasized, that the strong tradition of states' rights in the United States—a legacy from our founders, a primary cause of the Civil War, and a source of still-unsettled controversy for over 200 years—does give us grounds to hope for successful decentralized control and operation of a child health service. On the other hand, it is the most visible obstacle to the creation and installation of any national project, since without previous state testing, state models, or state pilot programs, national programs languish in congressional committee. There is hard common sense and scientific validity to this, of course. Why should we put profoundly unsettling social programs into effect on a national scale without having tested their worth? Would we not be leaving ourselves wide open to their deficiencies, their unsuspected dangers and traps?

FINANCIAL CONSIDERATIONS

Financial aspects are more easily dealt with. The social support cost is very high. In France, for example, it is over 4 percent of the gross national product, in Holland, over 3 percent. Preventive services are much cheaper, the total coming to something under $40 per child per year. In the United States this would total nearly $3 billion, just about what the U. S. government is now spending for child health and medical care services. If we adopted the European financing model of part personal contribution (dues to a Cross agency in Holland) plus municipal (similar to school support) tax funds, state support, and federal contributions, financing a preventive system would be simple and easy.   Financing a curative system, however, would still be difficult, given the current debates and program suggestions.

Chapter 5

The American Way

In general, these considerations offer a hopeful view on the possibilities of creating in America a national program for child health, a program aimed at comprehensive care of the health of America's children—compulsory, yet requiring voluntary participation and cooperation; public, yet fostering private initiative; nationally standardized and supervised, yet locally designed, operated, and controlled.

This tangle of seeming contradictions closely approximates American traditional forms, reflecting the pluralistic nature of American social and political structures. Challenges to our traditional thinking permeate the texture of a possible solution: separation of preventive and curative medicine (a rejection of a classical professional shibboleth); granting responsible leadership to the nurse rather than to the physician, even in quasi-medical matters; the primacy of the child's interests rather than of the parents' rights; intrusion of government into family affairs. Will we give legal sanction to a court or social agency to decide on disposition of services important to a child's health if a family is *not* poor, *not* dependent on public welfare, *not* a suppliant for social services?

The problem of child health services for the United States is of such complexity that there is no simple, direct way to approach a solution. The questions of children's allowances and family income policy have social ramifications that ought not be mingled with the more clearly health aspects of social policy, despite the recognized and unassailable fact that the health and social factors are inter-dependent. The deep-running and strongly held feelings regarding independence of the family and family control of, and responsibility for, children can be challenged only at peril of jeopardizing any health program. The United States' lack of strength in three essential areas makes for a shaky foundation upon which to build a new and effective child health program. There is no strong national public health system for leadership, no strong private network of child health services to be broadened or assimilated, and no national public constituency for children. Another negative factor, in addition to natural inertia, is the powerful professional bloc that sees much to lose and little to gain in modifying or exchanging the status quo. And finally, despite the fact that relatively small amounts of public and private money are invested in child health care, the total is a goodly sum. There is then, some resistance to added appropriations. The whole of these considerations suggests that new programs must be phased in, and the phases must encompass social philosophy, traditional attitudes, professional concerns, and public and private funding. Not everything that needs to be done, ought to be done at once, everywhere.

If we are going to violate some of the traditional social customs carefully preserved over the years, we can do it only if we can show, from the limited evidence presently available, not only that the health of the child will be enhanced, but also that the social link-ages—of parents to one another and of parents to children—will not be damaged.

We are asking Americans to adopt a social support program at a level of financial investment they do not yet agree is either necessary or desirable. If money is the most important contribution that can be made to child health, then discussion of any carefully constructed system of preventive and medical care is a waste of time. But if financial investment is only a part of what is needed, and since a strong, effective system of preventive and curative services will be needed in any case, we should proceed with what is possible, with what is feasible in political *and* financial terms and adopt this plan as quickly as possible. This in itself may help bring about the social support we desire and consider important.

If we agree to this approach, a great many of the contradictions resolve themselves into more readily adjustable considerations.

- All children are vulnerable, although not equally so. It is important to deal with *all* children on a preventive basis in the beginning, identifying and giving priority to those more vulnerable—physically, emotionally or socially—without regard to family income. Parents may be classified by income for tax purposes, but not for child health reasons.

- The Dutch and Scandinavians are no less committed to democratic principles than we are and no less sensitive to encroachments on their liberties by government. Yet they allow for government intervention when it means discovery and treatment of handicaps in their children and welcome such benevolent intrusions. For the prevention of disease, disability, and death in their children, government concern is welcome.

- We have no good evidence that the complex of preventive services will help children to be healthier, learn better, or be more competent adults. However, evidence is accumulating that learning capabilities are associated with good nutrition and good health. We do know that lack of immunization means greater susceptibility to epidemic childhood disease. We do know that not finding and treating handicapping conditions in children means permanently handicapped adults. And we know that a haphazard approach will not ensure immunization of all children or guarantee that children's handicapping conditions will be found and treated. Outreach services to families may or may not play a useful part in preventing abuse, neglect, or psychological damage of children, but such outreach services are essential to guarantee case finding, immunizations, and follow-up treatment.

Since all children have similar needs and only systematic program efforts can ensure meeting those needs, a program of preventive services for *all* children is critically necessary. Providing a program for *all* handicapped children is to provide a program to prevent handicapped adults. The traditional and artificial efforts to deny children services on the basis of parental income endanger programs for *all* children.

Chapter 6

A Recommended Program

I find that most of the "daring" proposals for reform and restructuring that emerged from my long and intensive reviews of our failures and others' successes, are staples of long standing. In a sense, like most innovation, the process is essentially a rediscovery of older values or forms dressed in modern clothes.

ORGANIZATION OF COMMUNITY CHILD HEALTH PROGRAMS

Community Child Health Programs are to be preventive units, based in local communities, supported in part from federal and in part from local tax funds, under the supervision, if not direct control of local health departments. A national child health service will plan programs and set standards, assist states in meeting standards and staffing clinics, and provide a locally based supervision and inspection service for evaluation and quality control.

Services provided must include prenatal and well-baby care; nurse visitations to the home; home help during and after childbirth; immunizations of the children according to a schedule; a modest maternity allowance to a pregnant woman upon registration; family planning services; preschool screening examination of children according to a schedule; assessment centers for evaluation of screened referrals; school-entrance and-exit examinations; medical and psychological care, as needed, in the schools; and school health education programs. Where possible, assessment centers should be associated with a local clinic, and strong liaison should be established with schools, for appropriate diagnosis of learning disabilities, and with social agencies, for appropriate family follow-up.

Staff for clinics will include at least one midwife for each 100 anticipated childbirths, at least one child health nurse for every 500 children, one public health nurse per 1,000 population, a supervising pediatrician for every 5,000 children, a supervising obstetrician for every 5,000 pregnancies, and physicians employed and paid by the session for work in the assessment centers (except that when assessment centers are operated as part of a hospital-centered program, the staff will be wholly salaried); and physicians, by the session also, for school health services. Midwives should be encouraged to continue assisting those patients who choose hospital delivery. Home childbirth should not be discouraged, provided sufficient attention to risk factors is maintained. Everyone employed in the preventive service should be salaried except per-session physician consultants, and salaries should be negotiated nationally between government and professional group representatives.

The system of preventive health services for children must be under the control of nurses with training in and enthusiasm for the preventive aspects of the work. The European experience is strikingly impressive. Where the system works best, the nurse has the predominant role. Doctors, pediatricians, and obstetricians especially, may be needed as consultants and must have a voice in the advisory councils, but the day-to-day operational controls must be in the hands of interested and enthusiastic professionals. Keeping prevention separate from treatment may sound heretical, but in reality, that is the way it is now, largely because prevention is ignored and neglected by physicians who have no real interest, or perhaps even belief, in the value of preventive services. Separating prevention and treatment, with nurses maintaining a strong liaison, may, paradoxically, improve the connection that is now so tenuous.

We have tried hard to make doctors change their orientation, to make them become more child and family oriented, more preventive minded, less categorically disease and organ/system oriented—but without real success. They can't change their way of thinking, looking, and feeling, not only because of the curative emphasis in their education, but also because success in the profession is measured by scientific standards that sometimes actually interfere with the business of providing satisfying services to people. To understand why physicians must play a secondary role in preventive services, one has only to think of the bondage to technology that obstetricians and pediatricians have accepted, isolating infants from mothers in the name of disease control and multiplying caesarean sections in the name of reduced infant mortality. *Prevention is a professional role that should be assigned to willing and expert professionals.*

A very important component of the local child health service should be the opportunity for community groups to organize their own clinic on a nonprofit basis, separate from the official health department clinic and supported, but not controlled, by local government agencies. While this proposal may appear startling on the face, it is well within traditional American patterns. As far back as the Rural Electrification Administration in the 1930s, incentives for cooperatives to form and provide a community service were legislated. The Economic Opportunity Administration fostered neighborhood health centers. Current legislation offers staffing grants to mental health centers, and the Health Maintenance Organization legislation offers special financial incentives to such health agency formation. The Dutch precedent of "denominational separateness," may bring about a latent recognition of the need for a degree of separateness among American groups.

In the early 1930s in London, a pair of prevention-minded physicians, with some private foundation support, built a health center whose ostensible purpose was recreation, but whose basic reason for being was to promote health. The Peckham Center charged a few pennies a month for family membership in a club that offered gymnastic, sports, swimming activities, and a bar(!) for family recreation—with one proviso. Each member of the family was to be examined once a year by the guiding medicos and to be made aware of the physicial, emotional, or social needs for care. However, no treatment was given at the center, only advice. The doctors considered themselves "ethologists" (students of the normal), not pathologists. The club was a great success and ended its health promotional career only with the Second World War. While not an exact model of what is suggested here, neighborhood grouping for health promotion and disease prevention is not an altogether novel idea.

In the United States in the late 1960s and early 1970s, the National Urban Coalition attempted to stimulate local health service improvement in poor and deprived urban centers. Four of the six cities in which the effort was made responded actively and enthusiastically with local energies to create and maintain neighborhood health activities. The services offered were not entirely curative, but also emphasized health promotion, family participation, and manpower development. The communities, even poor communities, can be stimulated to develop autochthonous health programs.

More important perhaps than the evidence of precedent, is the growing evidence of *need* for community participation to strengthen community services and reduce bureaucratic impersonality in the delivery of personal services. Decentralization that operates only to implant smaller bureaucracies, without local participation, is little more desirable or functional than larger bureaucracies. There is a growing realization of the people's need for cultural identity. This identity can find its expression in neighborhoods' racial, ethnic and religious groups, and language clusters' self-determination of community services. Who can better appreciate the kind and volume of service they need? In this kind of health system particularly, where so much depends on reaching parents and influencing the parent-child relationship, such community grouping is essential.

Members of private groups would be expected to pay a modest annual membership fee, but the budget (essentially similar throughout the United States because of standardized salary schedules for staff and formal description of services) would be met by contributions from the local child health department budget.

To ensure equality, each local child health department should have an elected child health board with responsibility for the collection of data and the disposition of funds. It would be the responsibility of this board to determine community groups' eligibility for budgetary assistance and staff qualifications. In case of disputes about service, staff, or funds, the board would also be responsible to act as a court of appeal.

Funds would be assigned from federal sources according to an agreed-upon formula that includes numbers of children under school-leaving age, numbers of births and rurality, using not state figures but local health area figures for this computation. States and local areas will be expected to match federal funds in accordance with this formula, and community groups seeking private operational status will have to pay a portion of the cost of operation through membership dues. Nevertheless, no person should be excluded from participation in a private community group for lack of funds.

The nurse focusing on children and family services must have a background and training consonant with this role. Prevention must be emphasized as a career, with nursing, midwifery, psychology, and pediatrics part of the background training. Also included should be training separate from hospital training—experience should include exposure to the schools and the courts. Career ladders must be available, based on performance as well as academic background. The job should have satisfying status and career goals.

Child health nurse training must include some education and experience in social work. Ideally, in the child health setting envisioned, a parallel social agency for family consultation, guidance, and follow-up is clearly indicated. However, until the welfare system is eliminated as such, so that determination of eligibility and investigation of cheating ceases to be social agency function, few agencies will have the resources to provide social services of this kind. When social workers can be staff members of family service agencies rather than of government control agencies, the parallel social agency envisioned will be closer to a reality, and the opportunities for real service will significantly increased.

CHILDREN'S HEALTH INSURANCE

Because of the current agitation for a national health insurance program and the multiplicity of legislative actions aimed at accomplishing this, it is not unlikely that a national health insurance program covering children (as a first step toward universal coverage) may emerge. The fact that the curative services needed by children are so far fewer and, therefore, so much cheaper than those needed by adults or the aged is a great incentive! In any case, a national program of paid curative services for children is essential if the preventive program is to be successful. A great deal can be done through an intensive, sharply focused preventive program such as the one already described. But it must be remembered that if case finding is not followed by treatment, parents will lose heart, becoming rebellious and frustrated, staff will lose interest, and the children themselves will not cooperate. And if the necessary procedures are not being carried out, follow-up will have no meaning. Economic barriers to medical care will only perpetuate the ineffectiveness of the status quo. In addition, the budgeting for the preventive services will suffer as more and more money is poured into the recognizably ineffective special curative programs for the poor. So long as prevention and care have to compete for funds out of the same pocket, preventive services will receive short shrift.

This curative service need not be so highly structured or too much different from the existing system, in the beginning. It is true that for long-range purposes, for improved service as well as cost control, America needs a completely reorganized medical care system, locally administered, with far fewer medical specialists, medical care institutions, and technological luxuries, and preferably staffed with salaried professional groups. But it would be criminal to wait for the arguments and experiments and social trials to be completed before undertaking a preventive health service for children. A curative insurance system for children, based on existing patterns, would be far from the most desirable eventuality. It would still provide imperfect access and imperfect quality while feeding cost inflation, but it is a necessary concomitant of a preventive service.

ADVOCACY

Mobilizing a constituency is essential for carrying out the program described and for maintaining the momentum necessary to ensure its survival and continuing beneficial operation. This cannot be left to chance or to some amalgamation of existing groups with broader interests. A formal group, with official status and sanction, needs to be created. The White House Conference groups, ad hoc, had no common thread of group representation or continuity.

Because of the importance of children's health to the future health of the nation, a national advisory conference on children should be established by Congress, funded, like the National Academy of Sciences, as a quasi-governmental, nonprofit organization. It is at this level that many of the practical policy problems of liaison with courts and social agencies; qualifications and training of professional personnel, and service content and effectiveness could be reviewed. The conference would be comprised of elected members from the local child health councils and state child health councils. The private, nonprofit child health groups would be encouraged to develop state-wide organizations and elect members of the conference as well. This conference would have an executive board that would act as the national advisory council on child health for the national child health service. Although Congress would be expected to provide minimal staff support, voluntary contributions and other child agency support would be solicited to allow the conference to hold regional meetings, support research and policy studies, and, in a sense, "supervise the supervisors."

This national conference group should also provide an official, or quasi-official, channel for the appointment and activity of ombudsmen for children. Official agencies engaged in providing services cannot be trusted to judge themselves and their actions. While self-inspections can catch bureaucratic misdemeanors or failures, the effectiveness of the services should be viewed from the outside as well. Complaints and grievances have to be monitored also. While every official agency should have a grievance channel, grievance procedures are not always sufficient. Court appeals are generally time consuming and expensive, and judges often legalistic rather than personally sensitive. A form of arbitration, personified by an ombudsman, might go far in achieving personally satisfying as well as professionally effective services.

Considering the torrent of books published in recent years on the *family*, the plight of the family, the disintegration of the family, the attacks on the family, and various other pessimistic analyses of the state of the family in the United States, a recommendation for a family effort on behalf of children may strike the reader as curious. For my part, while I recognize the baleful influence of social forces on the stability of the modern family, I do not share the view that the family is on the verge of collapse. Under stress, yes; disintegrating, no! Also, while the analysis derived from my own work might lead to the conclusion that the American family is hardly eager to carry out activities on behalf of children, again, that analysis does not portray a hopeless situation.

In my opinion, focusing on a helping approach to child care, offering the family a positive and useful role in child care, may be the very thing needed to strengthen and rejuvenate the family. One can argue that the weakening of the family tie is a result of lack of sufficient family role in child care and that the need is not so much finding ways to strengthen the family that will help children, as it is finding ways to help children that will strengthen the family.

This program offers a vehicle for support of the family through a focus on services for children.

GETTING OFF THE GROUND

With the best will in the world, selling this program and nursing it through public, legislative, and professional channels could well take a lifetime—by which time the proposal would probably have been superseded. It isn't sensible, or in the American grain, to undertake a huge national program, so opposite our traditional forms and structures, without any more evidence than the logic (if such it is) inherent in the arguments presented here.

The proposal needs a field trial.

With the help of Congress and the executive branch, one or more states could, with the use of waivers allowed by existing law, utilize funds from Title V and Title XIX of the Social Security Act, additional funds granted under Public Health Service legislative authorities for support of community health activities, other welfare funds, and perhaps some foundation support, and begin now to carry out a program along the lines described.

The personnel exist—pediatric nurses and child health nurses as well as physician assistants, pediatric associates, midwives, and interested and cooperative physicians. Hundreds of centers for preventive services for children now exist—the well-baby and pre-natal units of local health departments, the specially funded mater-nity and infancy and children and youth centers, OEO neighborhood health centers, and the successor neighborhood health centers and networks developed since OEO times. Hospital clinics must be avoided for several reasons. They are overly expensive to operate, sharing in the inflated overhead of the mismanaged hospitals as it is. They also tend to share the hospital ethos, serving the institution and medical education rather than the patient. Finally, they are disease and treatment oriented. Perhaps some assessment centers could benefit from hospital association, but not preventive units.

Private groups—church and fraternal organizations, boys and girls clubs, ethnic groups—all with family interest and concern, also exist in large numbers. Through a public education program they could be enlisted into nonprofit community child health center organizations.

The proposed trial by states could have important effects in addition to demonstrating the viability and feasibility of such a program. It may educate families in ways of preventive thinking. It may bring before the public more knowledge about vulnerable families, child abuse, and child neglect and what can be done about those problems. It may stimulate more knowledge about the values of different medical care insurance or service programs and bring the national debate on that issue into focus.

One profitable asset of this approach—the single or multi-state trial—will be the evidence it provides that a totally different approach to design, organization, and reimbursement can success-fully form a comprehensive health service. Many people have noted the hopelessness of trying to introduce national health insurance based on the presently structured medical practice form. And the equally hopeless possibility of radical change, with professions op-posed, leaves Congress reluctant and the people puzzled and unsure. So an experiment of this kind—a service focused on prevention, heavily staffed by nonphysicians, on a salaried base—may give pause to the planners. Maybe civilian control of the medical profession is no more unreasonable than civilian control of the military, and a salaried service for the medical professionals no more impossible to attain than a salaried hospital staff. The experiment, if successful, can prove salutary.

The opportunity is there, the funds and personnel are there, the program is there. The choice is ours.

Part II

Child Health in America

Chapter 7

Child Health in America

CONCERN FOR CHILDREN: AN AMERICAN DILEMMA

All is not well with America's children. We hear this more and more, and on all sides, from professionals and nonprofessionals, radical and conservative politicians alike, students of the matter. Of course the nature of that "non-wellness" is defined in different ways by different groups.

Psychologists, sociologists, pediatricians, and politicians have taken up arms against the mistreatment and neglect that they feel is typical of the child's fate in America today. Keniston, for the Carnegie Council on Children, writes in "Do Americans Really Like Children?" that for all our boasting about being a "child-centered, child-loving people," the facts do not bear this out. So much poverty is permitted to exist, and more children are likely to live in abject poverty than adults. Family life is threatened: "Divorce rates have risen more than 700 percent in the last half century ... proportion of children in single-parent families has increased astronom-ically . . . half the mothers of school age children work outside the home . . . ." He goes on to describe the inadequacies of the schools and the educational system. And he emphasizes the glaring dis-crepancy between our wealth, our resources, and our pitifully poor record in the health of children.[1]

Vice President Walter Mondale, then senator, told the Senate: "Our national myth is that we love children. Yet we are starving thousands. Other thousands die because decent medical care is unavailable to them. Forty-five percent of children born in U.S. hospitals do not receive prenatal care which could prevent some of the handicaps; 3.7 million handicapped children ... are not receiving the special educational services they require; 1.3 million children who need mental health services ... are not getting them; 1 million educable mentally retarded children who will never get the help they need ..." He names the victims of neglect: 1 million migrant children; 10 million Indian, Chicano, Puerto Rican, inner-city children; and 7 million handicapped children, nearly 5 million of whom are not receiving the help they need.[2]

There are others. Milton Senn, elder statesman of pediatrics and child care, writes in *Speaking Out for Children*, "... Americans ... know from firsthand experience ... that the inadequacies of contemporary society adversely affect the lives of most American children in one way or another, regardless of their economic or social status."[3]

Grotberg, in the introduction to *Two Hundred Years of Children*, a somewhat self-serving government document that puts the best possible construction on the status quo, especially as regards government efforts in child care and child health, writes, "Life in 1976 is still difficult for some children, particularly those children from families with low incomes and children from minority groups. These children have shorter lives, less education, less opportunity for advanced education or higher paying jobs. Another vulnerable group is the disabled, whether the disability is mental, physical, emotional or developmental."[4]

In a compilation, recently put together by the Office of Child Health for the secretary of HEW, the statistics are carefully laid out. Our maternal and infant mortality rates, despite laudable gains in recent years, are still lamentably high compared with other economically and technically advanced countries (We rank 16th in infant mortality worldwide.) The report lists the deficiencies attributable to poverty: higher infant and maternal mortality; smaller children; lower hemoglobin; more skin and intestinal diseases, greater infestation with worms. Lead poisoning and rat bites are more common among poor and minority children who also miss more days from school.

"Poverty" is an elastic state, with many definitions. In a document published by the Congressional Budget Office, weighted average poverty thresholds were calculated (by age of family head, whether the family head was male or female, number of children, and so on), and it appears that nearly 30 percent of the families in the United States are at or below the poverty level. However, in calculating benefits provided these families by one or another federal program—cash assistance, social insurance, food, and medical benefits—the agency calculates that fewer than 7 percent are actually below that federally determined poverty line. Nevertheless, there are others who argue that the Bureau of Census definition of "poverty" is artificial to start with, and sets much too low a standard, so that despite government benefits and considering inflation and food costs, a fairer statement of the degree of impoverishment in the United States would be 20 percent.[5]

Over 200,000 children with congenital handicaps and defects are known to be born each year. There are many more, of course, not discovered until later because we have little or no examination in many situations and for some social classes.[6]

Those who are not impressed by infant mortality data may possibly be more impressed by child suicide rates, exceptionally high in the United States,[7] or by the death rates of children under five.[8] Teenage pregnancy is increasing, endangering the life of mother and infant (the risk of infant mortality and maternal mortality is greater if the mother is very young.) Also, the biological immaturity may be accompanied by psychological immaturity, raising questions about the future of mother and child, even if both survive. Finally, the economic consequences—social dependency—are also heavy.

And there are some grim reminders of new developments in problems of young people: In 1974, over 12,000 cases of gonorrhea were *reported* in children under 15; there were 20,000 emergency room admissions for drug abuse in teenage children (some as young as 10).[9]

Table 7-1   Infant Mortality: United States 1975

All races	16.1
White	14.2
Other	24.2
Black	26.2

Source: National Center for Health Statistics, Health Resources Administration, U.S. P.H.S., Department of Health, Education and Welfare.

NEGLECT AND ABUSE

There are other new, or newly recognized, problems in child health. One gets a disturbing sense of this from the amount of violence perpetrated against children and the apathy of society toward this cruelty. In *The Battered Child*, Helfer and Kempe estimate about 75,000 cases and 2,200 deaths a year. Because of Americans' apathy and their tendency to condone parental crimes against children no one knows exactly how many battered children there are.[10] As Radbill points out in this same book, "Maltreatment of children has been justified for many centuries by the belief that severe physical punishment was necessary either to maintain discipline, to transfer educational ideas, to please certain gods, or to expel evil spirits."[11]

There is no "hard" data on the prevalence of this social disorder. Some professional observers question Fontana's contention that child abuse is the "leading cause of death of children under five." Others feel this is an *under*statement. In a March 12, 1976 letter to the *New York Times*, Eli Newberger, a family specialist at Harvard, makes the point that many more than the cases reported must occur, and cases reported grew from 8,000 in 1967 to over 100,000 in 1974! He points out how reluctant doctors are to regard, let alone report, childhood injuries as parent inflicted; how poor children only marginally in touch with the medical care system may escape professional observation of their injuries; the public's view of the failures of protective services, which makes them hesitant for fear of yielding the abused child to an even worse fate; as well as the general acceptance of the "right" of parents to "discipline" their children.[13]

Estimates of child abuse range (officially) from 200,000 to 4.8 million, some of which is hidden in the extraordinarily high rate of accidents among children. Accidents are the leading cause of death of children at all ages.[14] Other "new" problems include drug abuse; over 21,000 young people between the ages of 10 and 19 were seen in hospital emergency rooms for substance abuse in the year April 1974-April 1975.[15]

The Newbergers and Richmond also report extensively on the whole range of problems that affect children, as they see it, unnecessarily. "*While great strides have been made to decrease the incidence of organic disease phenomena, both mental illness and risks to children deriving from their physical and social environment have been largely ignored and seem to be increasing.*" (emphasis original)[16]

Malnutrition continues to be, in the United States, a serious problem for children. Since more than 20 percent of children live in families whose income falls below minimum standards, it is clear that there will be hunger and malnutrition among millions of them. Despite federal food programs, only a third of the poor children attending public school were in the school lunch program, and only a third of poor families participated in food stamp programs.[17]

The *U.S. Nutrition Survey* emphasized the failure of federal food programs.[18] Earlier bleak evidence can be found in *Hunger USA*[19] and in *Heal Yourself.*[20]

We know from earlier Selective Service data that many childhood health needs are not met, as the adolescents who appeared for their induction physical examinations were found to have untreated (and previously undiscovered) defects and handicapping conditions.[21] We know from state reporting that immunizations of children have been declining,[22] the visible impact of which is the occasional explosion of heretofore controlled epidemic childhood disease, such as the diphtheria epidemic in San Antonio, Texas in 1970.[23] In that epidemic, the poor and minorities suffered disproportionate effects, the disease being 12 times more prevalent among the poor and brown than among the well-to-do and white.

Special, more refined studies show a definite parallel between susceptibility and lack of care. Between 1965 and 1972, there was an increase in reported cases of diphtheria and measles, diseases preventable by immunizations. Hallstrom reports an inverse correlation between the rates of immunization at different income levels and the disease incidence rates.

Immunization by Income Level

Percent Immunized Against	Central City Children	Suburban Children	White	Nonwhite
Polio	68.6	83.3	82.3	68.6
Diphtheria	42.3	60.1	57.4	40.7
Measles	65.5	75.8	74.2	61.8

Source: Betty J. Hallstrom, "The Provision of Health Care to Children," mimeographed (Minneapolis: Minnesota Systems Research, Inc., 1972).

She also estimates that while one out of three school age poor children needed care for emotional problems, only 5 percent of those children received it.[24]

In "Health Care of Children and Youth in America" Arden Miller recites a litany of neglect of children's medical needs: "Five million of the nation's six million retarded are never reached by any service developed specifically to meet their needs;" and he writes further, "Three-fourths of the nation's retarded children are found in impoverished, rural and urban slums. A child from a low income family in these areas is 15 times more likely to be diagnosed as retarded than a child from a high income family."[25] It does not take too much thought to realize that in addition to failures of omission, there are failures in commission.

Miller emphasizes the patterns of discrimination that intensify the neglect and lack of care and thus add to the burden of illness, suffering, and early death among poor and minority children.

Disability due to illness or accident is 50 percent higher for the poor than for the non-poor ... tuberculosis, untreated middle ear infections, iron deficiency anemia, lead poisoning, malnutrition ... [so prevalent among the poor as to be termed "diseases of poverty"]

Between ages one and four a non-white child is three times more likely than a white child to die of influenza or pneumonia—and twice as likely to die an accidental death.

Infant deaths among Indians and Alaskan natives are nearly twice that for other races.

Only about one-third of migrant children have an immunization record, and only half of these records indicate adequate immunization. Among migrant children one in ten failed to pass a vision test and over one-half required dental work.

Among children 6 to 11 years of age, those from families with incomes under $3,000 per year average 3.5 carious teeth each; children from families with incomes over $15,000 average less than one carious tooth per child.

In the South, 15 percent of young adults 15 to 24 years of age have never seen a dentist.[25]

Lowe, distinguished pediatrician and government official, adds: "Nearly five million children under 15 have no source of medical care and nearly 40 million children under age 17 have not had a routine physical examination in the last two years."[27] In an earlier HEW document, "A Program Analysis of Maternal and Child Health Services," it was shown that poor and minority children suffer most from the failure of the medical care *system*, but all children benefit less from medical care than our present state of knowledge and capability should allow.[28] More recent data show little change in this situation.[29]

Children from high income families are more likely to see a pediatrician, receive well-baby checkups, get immunizations, and be born to mothers with adequate prenatal care.[30] Fewer doctors practice in poor and rural areas or in areas where minority groups are concentrated, and there are fewer medical resources there. Fewer poor families have health insurance with which to pay for medical care. Low-income people live farther from medical services and wait longer to see a physician.[31]

Medicaid may have closed the gap between use of physician services by rich and poor, but not for children. The equalization of use of ambulatory services by low- and high-income groups extends only to adults. Low-income children still use necessary medical services less.[32]

The value of children to a society may be reflected in the relative priority given expenditures for their care—public and private, and the various economic levels. If three million children known to have visual defects requiring correction by eye glasses do not have those eye glasses, that tells us something about family priorities, and perhaps public priorities as well.[33]

Of the $120 billion spent for personal health services in the United States in fiscal 1976, $18 billion was spent for children under 19. This was 15 percent of the money spent, for 33 percent of the population. On the other hand, $34.8 billion was spent for those over 65, 10.5 percent of the population. Granted, old people have greater needs for medical services, and for expensive medical services at that—hospital and nursing home care. Still, this is a wide discrepancy. The public share of these expenditures was $4.7 billion for the young and $23.6 billion for the old. The public accepted 68 percent of the cost of care for old people and only 26 percent of the cost of medical care for the young.[34]

It may be easier to establish actuarial insurance bases for hospital and specialist services, which old people use, and more difficult to establish effective reimbursement schemes for the office services most children use, but the result should be obvious. Whether because their families are poor, or because the locations in which they live cannot attract sufficient medical resources, or because the insurance scheme does not adequately cover the specific services they most need, children are deprived of medical care under any of the circumstances in which money makes a difference.

Preventive health services are particularly lacking for children. It should be clear that adults use preventive services much less than curative services. For children, illness is acute, and while frequent, rarely requires the armamentarium that adult disease requires. It certainly involves less in the way of expensive resources, such as hospitals and costly technological diagnostic and therapeutic instruments. For children, prevention is all. Yet there is no major American effort to develop a systematic approach and allocate specialized resources to this end. Epidemics of preventable disease occur, and immunization levels are nowhere near 100 percent. Again, to quote the Newbergers and Richmond, *"Where the means exist to ameliorate or eradicate health problems, such means do not equitably reach and serve the poor and non-white."* (emphasis original)[35] If there were really great social concern, one would think more of the cost would be met from public funds, given the relatively low cost of child care and the grave evidence of need, of sickness, and of premature death—particularly among poor children.

So the uncomfortable question is raised more and more frequently: "How is it that in a self-proclaimed child-oriented society, spending billions of dollars for child health services, including a very heavy investment of federal funds, child health is so poor?" We do not lack for explanations—or excuses. The commonest one is that the United States is the last industrialized Western country without a national health program. Another explanation is that child health services are lacking. There are great gaps in the distribution of our medical care resources. A whole literature has grown up on the maldistribution of medical care services, medical care manpower, and medical care financing. This maldistribution does have an especially baleful effect on children, affecting not only their current health, but also their future health and social usefulness. And since this disproportion of care and service availability falls most heavily on the poor, it will fall most heavily on poor children, and a disproportionate percentage of the poor are children.[36] As Ginzberg and Solon point out, "Prolonged neglect is costly. Most social problems do not fade away, they become more acute when neglected."[37]

It is difficult, reviewing the grim statistics, not to accuse Americans of lack of concern, of indifference to the needs of American children and the tragic consequences of neglect—not to pass judgment on the American people. But it is important to view "neglect" in the appropriate context. Most of us do have love and affection for our own children and do attempt to cherish and protect our own. We speak here of *national* neglect, not personal neglect. It is not my intention to accuse Americans of personal, *deliberate* neglect.

True, there are some observers who do. Arden Miller, paraphrasing a comment made to him some years ago by an older American pediatrician, writes, "We pretend to be a child-oriented society, but we neglect, abuse and exploit our children."[38] In a newspaper report of a conference on the quality of life held in Florida in 1975, even stronger statements were made. "The United States is a nation of people who worship being young, but (in many cases) hate kids ... or treat them as toys for adults." Dr. O. J. Keller of the American Correctional Association said, "Are we really a child-loving nation? I don't think so." He continued, "Look at child beating. Fifty thousand kids a year are killed by their own folks in this country—more than all the children who die from childhood diseases. And half of them are under four years of age." Dr. Fred Seligman, a psychiatrist at that meeting, added, "the quality of life of children takes low priority in our culture."[39]

Apparently, even outside the health field, those working with children sense that society has less than an amiable concern for troubled and sick children.[40] A lawyer with some experience in the juvenile court system writes, "Working on juvenile cases was like picking up a damp, flat rock and finding thousands of slimy, crawling things under it."[41]

Some idea of the magnitude of the problem with which we are dealing when we slip into such innocuous terminology as "child care needs" or "child health programs" can be outlined with a few figures. By age 11, 18 percent of all children tested have some visual defect, 21 percent have some orthopedic defect, 8 percent hearing difficulties, and 9 percent speech problems.[42] Lesser reports that the number of children with congenital heart defects increased from 2,200 in 1950 to 35,000 in 1969![43]

Oglesby, reporting on handicapped children, lists the following distribution of defects in 1970:[44]

5.5 million emotionally disturbed (under 18)
2 million mentally retarded (under 21)
10.5 million with eye problems (age 5-17)
2 million with orthopedic difficulties (under 18)
2 million with hearing defects (under 21)
400,000 with cerebral palsy (under 21)
400,000 with epilepsy (under 21)
2.5 million with speech defects (age 5-20)
100,000 with cleft palate (under age 10)
50,000 born each year with congenital heart disease

Schlesinger writes that 25 percent of all children attending school have some degree of visual impairment.[45] A follow-up study reported in the HEW Program Analysis implies that 5 percent, or almost 3 million of them, don't have the glasses required to correct those impairments.[45]

Where specific federal action has been undertaken to help correct some program deficiencies, as in Title I of the Elementary and Secondary Education Act (special grants to school districts for health services), very little has been accomplished in actual health services. Millions of dollars were spent, but little done to augment the missing health services.[47] As interested partners, the states do little for themselves when federal support is lacking.[48] In *Child Health and the Community*, Haggerty, Roghmann, and Pless note that "The well-baby care received by the indigent population in Rochester is poor compared to what is considered optimal."[49] And the situation doesn't improve with time. "The main finding from our comparison of the volume of child health services and the utilization rate per child per year is a trend toward decreasing utilization."[50]

The accumulation of facts and impressions raises the issue of whether the scandalous poor health and lack of effective health services for American children is systematic or accidental. "Neglect" implies the need for some positive action: to know what is needed to be done and then overtly fail to do it. Is that the case with America's neglect of children?

THE YALE HEALTH POLICY PROJECT

Puzzled by the apparent contradictions—a nation rich in resources, poor in performance; child-loving and child-neglecting; committed to social justice, yet treating its offspring unjustly—I sought illumination. Was there an invisible block to performance, a gap or defect somewhere, that if found and corrected would resolve the contradictions? Could we by a judicious move, a touch here or there, reduce the inequities, provide the services, eliminate the unnecessary sickness and suffering and early death?

The Yale Health Policy Project was established to review the steps along the way to see if a cause (or causes) could be found and, if found, corrected. Every step along the way would be examined: the public discussions, such as the White House conferences; the political discussions, such as the congressional hearings; the actions of Congress and in the executive branch; what happened between the federal government and the states when the money and the authority was passed on; and what happened in the states. We would try to find a key in the public thoughts, speeches, and acts.

The Federal/State Relationship

Speculation on the cause of the difficulties was not new. By and large—except that it should make more money available to create more programs and to carry out existing ones more effectively—the federal government was excluded as the culprit. If there was blame assessed, it usually was directed at the "bureaucrats," meaning officials at the state or local levels, who were felt not to be as competent as the federal officials.[51] Not everyone shares this view of the states' incompetence. But it is prevalent, among professionals and politicians alike. Attitudes and expectations regarding state government are deprecatory bordering on the contemptuous:

> The states vary enormously in the effectiveness of their executive and legislative branches. A mere handful are able to fulfill the wide-ranging responsibilities for domestic government that are inherent in the concept of federalism. The remainder require very serious measures to bring them up to a tolerable level of government functioning. To place increased power or money in their hands, without at the same time providing for drastic steps to raise their effectiveness, would be the worst kind of folly.[52]

> The shared relationship between levels of government does not seem to be working well. The infusion of federal monies into state and locally administered programs has not brought relief to urban problems—indeed, sometimes it seems to exacerbate them.[53]

An occasional writer does recognize associated difficulties, implying that there may be something more than state ineffectiveness at the root of the problem.

> ... it would better equip the states to hold up their end of the job, both in the broad sense of making them more effective units of government and in the narrow sense of enabling them to meet the matching requirements of the functional grants. In other words, minimum-strings assistance to the states would serve, not thwart, the national purpose.[54]

But the assumption of inadequacy remains.

No one really questioned that the *system*—or lack of it—was critical. It was thought that a national health insurance program, by improving the ability to pay for medical services for children, would be the answer. Or perhaps more money for specialized programs to reach the special-risk children would do the trick. Most explanations assume that the United States as a nation *is* concerned about child health and aims to make and keep the children of the country healthy, but is frustrated either by cost, incompetence, or confusion. A few more dollars, a little straightening of the sails, and our goals would be in sight.

At the time the study was begun, in 1972, the time was ripe for review. The federal/state relationship was at the top of the agenda; block grants and revenue sharing were being discussed extensively, and there was even legislation aimed at strengthening state efforts. In the area of child health, there was an amendment to the Social Security Act[55] and there was the Revenue Sharing Act.[56] If worthwhile federal efforts were usually frustrated at the state level, this would be a good time to find out, and child health was an excellent vehicle for that discovery.

It would be interesting to find out if the states were really the inert, incompetent masses so many people believed them to be, immovable except by federal initiatives. Some studies on the federal/state relationship did exist; welfare had been looked at,[57] the poverty program,[58] and Medicaid.[59] But comprehensive analyses of child health services, aside from inventories, were scarce.[60]

In short, over a four-year period, the background and operations of federal child health programs as they were delegated to the states were examined in documents and interviews. An investigation of exactly how and how well the programs cared for children was not undertaken, involving, as that would, recourse to specific health records, results of physical examination of children, and clinical materials that could very well overwhelm a policy study. Such program investigations would be useful, though, and may very well need to be carried out in the future. But for our purposes, the discovery of how the machinery worked right up to the care of the child was our field of examination.

The findings are of some interest, because they underline the steps that have to be taken if an effective, comprehensive child health program is to be developed for American children. It does not seem worthwhile to list all the techniques and methods employed in obtaining information and collecting data. The interested reader may write to the Yale Health Policy Project and obtain a copy of the final report, *Politics and Social Policy: Failure in Child Health Services.*[61]

Federal Child Health Programs

First, a little background on federal child health programs is necessary. It is only in the 20th century that the federal government began to concern itself with domestic welfare in any serious way. The establishment of the Children's Bureau dates from 1912 and grew out of concern about the ill effects of child labor. Its establishment was the result of a series of agitations and was assisted by President Theodore Roosevelt's calling a White House Conference on Children three years earlier in 1909. In those days, opposition to federal "interference" in the sacred family relationship, or to intervening between parent and child, was strong, so that in 1921, the first federal legislative effort to promote child health ran into a storm of controversy. A bill was finally passed, but it was a modest one. The Sheppard-Towner Act provided relatively small sums to the states who agreed to participate in a program to improve the health of mothers and children. It lasted only until 1928, and some states never did participate in the program.

With the passage of the Social Security Act in 1935, an important precedent of federal grants to the states for health services was established, and Title V of that act became the mainspring of philosophic and financial support in the federal underpinning for child health services. Since then, other federal programs supporting child health services—general programs such as Medicaid and categorical programs such as immunization programs—have passed the Congress and been added to the books.

To review federal health programs for children properly would require attention to a very large number of government health and health-related programs.[62] Because of the multiplicity of federal programs, an examination of federal health policy in other than the child field might have been difficult, if not impossible. Ruth Roemer and her colleagues subtitled their study *From Jungle to System* for that very reason.[63]

Aside from Title V and Title XIX of the Social Security Act, the programs are relatively small. These two programs of themselves amounted to nearly $3 billion in federal funds in FY 1977. Substantial numbers of people are involved in the spending of this money at all the levels of government and in the private sector.[64] Title V of the Social Security Act provides for formula grants to the states for promoting the health of mothers and children and for identifying and treating crippled children, especially in rural areas or other areas suffering from economic distress. Since 1935, other items have been added: research, training, and service project grants to institutions or agencies, grants that bypass the states. Title XIX of the Social Security Act (Medicaid) became law in 1965 and provides for federal financial assistance to the states according to a sliding scale of reimbursement, varying with a formula based on the state's income level.

The opening paragraph of the child health title of the Social Security Act (Title V) reads, "For the purpose of enabling each State to extend and improve, as far as practicable under the conditions in each State, services for promoting the health of mothers and children . . . ." A great principle and a noble intention. How does one go about it? Many scholars have devoted themselves to analysis of the mechanisms whereby policies are born, of how the various competing interests compromise their needs and wishes so as eventually to produce a law. Few scholars have devoted themselves to an analysis of what happens after a law is passed.[65] There have been fairly narrow studies, although in considerable depth, by Wildavsky and some of his students, in which the findings are a bit surprising (counter to the accepted belief) and wryly and pungently described.

> Divorced from problems of implementation, federal bureau heads, leaders of international agencies and prime ministers in poor countries think great thoughts together. But they have trouble imagining the sequence of events that will bring their ideas to fruition. Other men, they believe, will tread the path once they have so brightly lit the way. Few officials down below where the action is feel able to ask whether there is more than a rhetorical connection between the word and the deed.[66]

Here there is a suggestion that perhaps the static world of "federal policy," in which failure is "state incompetence," might be worth investigating for a new, more dynamic explanation. Perhaps what should be questioned is the clarity or viability of the federal policy itself.

Connecticut and Vermont: Case Studies

The academic process by which the staff of the Yale Health Policy Project collected information and analyzed the material deserves note only in that everyone in the field was extraordinarily cooperative. This is said in advance of the critical comments that will have to be made on the lack of data and important kinds of information that should be offered. The information came from the two states studied intensively, Connecticut and Vermont. The health commissioners, welfare commissioners, and all other officials with whom we dealt were agreeable and helpful. The problem is that much of the data that would be useful in establishing exactly what was done and how are not customarily collected. So the first conclusion we came to was that to determine the effectiveness of the programs, more and different kinds of information would have to be collected— not for investigators such as our team, but for the operating agencies, so that they will know what they should do and whether they have done it. For the most part, such data does not now exist.

The two states, Connecticut and Vermont, differ considerably, despite a common political heritage. Both are small, but Connecticut's population is 3 million as compared to Vermont's 400,000.

Connecticut is wealthy (highest per capita income in the United States), Vermont is poor. Connecticut is urban and industrial, Vermont rural and agricultural. Vermont is sparsely populated, Connecticut densely. Vermont is predominantly Republican and has a tradition of a strong legislature and a weak governor. Connecticut on the other hand, is politically independent, and characteristically has a strong governor and a weak legislature.

Vermont spends more money proportionately for the general welfare despite its relative poverty. But in health resources, doctors, hospital beds, and the like, the two states are quite similar. Both states spend about the same for Medicaid, although Vermont receives more federal matching toward its expenditures (83 percent to Vermont, 50 percent to Connecticut). Since both states incorporate the federal money into state revenues and then "appropriate" a total budget, average expenditure is therefore that total, which means that Vermont actually spends proportionately less state money for Medicaid than Connecticut.

In recent years, Vermont has attracted large numbers of young people seeking "nonestablishment" lifestyles, people who find the atmosphere of Yankee agricultural independence congenial. There is, probably in consequence, a very strong consumer movement in Vermont, and the Vermont Public Interest Group has exerted important pressures for social legislation. Connecticut has not shown comparably strong consumer activity.

Infant mortality in both states was slightly lower than the national average. The decline in infant mortality in Connecticut began earlier and continues more precipitately than in the United States as a whole.[67] This decline is statewide and bears no relation to Title V programs, since the decline is not limited to areas such as Hartford or New Haven, where the heavily (federally) subsidized maternity and infancy care and children and youth programs (projects under Title V) exist. It is true, however, that where there is a higher-than-average infant mortality rate within a state subdivision, there is associated poverty.

The review showed that insufficient federal support could not be used as an explanation for the states' failures to carry out effective child health programs. It was clear that the states were making little systematic effort to reach every child. There was no evidence that the states tried to or wanted to collect information that would identify the areas and children in need of services, and no evidence that the states knew what children were being served and whether they were those most in need of services. Finally, there were no clear programs aimed at meeting children's needs.

Following up on that, it was clear that the federal government itself made no systematic effort to compel or cajole the states into identifying the needy areas of children. In fact, it made little effort to find out what the states were doing and whether the programs actually met the federal specifications. The report forms didn't even ask the kinds of questions that would have produced useful answers.

Looking back over the history of the federal/state relationship, it is easy to see how the United States could have reached this stage 40 years after passage of the act that was aimed at "promoting the health of mothers and children." The state failures to carry out the federal intention were not accidental. But they were not planned to fail either. It is simply that the entire structure was not geared to succeed. No goal was set, therefore, no measure of success was possible. In the process, every conceivable obstacle to effective performance that could be put in the way, was put in the way. This complex federal/state system was a perfect candidate to fall victim to Murphy's Law: "If anything can go wrong during an experiment, it will go wrong." And its corollary: "If there is some particular element whose function is critical, that element will fail."

To summarize the analysis and findings in the four-year study of the operation of child health policies in Connecticut and Vermont will help underline the limitations of the present system of child health services and programs, from the top (federal government responsibilities) to the bottom (local provision of such services). Granted, these two states may not be representative of the United States as a whole and, because of their history, will be organized differently from the southern states and certainly differently from the relative newcomers, the western states. Still, the functional approach and, therefore, the systemic lack of effectiveness will not be much different. Every state in the Union depends upon the federal Social Security programs, Title V and XIX, to provide the basic funding for the major child health efforts. All the states have to match these funds in order to obtain them. The rules of the game provide that a certain state structure is required to make the state eligible for federal funding. It is unlikely then that there will be very much difference in the structure of the various states' child health systems. The general conclusions drawn from the evidence of policy ineffectiveness or failure in the two states studied should be applicable to all the states. Accomplishments may vary, in accordance with the wealth of the state or, more surely, in accordance with its contribution beyond the required federal matching. Perhaps some states have achieved more by virtue of better state management and control. But the differences will be of degree; the basic flaws remain.

We might group the results into problems related to policies at the federal level and those related to policies at the state level. Beginning with the federal level, one might start immediately with the law's definition of purpose and its ambiguities: "promotion of the health of mothers and children." What constitutes "promotion"? Does "mothers and children" mean *all* mothers and children? To what age is one still a child? In the "crippled children" section, what are the crippling conditions for which the program should be responsible? All of them? What is a "crippling condition"? And if there isn't enough money in the federal grant or in the combined grants of the federal and state governments, what shall be the priorities of the organization set up to "promote the health of mothers and chidlren" and to take care of the "crippling conditions"?

Some History

There is some historical basis for the ambiguity. Concern for child health received national prominence with the first White House Conference on Children in 1909. These have been held every ten years since, the last in 1970. These conferences have tended to make vigorous statements, the gist of which is repeated every ten years. Unfortunately, this leads to the suspicion that not much was accomplished in the years between. While the statements are bold, legislative follow-up is weak or nonexistent.

Child health legislation passed in 1935 as part of the Social Security Act is often pointed to as an example of social concern and federal involvement in child health services—proof that we are a child-oriented society. The inclusion of this legislation (Title V) was the result of tremendous behind-the-scenes intrigues and lobbying, numerous efforts to forestall a national health insurance title, intense professional antagonisms, and considerable political maneuvering—hardly solicitude for the health of children! Some of the story is told in Witte's memoir on the origins of the Social Security Act,[68] and

some in Hirshfield's account of the battle for national health insurance at that time.[69] It is clear that concern for child health was not
the major reason for the inclusion of a child health title.[70]

After Congress passes a law, often deliberately ambiguous, the
federal agency charged with carrying out the law is supposed to
write specific regulations that spell out the intentions of the Congress
in sufficient detail so that the states can understand and comply, and
Congress will agree that this is what they meant. Ambiguity in the
congressional language may be necessary to assure applicability of
the law in 53 jurisdictions (50 states, the District of Columbia, Puerto
Rico, and the Virgin Islands). Definitions may have to be stretched
to fit, and qualifications tailored to the needs and capabilities of the
various jurisdictions. But when the regulations were written (two
years after passage of the act), they were mysteriously almost as
vague as the law itself. Age, for example, was not defined, and states
adopted their own definitions of the age at which a child became an
adult. The state definitions eventually became federal definition. As
to who should be eligible, or what a crippling illness is, the federal
regulations still do not say.

In a word, states were left to do what they had been doing, only
now with some federal money to replace their own expenditures. The
regulations' lack of clarity made it possible to circumvent the so-
called "maintenance of effort" clause, which charged states to use the
federal money only on top of what was already being spent. There
was also little constraint on what sorts of new programs states could
develop or how they could develop them. This was not exactly a blank
check perhaps, but far from federal control and standards. For
example, federal regulations required that the states submit a state
plan in order to qualify for funding. Most states did not file a plan
until much later. More often than not, the plan, when filed, was as
vague as the regulations. Connecticut's plan, for example, still does
not spell out eligibility. Of course, it isn't only in the area of child
health that states act as independent and distinct entities. Connecticut was not exactly stampeded into meeting federal requirements in other matters either. The Bill of Rights wasn't ratified in
Connecticut until 1939.

There is more than a suspicion that the result was not altogether
unanticipated or undesired. In the late 1920s and early 1930s, when
the battles for health insurance, social security, and a child health
program were being fought out, a professional struggle to define

"public health" was going on. That contest to define "public health" was very important in eventually deciding the content of child health services. The argument centered around the need for establishing effective structures to carry out public health activities (The sanitary revolution was not yet considered over!). Haven Emerson, physician, public health philosopher, and teacher at Columbia University, was pitted against Charles-Edward Amory Winslow, New England Brahmin, epidemiologist, and public health statesman ensconced at Yale. Emerson took the narrower view of public health, as a responsibility for the care of masses of people only; private medical care matters belonged to the physician and the medical societies and were none of the concern of public health. Building strong local health units on this base was, in his view, the essential public health function.[71] Winslow, on the other hand, saw all of health, including medical care, as the public health area, and had already espoused compulsory national health insurance as a public health goal.[72] (In this case, the Brahmin was a bit of a populist.) In the struggle for definition and decision in the public health movement, the Emerson forces eventually won the day.[73]

Winslow's approach to public health was essentially the alternative we view more sympathetically today—the "systems approach," through comprehensive care, neighborhood health centers, and the merging of preventive and curative services. During the struggle, a New York state health officer, Hermann Biggs, provided a "political" face to the Winslow position by introducing (unsuccessfully) a comprehensive health care bill into the New York state legislature.[74]

It appears, then, that the idea uppermost in the minds of the framers of the child health section of the Social Security Act, and in the minds of those who were to carry it out at both the federal and state levels, was *to build health departments*. With a health department structure in place, then child health services could be delivered. So building the structure was the first order of the day. The regulations were written to facilitate this. And building state health departments has taken place. The law, by that definition, seen in that perspective, has not been a failure. It has been a great success. It is only that a great many other factors have supervened, interrupting the steady flow of the process and making the final product, child health services, still a distant hope.[75]

The states have used the money provided through Title V to structure health departments along classic lines adopted from the winner of the definition contest, Haven Emerson: narrow, not related to comprehensive health services, and program oriented rather than child oriented. Of course, hindsight may not offer the same view the best-intentioned public health workers of that time had. An effective structural base for public health work in the United States *was* lacking. True, the child health legislation now on the books was passed as a sop to the militant proponents of national health insurance in 1935, when that issue was laid to rest.

So the maternal and child program was neither a breathless crusade by federal policy makers to relieve shortages of health services nor naive in its limited funding levels. The hardest policy issue dilemma for the Committee on Economic Security had already been solved when the Roosevelt administration realized that compulsory health insurance was not politically feasible. The health programs in the Social Security Act were a far more restricted, series of alternatives.

The intent of Title V, then and for future interpretations, was not aimed at helping children *directly*, but at building public health services, so sadly lacking in the country, and to build them on the Emersonian design, which might eventually help children, but *indirectly*. Not child health services, but community health education and preventive medical services—with a good system of data collection and capacity for analysis—was the goal.

Shortcomings in the Federal Role

It is only by current standards and expectations that the program may be judged a failure. And a qualifying "modest" may be added, because federal appropriations never did measure up to the needs, even as originally defined, leaving a fiscal deficit that made full accomplishment unattainable. True, the states may be faulted for not having added the measure of funds to make up the difference and even for having used federal funds as a substitute rather than a supplement. But then, perhaps that, too, was part of the hidden intent that the federal contributions should eventually make up the bulk of public health funds.

Inflation and annual salary increments also took their toll, as did increasing demands on health departments for other than service programs—consultation, licensure, inspection, and the like—without a corresponding increase in funds for personnel. Under such circumstances, the state should not be faulted for acting in accordance with the latent intent of the law, even if that intent is not in accordance with obvious current concerns.

If building health departments was the real motive for Title V, Title V must be acounted a success. It built state health departments, and it is still building them. Even today, it appears that a large part of the money that comes into Connecticut from the federal government designed to provide preventive services for infants and pregnant women, goes to maintain the personnel of the Connecticut State Health Department in Hartford. At that, in constant dollars, the health budget for children has increased only four times, while the budget for the rest of the health items has increased 20 or more times since 1935. This is done with the full knowledge and consent of the federal government and the regional representatives that monitor the expenditures. The funds are being used—legitimately, as perceived—to accomplish the implied purpose of child health legislation: to build and strengthen state health departments.

A long-time federal official and honored pediatrician charged with development and supervision of child health programs in the United States, in commenting on the draft of the report on Connecticut, wrote, somewhat somewhat indignantly, "Federal law and regulations do not say that the primary purpose of the money is for direct services. There is no basis in federal policy that would lead one to use numbers of children served (out of total need) as a measure of program effectiveness."[76]

To sum up, history dictated that states would be free to define the use of the federal money made available through the Child Health Title of the Social Security Act, and history also dictated the terms of that definition. Federal legislators, who are really state representatives in the national arena, as a rule not only consent to, but demand that kind of freedom in legislation. Delicacy and ambiguity in legislative language is desired, not avoided. What is sometimes described as "incompetence" at the state level may be the result of carefully orchestrated pluralism at work at the federal level.

Given this approach, the federal/state relationship can be seen more as a series of subtle interactions, constantly adjusted and modified as the legislative intent becomes more visible in official actions. The quality of the personnel at federal and state levels is not necessarily much different, and the contemptuous belief that the quality deteriorates as you go further down the bureaucratic line is not necessarily valid. The character of the bureaucracy, therefore, may not be different at the different levels either. There may be another explanation for what is interpreted as bumbling, in-effectiveness, and bureaucracy: that behind the high-sounding phrases of the federal legislation may be a "gentleman's agreement," a shared understanding of the real goal. The role of the Congress is not necessarily to lead, nor to drive the states, but to prepare *acceptable* legislation so as to meet states' needs, and incidentally, to get Congressional representatives re-elected.

Before making a judgment on the quality of program management, therefore, one ought to be certain that the aim of the legislation as initiated was what we today consider it to be. There is a question as to whether the ambiguity of the regulatory language was or was not deliberate. It is quite likely that the framers thought that "child health improvement" would be more attractive to the Congress and the people than the bland and bureaucratic term "strengthen local health departments." Of course, they also may have felt that strengthening local health departments was bound to lead to improved child health. The point is, that to evaluate the impact from the standpoint of what the "congressional intent" was in 1935 is difficult and perhaps impossible. It is likely though, that the phrase, "improving child health" didn't really mean finding out how many kids were in need of care and then seeing to it that they got it.

One aspect of the federal role that is frequently overlooked is that of the regional offices. All the cabinet offices (departments) have been "decentralized" to some degree since the 1930s. The "decentralized" is in quotation marks because as the initiated know, the regions are hardly powerful enough to be centers of power. To some observers, the regions are populated with "remittance men," exiles in positions of presumed authority who are kept out of the real center—Washington—and supported by the patronage of local political appointees.

In a magazine article aptly entitled "Sisyphus in Chicago," Douglas Bauer writes about bureaucratic reaction in the regional office of the HEW there. He quotes the second in command: "I very rarely look at the [federal] regulations. Once in a while, if I really don't want to do something, I'll say, 'Find me something in the regs that makes it impossible for me to do this.' "

In addition to this bold declaration of independence from federal control, the bureaucrat quoted emphasizes that maintaining the size of his empire is his major concern and that any effort to deploy funds toward services and away from employing aides is resisted, even to the point of a newspaper attack on the local congressman.[77]

It is this kind of arithmetic in the regional offices that diverts federal expenditures from services to management of the structures theoretically devoted to providing services.

The regions could be useful resources for decentralization. Decentralization is a powerful tool for reducing bureaucratic neglect because it places the program controllers and the people it affects closer together. The danger, however, is two-fold. First, regions can and do become the state's voice in Washington rather than the federal voice in the states. It is inevitable for regional offices to represent the states and be their advocates in Washington, rather than attempt to be the Washington advocate in state capitals. Representatives and senators who receive a message from "back home" about uncompromising or ununderstanding HEW officials in the regional office are bound to have an influence on the views of the secretary of HEW. A regional officer will learn quickly that promotion and advancement follow friendly cooperative relationships with the states and that exile and demotion are the fruits of conflict. One important purpose of national programs is to bring national standards to otherwise backward or reluctant areas. So long as the regions can be manipulated in this way, by Representatives and Senators, either directly or through the governor, the regions will be more responsive to local than to federal pressures.

The second danger is an opposite one. Without an elective base, regions can become dictatorial and completely unresponsive to local needs. There is little use in a regional decentralized activity that does not report back the failures or need for flexibility discovered in the process of fulfilling a federal mandate.

Perhaps, if decentralization is to be the wave of the future, more thought should be given to using our oldest and already time-tested (even if often the test has been failed) regional apparatus—the state. It may be more difficult in the long run to establish smoothly running, democratic regions than to modify state behavior so as to accomplish that end.

STATE ACTIONS AND CHILD HEALTH

Federal laws are written by Congress and implemented by state executive bodies whose contact is with the federal executive bodies and not the Congress. State legislatures learn about what the federal law is from publications and interpretations put upon those publications by the state executive bodies—the governor and his cabinet officers. In many instances, the state has to pass conforming legislation or react to the federal legislation by, for example, appropriating matching funds. Yet state legislatures are completely dependent upon the executive branch of the state government for information and direction.

Committees of the legislature generally have no staff. The legislators are poorly paid, meet infrequently, and have to pay attention to other business matters to get ahead economically and even politically. If there is hostility between the executive and legislative branches, or if each is under different political party control, the adversary relationship will obstruct complementary legislation or funds. Even when the governor and the state legislative body are of the same party, the lack of staff and liaison may cripple compliance.

Legislatures are most sensitive to tax increases and seek to avoid heavy cost responsibilities. Since the federal government will match Medicaid costs, for example, it is considered wiser to obligate the heaviest costs to the federal net. For that reason, and others, children tend to be the least likely to benefit from Medicaid because the program priorities favor heavier institutional costs rather than doctor's office costs, and so nursing homes and hospitals soak up the bulk of Medicaid expenditures. The deprivation affects more children in "medically needy" families—the working poor—as opposed to children in families receiving cash assistance.

Overall, the Connecticut state legislature has not concerned itself very much with matters relating to child health. Only 3.6 percent of the bills offered since 1967 have concerned health as such (omitting financing bills for hospitals and doctors), and only a third of these—about one percent of the legislative load—referred to children. In Vermont, the number of health-related bills was three times greater, and even included issues of environmental health. Yet only ten percent of the 10,904 bills proposed dealt with health and welfare, and of those, only 332 pertained to children. Vermont legislators were more likely to consider measures that would apply to all children, probably because Vermont, a poorer state, had a much greater number of poor children and could blanket in all children without much difficulty or added expense.

Legislative function in the state legislatures are pale copies of congressional actions. Part-time legislators and little staff make for economy of action. "Bills" hardly more than a few sentences of proposals are in the clerk's hands as the session opens. Hearings are uncommon. Little effort is made to involve the experience of citizens or academic community members in review of the bills.

In Connecticut, as in other long-settled parts of the eastern seaboard, the county system of government has waned. Counties no longer exist as administrative structures, and public health is solely a town responsibility. In looking over the official town health structure, there is obvious unevenness in the distribution of talent. Equally obvious is the ability of the better trained and qualified health officers, where there are such, to obtain outside funds (generally from the federal government) through successful grant applications. The state legislature knows nothing of this and does nothing to help equalize the resulting disparities among towns.

Neither the state planning body nor the area planning agencies have collected information about child health needs or specific aspects of maldistribution of resources for child health services. The health department's own records are inadequate to provide data on this subject or even data on the type and distribution of services, or what classes and categories of children receive the services.

More functions have been added to the state health department, but without sufficient financial support. The lack of information intensifies the weakness of the department and its inability to establish priorities for action. Lack of field nurses and other professionals prevents adequate follow-up on cases found in clinics or schools. Poor communities are not encouraged to do more since the state also imposes a matching requirement for the state funds passed on from federal funds for the poor. So those who most need aid are least likely to obtain it.

Despite strong immunization efforts, actually the most emphasized state child health program, immunizations lag. Connecticut's measles rate is one of the highest in the northeast and in the country. Vermont does a better job on immunizations, no doubt because of its more generalized child health program. However, because Vermont collects more information, it is also easier to recognize the declining volume of services provided by the Vermont Health Department over the past 20 years. Although the child population of the state had grown from approximately 150,000 to 180,000 between 1955 and 1970, for example, state maternal and child health programs served 34,000 in 1956 and 23,000 in 1970, a fall from 22 percent of the eligible population to 12 percent. In both states, despite the fact that public programs provide the only access to many types of health service for some children—those whose needs are greater than their parents can afford to pay for, or more complex than the existing local programs can provide—the maternal and child health programs are reaching decreasing numbers of children.

The decline in crippled children's services has been attributed to the fact that increasing numbers have been cared for under Medicaid since 1966. However, the decline started before that. There is no way to prove this from the Medicaid data, since the record keeping on Medicaid data is insufficient to indicate the family economic situation and eligibility for crippled childrens' services cannot be elicited. Therefore, there is no way to determine exactly how many crippled children the Medicaid program actually serves.

Over time, state-funded well-child conferences have declined to pre-Social Security days. Connecticut had initiated "well-child conferences" in 1923, dental hygiene programs in 1924, summer "round-ups" (preschool physical examinations), and May Day health programs in 1926.[78] Many of the well-child clinics today are entirely dependent on local financing. This puts poor communities, where the need is greatest, at a particular disadvantage, since state aid has declined.

The extensiveness of school health services is difficult to verify because there is no state-mandated supervision by any authority; local communities are expected to provide school health services. Interviews showed little in the way of examination, case finding of defects, follow-up, immunizations, or comprehensive programs of any kind.

Immunization data are misleading. For the health department to report that, say, 76 percent of the children reaching their sixth year are immunized against various diseases, is of little value. Measles or diphtheria strike in children's first, second, or third years, when the immunization rates may be as low as 25 percent. The rate rises to the level it does at age six because of the pressures put on the parents when they must report immunizations on school admission forms.

A variety of bureaucratic traps ensnare child health as well as services. The multiplicity of programs emanating from Congress

since around 1967 has intensified bureaucratic difficulties in administration. Old programs never die. They are superseded, but remain as
enclaves. When programs are controlled by two different agencies of
state government, for example, welfare and health, the task is
impossible. Not only the territorial imperatives of the officials, but
rival professional concepts clash.

Because the traditional public health dogma of absolute separation of preventive and curative medicine was so widely accepted, the
welfare departments assumed control of payment for curative functions and medical care programs. The division of responsibility is
different at federal and at state levels. Welfare and health funds are
both under the control of the secretary of Health, Education, and
Welfare at the federal level, but in separate departments at the state
level. Health and welfare bureaucrats struggle over policy decisions
at the federal level. Worst of all, the feuds originated above are
continued below. Congress blandly disregards this. "A single state
agency" is prescribed in most programs.

Sometimes Congress assigns responsibility to two agencies. In
assigning responsibility for the program aimed at finding and
treating handicaps in poor children (early and periodic screening,
diagnosis, and treatment, familiarly known as EPSDT), Congress
generously provided two conforming amendments, leaving it to the
federal, and eventually to the state, bureaucracies to fight out.[79]

In short, it seems that a pattern of tentative, inadequate child
health services was inevitable. The federal legislation is intentionally
ambiguous to provide the widest latitude for states to comply.
Executive agency directives are equally ambiguous. The staffs of the
HEW regional offices interpret guidelines and supervise compliance
with great flexibility. And if this were not enough to render
effective performance in "promotion of the health of mothers and
children" an impossibility, added financing and budgeting intrigues
within the state bureaucracy ensure failure.

It would be fair to assume then that "federal" programs become
"state" programs very rapidly in those instances where preexisting
state programs were already on the books, so that federal leadership
is essentially a matter of providing funds, not policy. We found that
expenditures for health in Connecticut were unaffected by the flow of
federal dollars. The percentage of state funds devoted to health
purposes declined despite increased federal contributions. Because
federal funds are incorporated into state treasuries along with other

contributions, and the state then establishes its own budget, federal funds within the expenditure budget are not easily identified. Finance officers have become masters in the art of circumventing federal intentions by using federal funds as substitute for, rather than supplement to, state funds.

Vermont and Connecticut started on different footings in 1935 when the first federal funds came through in the Title V program. Both had had child health programs long before that—Vermont in 1914 and Connecticut in 1919. Because the original health activities were the result of a polio scare, crippled children programs were the earliest of the state measures in the field. Vermont has maintained strong services in this area ever since. But in both states, attention to "soft" areas, well-baby and prenatal care, declined as federal money became more abundant. It is difficult to retrace the exact steps by which the retreat was undertaken, but the evidence is in the annual reports. Increased attention to nonservice responsibilities certainly played a part; increased costs of surgical and rehabilitative procedures for handicapped children must have been a factor as well.

Connecticut is much the wealthier state, but the percent of the state budget devoted to health services and the average expenditures for poor children are less than in Vermont. In both states, "health" is considered more remedial than preventive. Vermont got better cooperation from physicians than Connecticut did—all of Vermont's pediatricians participated in the Medicaid program, only 38 percent of Connecticut pediatricians did.

OVERVIEW

Standing off a bit to consider the actuality and consequences of the major national effort to look after children's health, the two titles of the Social Security Act, it is evident that the laws are not working to the desired end. There are complex and interesting forces at work, even beyond those mentioned, that influence (usually unfavorably) all kinds of federal programs, child health programs not excepted. The flow of funds to the states generally is regulated by formulas that almost invite failure. If more money is put into Medicaid programs in the hope of attracting physicians and other medical resources to underserved areas, the effect also is to assure that more money will flow into places where there is a heavy concentration of resources, even though there may be fewer poor people there. Tightening the budget doesn't move those already in place in the heavily doctored areas, but it does discourage movement into the under-doctored areas.

In the American political tradition, political action is the result of forces projected by competing interest groups. The nation is seen as clusters of small interest groups, each a minority, so to speak, who achieve their ends by aligning themselves with enough other minority groups to become a majority. In the process, some of their demands are reduced, others are met; laws get passed or appropriations made. It is the economist's "optimizing" as opposed to "maximizing" gains. But children have no interest group. It is said that parents are the children's interest group, but parents are busy with their other minority clusters—racial, religious, or ethnic, labor or capital, urban or rural, hawk or dove. Professional interest groups rarely intervene in the political process except for their own economic or professional interest. Doctors lobbied for or against insurance measures, pay scales under Medicaid, and representation by medical societies or Blue Shield, but they didn't need to demand or lobby for control of medical affairs in the state.

In Connecticut, for example, lobbying by the state medical society is unnecessary because over the years the society has become the controlling element in the committees that make the decisions. It is no longer necessary to buttonhole state legislators. The location of prenatal clinics, standards and fees, the selection of the participating physicians, the preparation of the state plans—all were cleared with medical society officials through formalized arrangements. (In fact, until 1973, the health commissioner had always been selected from a list of names approved by the Connecticut State Medical Society.) The Connecticut State Medical Society was permitted to regulate the availability of physicians for well-child conferences, and standards and regulations for well-child conferences were drawn up and approved by the Public Health Committee of the Connecticut State Medical Society.

Consumer groups that might influence legislation tend to belong to the Disease of the Month Club and lobby enthusiastically for funds to set up competing organizations to fight one or another disease, apparently without recognizing the cost-effectiveness of a comprehensive system of child care. Such a system could be geared toward prevention of, treatment of, and even research into, the whole range of these diseases. The power of interest groups, not only to obtain their own limited objectives, but, in so doing, also to distort and frustrate the whole medical care system, is the subject of an interesting book by R. R. Alford entitled *Health Care Politics.*[80]

Federal Grants-in-Aid ($) per Poor Person, FY 1970

	Title V Total	Total Health Excluding Medicaid	Title XIX (Medicaid)	Total Health Including Medicaid
U.S.	6.62	36.12	93.20	129.32
Ala	7.17	30.23	32.04	62.27
Alaska	10.20	63.00	0	63.00
Ariz	4.43	54.73	0	54.73
Ark	4.47	20.01	5.89	25.90
Calif	5.39	32.64	240.94	273.58
Colo	15.47	66.60	85.82	152.42
Conn	9.47	67.71	193.88	261.54
Del	7.76	37.76	40.57	78.33
D.C.	37.41	109.75	103.45	213.20
Fl	7.31	26.53	16.01	42.54
Ga	5.74	28.80	56.93	85.73
Hawaii	16.67	112.45	109.62	222.07
Idaho	7.97	39.18	63.10	102.28
Ill	8.15	33.47	90.44	123.91
Ind	4.97	38.15	23.73	61.88
Iowa	4.83	41.20	44.68	85.88
Kans	5.50	42.76	89.35	132.11
Ky	4.04	28.27	55.46	83.73
La	2.91	21.82	39.77	61.59
Maine	5.24	35.30	55.78	91.08
Md	15.58	50.59	101.95	152.54
Mass	13.86	65.32	280.82	346.14
Mich	10.28	56.37	133.47	189.84
Minn	7.92	38.61	160.79	199.40
Miss	3.31	17.89	7.54	25.43
Mo	6.33	41.15	48.82	89.97
Mont	7.73	46.16	64.13	110.29

Federal Grants-in-Aid   continued

	Title V Total	Total Health Excluding Medicaid	Title XIX (Medicaid)	Total Health Including Medicaid
Nebr	11.16	43.10	53.42	96.52
Nev	11.91	39.14	87.91	127.05
N.H.	7.95	46.03	60.48	106.51
N.J.	4.06	36.28	45.93	82.21
N.M.	5.55	43.70	41.61	85.31
N.Y.	8.71	40.67	273.69	314.36
N.C.	5.71	35.45	19.89	55.34
N.D.	4.86	40.59	87.84	128.43
Ohio	9.32	43.78	51.17	94.95
Okla	2.63	26.20	133.64	159.84
Oreg	7.51	41.56	41.89	83.45
Penn	6.20	50.86	99.38	150.24
R.I.	6.54	41.35	170.80	212.15
S.C.	4.49	24.39	38.98	63.37
S.D.	3.81	28.94	42.04	70.98
Tenn	5.09	30.46	15.60	46.06
Texas	4.23	22.52	43.54	66.06
Utah	6.65	61.92	88.88	150.80
Vt	7.27	75.60	163.19	238.79
Va	5.88	28.23	26.14	54.37
Wash	8.61	34.87	115.71	150.58
W. Va	4.27	26.23	32.91	59.14
Wisc	5.30	39.43	194.71	234.14
Wyo	9.32	57.42	24.32	81.74

Sources:

Grants-in-Aid: U.S. D/HEW, Maternal and Child Health Services, *Apportionments to States, Fiscal Year 1970*, Unpublished, Washington, D.C. 1970; U.S. D/Treasury, *Federal Aid to States, FY 1972*, pp. 8-9, Columns 46, 47, 48, 49, and 50 (excluding territories), Washington, D.C. 1973.

Number of Poor Persons: U.S. Bureau of Census, *Statistical Abstract of the United States: 1973* (94th ed.), Washington, D.C., 1973, p. 337.

Prepared by Milton Chen Ph.D., March 1976.

The final result of the lack of clarity of the legislation, the bureaucratic entanglements at the federal/state interface, the lack of data, and the lack of a child advocacy group, is the lack of a child health service. In fact, services for children are actually diminishing. The reason we have failed to achieve the level of health among our children that twentieth century scientific and medical knowledge could allow us to achieve and that other countries have achieved, is that we have failed to develop a systematic approach.

The almost total absence of data on the effectiveness of national services renders Congress and the people helpless. National child health programs continue, receiving more funds to accomplish less and less. There is little correspondence between the federal allocation formulas on the one hand and the health needs or fiscal capacity of a state on the other. For example, closed-end grants like the Title V formula grants favor rural and farm states, regardless of need. (See Federal Grants-in-Aid table.) The project grants section of Title V is also discriminatory in its operation. According to a comptroller-general's report, "... a major part of the funds for the special grants projects has been concentrated in a few states, primarily for projects in major cities."[81]

Karen Davis points out that "The limited data available suggest that at least in recent years the program has not concentrated on the health problems of women and children in rural areas." And further, "State programs ... provide less than proportionate share of services to rural residents." [82] Naturally, specific need of poor areas in wealthy states are lost in this coarse analysis, but it is clear that a new grant-in-aid program design is needed—one more like revenue sharing, one that takes into account service needs, health needs (existing resources vs. current health needs), and state fiscal capacity.

Other inequities in the allocation of federal health funds occur because the federal agencies do not review the state budgets in determining future policies. For example, in Connecticut, in a ten-year period, the total state budget quadrupled, as did the federal health contribution. But the state health budget only doubled! The largest increase in health department expenditure was for administration.[83]

In 1967 Congress enacted the amendments to the Social Security Act calling for early and periodic screening, diagnosis, and treatment (EPSDT). It was an effort to provide the United States for the first time with a comprehensive health program, although for a limited segment of the child population. That program must be considered a failure.[84] An attempt to build a comprehensive child health program for the United States on the existing program structure is doomed to failure.

CONCLUSION

A variety of bureaucratic hazards undermine the accomplishment of the basic national child health objectives: the elimination of unnecessary morbidity and mortality in childhood. The legislative and executive branches of the federal government and of the state governments, by reason of their inter- and intra-agency rivalries and conflicts, obstruct effective performance even when sufficient resources are available. For the most part, however, sufficient resources are not made available because the necessary information about the exact nature of the gaps is neither asked for nor collected. The fact that so little demand for information is made on the states tends to confirm the theory that the federal government really gives the states funds for state programs rather than for national programs to be implemented in the states.

When this material was presented to various professional groups, the criticism was made that other dependent classes of society—the aged, and poor, generally—are also the subject of neglect and indifference, as much as or perhaps more than children. It may be that social neglect is a response to the helplessness of all segments without power. But in this case, whatever the cause, or whatever may be the similarities between children and other suffering groups in our society, the *system* set up to provide a base for the elimination of unnecessary death, disease, and suffering is hopelessly incompetent. More money does not seem to be the answer.

Health departments are so structured that the resources expended on their administrative, nonservice responsibilities far outweigh those spent on providing services. Furthermore, any more federal money that is added—even if the clever financial manipulators at the state level will permit it to filter in to the health department operating structure—will be swallowed in a maze of added nonservice activities. However important inspections of facilities and licensing of activities may be, they will not compensate, in terms of lives saved or diseases prevented, for personal services to families and children. In the days of the sanitary revolution, mass services, large-scale actions, were vitally necessary. Today, mass action needs to be aimed at preventing pollution of air, water, and the work place. And yet such action cannot substitute for the personal attention to each pregnant woman and child that is the building block of the health of each generation.

Consultation and guidance have helped communities to provide more and better care. Better licensing procedures have improved health care quality. And there *is* greater public awareness of health needs and resource lack. But the dwindling well-child services, reduced crippled children's services, and immunization deficits are reflected in our too-high infant mortality rates, our too-high death rates of children under five, the epidemics of preventable disease, the undernutrition of large segments of the child population, and our child abuse records.

Those observers who look at other countries are beginning to castigate the United States as uncaring about children—an attack opposite from the one usually made that the United States is too permissive with and overly indulgent of children.[85] Other countries much poorer in substance and without expressed dedication to democratic principles pay much more attention, socially, to the needs of children. Poorer countries than ours provide special allowances for families with children to assure that poverty alone will not prevent children from achieving their potential. Most countries in our stage of development provide centers for the care of preschool-age children of working parents or children with only one parent, and centers for the care of school-age children before and after school. These children, then, do not lack supervision and opportunities to learn and play. Nourishing food is served in schools and in these centers so that no child shall go hungry or become malnourished. Health services specifically for children are provided in these same countries without charge, or as part of a system of national health care to ensure that no illness, malady, or handicapping condition shall go untreated. Again, this is to guarantee, as far as possible, that children are not obstructed from achieving their potential. But it is not so much that they invest more money; they have a more coherent system.

Perhaps there is some validity to the charge that we Americans do not care as much for children—in the mass, let us say—(I am not pointing an accusing finger at parents and saying that they do not care for their own children!) as people do in some other countries. Keniston points out that children are an economic liability on the American scene today.[85] T.J. Espenshade, in his critical analysis comments, "If this logic is correct, we should expect to find that American parents perceive very little in the way of economic benefits from children. On the other hand, they should be extremely conscious of costs.... " His study confirms this. "....a family's standard of living measured in terms of current consumption typically declines as the children grow older, these declines being more rapid and more prolonged the greater the number of children....[87] In our time, there is a growing tendency toward self-realization, which in many instances soon becomes a narrowly centered individual straining for self-gratification. Parenthood, in such circumstances is less and less appealing. And the cost of child-bearing and child-rearing becomes an added irritant and disincentive.

Neglect is costly, both financially and socially. Neglected children become sick, handicapped, socially dependent adults who need social and welfare support, and who need expensive hospitals, convalescent homes, and other institutional and rehabilitation facilities. The death and crippling of children also takes a tremendous emotional toll. Whatever our feelings about children, perhaps we would seize upon a more rational and effective child health if only to avoid the excessive costs of neglect.

In brief, the dilemma is that, as bad off as we are, to make change, we have to change a system of care, now almost 50 years old, that is unresponsive and insensitive to need. That change will require a change in public attitudes toward child health, which in turn demands—and must in turn result in—a powerful advocacy group devoted to children's interests, including health.

Is there somewhere a model of what this program should be? Are there directions to follow that will bring us an American child health system that will be effective, responsive, efficient, and satisfying to public, professionals, and politicians alike? Handicapped children grow into handicapped adults. Can that chain be broken?

Figure II-1   Infant Mortality—Poverty Areas

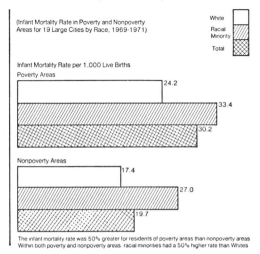

(Infant Mortality Rate in Poverty and Nonpoverty
Areas for 19 Large Cities by Race, 1969-1971)

White
Racial Minority
Total

Infant Mortality Rate per 1,000 Live Births
Poverty Areas

24.2
33.4
30.2

Nonpoverty Areas

17.4
27.0
19.7

The infant mortality rate was 50% greater for residents of poverty areas than nonpoverty areas
Within both poverty and nonpoverty areas, racial minorities had a 50% higher rate than Whites

Source: U.S.P.H.S., National Center for Health Statistics, Series 21.

Figure II-2   Infant Mortality—Socioeconomic Measures

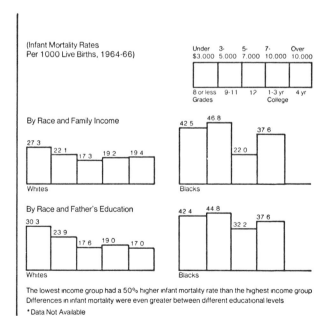

(Infant Mortality Rates
Per 1000 Live Births, 1964-66)

Under   3-   5-   7-   Over
$3,000 5,000   7,000   10,000 10,000

8 or less   9-11   12   1-3 yr   4 yr
Grades   College

By Race and Family Income

27.3
22.1
17.3   19.2   19.4

Whites

42.5   46.8
                37.6
        22.0

Blacks

By Race and Father's Education

30.3
23.9
17.6   19.0   17.0

Whites

42.4   44.8
                37.6
        32.2

Blacks

The lowest income group had a 50% higher infant mortality rate than the highest income group
Differences in infant mortality were even greater between different educational levels
* Data Not Available

Source: U.S.P.H.S., National Center for Health Statistics, Series 22, No. 14.

**Figure II-3   Infant Mortality Rates by Race: Selected Years,
1950-1975**

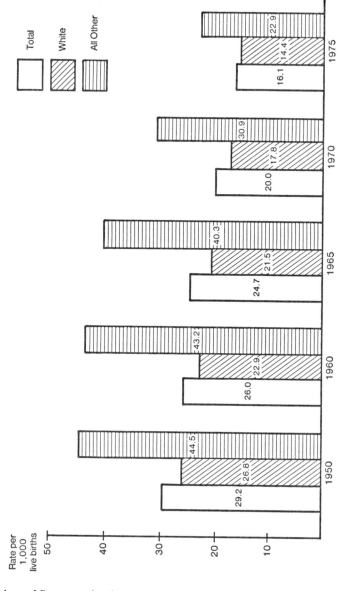

Source: Annual Summary for the United States, 1975. *Monthly Vital Statistics Report* 24:8, June 30, 1976. (Reproduced from *Socioeconomic Issues of Health 1977:* Center for Health Services Research and Development. American Medical Association. Chicago, Ill., 1977.)

REFERENCES

1. Kenneth Keniston, "Do Americans Really Like Children?" (Talk given to the American Orthopsychiatric Society, Washington, D.C., March 23, 1975). There is a more extensive presentation in this vein in Keniston's book *All Our Children* (New York: Harcourt Brace Jovanovich, 1977).

2. Walter F. Mondale, "Justice For Children," *Congressional Record*, 116, 197 (December 9, 1970):420.

3. Milton J. E. Senn, *Speaking Out For Children* (New Haven: Yale University Press, 1977), p. xiii.

4. Edith H. Grotberg, ed. *200 Years of Children* (Washington, D.C.: Department of Health, Education and Welfare, 1977), HEW pub. no. (OHD) 77-30103, p. 7.

5. Congressional Budget Office, "Poverty Status of Families under Alternative Definitions of Income" (Washington, D.C.: Congressional Budget Office, February 1977), Background Paper #17.

6. Office of the Assistant Secretary for Health, "A Proposal For New Federal Leadership in Maternal and Child Health Care in the United States," mimeographed (Washington, D.C.: December 1976), pp. 1-16.

7. R. H. Seiden, "Suicide Among Youth," *Bulletin of Suicidology* Supplement, December 1969.

8. National Center for Health Statistics, *Vital Statistics of the United States 1970*, vol. II, "Mortality" (Washington, D.C.: Government Printing Office, 1971).

9. Office of the Assistant Secretary for Health, "A Proposal for New Federal Leadership," pp. 1-16.

10. R.E. Helfer and C. H. Kempe, eds. *The Battered Child* (Chicago: University of Chicago Press, 1974), p. 232.

11. Samuel Radbill in *The Battered Child*, p. 3.

12. Vincent Fontana, quoted in *Hospital Tribune*, 9 July 1974. Dr. Fontana was then director of the New York Foundling Hospital.

13. Eli H. Newberger, letter, *New York Times*, 12 March 1976.

14. E. H. Newberger, C. M. Newberger, and J. Richmond, "Child Health in America," *Health and Society*, Summer, 1976, pp. 249-298. Similar material appears in "A Proposal for New Federal Leadership," Office of the Assistant Secretary for Health.

15. Office of the Assistant Secretary for Health, "A Proposal for New Federal Leadership," p. 21.

16. Newberger, Newberger, and Richmond, *Health and Society*.

17. Ibid.

18. Department of Health, Education and Welfare, *First Health and Nutrition Examination Survey* (Washington, D.C.: Government Printing Office, 1974).

19. Citizens Board of Inquiry into Hunger and Malnutrition in the United States, *Hunger USA* (Boston: Beacon Press, 1968). See also Senate Select Commission on Nutrition, *The Food Gap: Poverty and Malnutrition in the United States* (Washington, D.C.: Government Printing Office, August 1969); and Nick Kotz, *Let Them Eat Promises* (New York: Doubleday, 1971).

20. Citizens Board of Inquiry, *Heal Yourself* (Washington: American Public Health Association, undated).

21. Department of Health, Education and Welfare, *Program Analysis—Maternal and Child Health Programs US* (Washington, D.C.: 1966).

22. E. Gold et al., "Immune Status of Children One to Four Years of Age as Determined by History and Antibody Measurements," *NEJM* 289 (August 2, 1973): 231-235.

23. E. K. Marcuse and M. G. Grand, "Diphtheria in San Antonio, Texas," *JAMA*, 224 (April 1, 1974): 305-310.

24. Betty J. Hallstrom, "The Provision of Health Care to Children," mimeographed (Minnesota Systems Research, Inc., 1972).

25. C. A. Miller, "Health Care of Children and Youth in America," *AJPH*, 65(April 1975): 353-358.

26. Ibid.

27. Office of the Assistant Secretary for Health, "A Proposal for New Federal Leadership."

28. Department of Health, Education and Welfare, *Program Analysis*.

29. Newberger, Newberger, and Richmond, *Health and Society*.

30. C. A. Miller, "Health Care of Children."

31. National Council of the Organizations for Children and Youth, *America's Children* (Washington, D.C.: National Council of the Organization for Children and Youth, 1976) p. 33.

32. R. Andersen et al., *Health Service Use* (Washington, D.C.: Department of Health, Education and Welfare, 1973) pub. no. (HSM) 73-3004, Table 6, p. 11.

33. Department of Health, Education, and Welfare, *Program Analysis*.

34. R. M. Gibson, M. S. Mueller, and C. R. Fisher, "Age Differences in Health Care Spending, Fiscal Year 1976," *Social Security Bulletin*, August 1977, pp. 3-14.

35. Newberger, Newberger, and Richmond, *Health and Society*.

36. Department of Health, Education and Welfare, *Delivery of Health Services to the Poor—Program Analysis* (Washington, D.C.: Department of Health, Education and Welfare, December 1967).

37. E. Ginzberg and R. M. Solon, *The Great Society: Lessons For the Future* (New York: Basic Books, 1974) p. 23.

38. C. A. Miller, "Health Care for Children."

39. *Philadelphia Inquirer*, 12 October, 1975, p.1.

40. Edward Zigler, former Director of the Office of Child Development, Department of Health, Education and Welfare, in the *New York Times*, 9 April 1976: "The single greatest impediment to our improving the lives of America's children is the myth that we are a child-oriented society."

41. P. T. Murphy, *Our Kindly Parent, The State* (New York: Viking, 1974) p. 15.

42. H. Goldstein, in *Maternal and Child Health Practices*, H. M. Wallace, E. M. Gold and E. F. Lis, eds. (Springfield: Thomas, 1973), Chapter 4.

43. A. Lesser, *Maternal and Child Health Practices*, Chapter 3.

44. A. D. Oglesby, in *Maternal and Child Health Practices*, Chapter 40.

45. E. Schlesinger, *Health Services For the Child* (New York: McGraw-Hill, 1953).

46. Department of Health, Education, and Welfare, *Program Analysis*.

47. National Advisory Council on the Education of Disadvantaged Children, *ESEA: A Review and a Forward Look* (Washington, D.C.: National Advisory Council on the Education of Disadvantaged Children, 1969).

48. Gary Clarke, *Health Programs in the States: A Survey* (New Brunswick: Center for State Legislative Research and Service, Eagleton Institute of Politics, Rutgers University, March 1975).

49. R. J. Haggerty, K. J. Roghmann and I. B. Pless, *Child Health and the Community* (New York: Wiley, 1975) p. 175.

50. Ibid., p. 192.

51. John Burns, ed. *The Sometime Governments* (New York: Bantam, 1971).

52. John Gardner, in *The Sometime Governments*, p. vii.

53. John Rehfuss, *Public Administration as Political Process* (New York: Scribners, 1973), p. 78.

54. J. Burns, *The Sometime Governments*, p. 2.

55. Public Law 90-248, Section 301 modifying Section 505 of Title V of the Social Security Act.

56. Public Law 95-512, the State and Local Fiscal Assistance Act of 1972.

57. Martha Derthick, *The Influence of Federal Grants: Public Assistance in Massachusetts* (Cambridge: Harvard University Press, 1970).

58. Sar Levitan, *The Federal Social Dollar in its Own Backyard* (Washington, D.C.: Bureau of National Affairs, 1973).

59. Robert Stevens and Rosemary Stevens, *Welfare Medicine in America* (New York: Free Press, 1974).

60. Macro Systems Inc., "Analysis and Inventory of Federal Programs Impacting on Maternal and Child Health." mimeographed. Washington, D.C., March 1975.

61. Yale Health Policy Project Summary Publication, *Politics and Social Policy*, mimeographed (New Haven: Yale Health Policy Project, 1976).

62. Department of Health, Education and Welfare, *Maternal and Child Health Programs (Legislative Base)* (Washington, D.C.: Department of Health, Education and Welfare, 1975), HEW pub. no. (HSA) 75-5011. See also Macro Systems, Inc., "Analysis and Inventory."

63. Ruth Roemer, C. Kramer, and J. Frink, *Planning Urban Health Services: From Jungle to System* (St. Louis: Springer, 1975), pp. 4-9. "The maze of programs in the field of child health. . . each program has its own requirements, the result of which is a patchwork of programs for selected children or selected conditions."

64. U.S. Budget, Fiscal Year 1977.

65. J. L. Sundquist, *Politics and Policy* (Washington, D.C.: Brookings Institution, 1968); A. P. Sindler, *American Political Institutions and Public Policy* (Boston: Little, Brown, 1969); and Eric Redman, *The Dance of Legislation* (New York: Simon and Schuster, 1973).

66. J. L. Pressman and A.B. Wildavsky, *Implementation* (Berkeley: University of California Press, 1973), pp. 136-137.

67. Yale Health Policy Project, Working Paper #15, mimeographed (New Haven: Yale Health Policy Project, 1973). Between 1885 and 1924 the infant mortality rate in Connecticut declined from 150/1000 to 69/1000.

68. E. E. Witte, *The Development of the Social Security Act* (Madison, Wis.: University of Wisconsin Press, 1963), passim.

69. D. S. Hirshfield, *The Lost Reform* (Cambridge: Harvard University Press, 1970).

70. It is reported that the failure of the presidentially appointed Committee on Economic Security to obtain a majority in favor of a national health insurance title

resulted in an alternative decision in favor of a child health title, urged by a group of children's advocates.

71. Haven Emerson and M. Luginbuhl, *Local Health Units For the Nation* (New York: Commonwealth Fund, 1945).

72. C-E A. Winslow, *The Evolution and Significance of the Modern Public Health Movement* (New Haven: Yale University Press, 1923) pp. 63 et seq. See also, C-E A. Winslow, "The Untilled Fields of Public Health," *Modern Medicine* 2(1920): 183.

73. A. Sheldon, F. Baker and C. McLaughlin, *Systems and Medical Care* (Cambridge: MIT Press, 1970), Chapter 6.

74. C-E A. Winslow, "The Contribution of Hermann Biggs to Public Health," *American Review of Tuberculosis* 20 (July 1929): 1-28.

75. Department of Health, Education and Welfare, *Social Security in America: The Factual Background of the Social Security Act as Summarized from State Reports to the Committee on Economic Security* (Washington, D.C., 1937), Government Printing Office, p 291: ". . .development of more adequate state divisions of maternal and child health and through them to build up improved health services to mothers and children. . ."

76. Arthur Lesser, personal communication.

77. D. Bauer, "Sisyphus in Chicago," *Harper's*, July 1976.

78. Connecticut Department of Health, *Annual Report 1926*, p. 311.

79. Public Law 90-248, Sections 301 and 302, modifying Section 504 of Title V of the Social Security Act.

80. R. R. Alford, *Health Care Politics* (Chicago, University of Chicago Press, 1975).

81. Comptroller General of the United States, *Report to the Committee on Ways and Means on Maternal and Child Health Programs Authorized by Title V of the Social Security Act* (Washington, D.C.: Government Printing Office, June 23, 1972). Similar concerns are expressed and similar recommendations made in the Georgetown Public Services Laboratory Report, *Services to the People* (Washington, D.C.: Public Services Laboratory 1973), p.33: "Reassessment is indicated of formula grants-in-aid in the department (HEW) to remove any unnecessary existing biases and to determine the match of distribution formulas with purposes of distribution including purposes of intervention in urban affairs."

82. Karen Davis, "A Decade of Policy Developments in Providing Health Care for Low Income Families," Chapter 5 in *A Decade of Federal Antipoverty Programs*, R. Haveman, ed. (New York: Academic Press, 1976). She shows that Title V funds are distributed unevenly with respect to rural/urban need as well as income level—and capriciously, at best.

83. Department of Health, Education and Welfare, *Report of Review of Grants Awarded the State of Connecticut for Maternal and Child Health and Crippled Childrens Services under Title V of the Social Security Act for a period July 1, 1964-March 31, 1971 by Region I, HEW Audit Control (#20019-01):* " . . five full-time general administrative personnel were charged to the MCH program although a substantial amount of their time was used providing indirect administrative services to all state and federal programs as needed." The same audit uncovered almost a million dollars of unused MCH funds returned to the federal treasury in that period.

84. A-M Foltz, "The Development of Ambiguous Federal Policy: Early and Periodic Screening, Diagnosis and Treatment (EPSDT)" *Milbank Memorial Fund Quarterly Health and Society*, Winter 1975, pp. 35-64.

85. Alvin Schorr, *Children and Decent People* (New York: Basic Books, 1974) illustrates this point in detail.

86. Keniston, "Do Americans Really Like Children?"

87. T. J. Espenshade, "The Value and Cost of Children," *Population Bulletin* (Population Reference Bureau) 32: 19 and 31.

Part III

International Comparisons

Chapter 8

Scotland

INTRODUCTION

International comparisons, whether in health service organization and performance, or in other areas, require a degree of circumspection. Social institutions tend to define themselves largely by their historical and traditional developments and cultural attitudes, as well as by characteristic economic and political structure. One speaks of "democracy," as if all democratic regimes were the same. Yet it is obvious on even the most superficial inspection that attitudes toward the most fundamental social values are quite different among the various "democracies." Among the most significant differences is that between the parliamentary and the representative form of political democracy. This particular difference is singled out here because of its important bearing upon the mechanism and techniques of policy formation and, in this particular context, on *health* policy formulation.

Elected representatives respond differently to the electorate and to important interest groups in that electorate, depending upon whether they must run for office as individuals (representative democracy) or on a party slate (parliamentary democracy). Legislators elected on their own records try to create a public image of themselves as representative of certain objectives or positions. These positions may or may not coincide with the positions of the party to which the politician ostensibly belongs. The representative types want to be elected as individuals, and support of the party is generally a secondary goal. The parliamentary types are "team players" who espouse party positions and hope to be elected as part of a slate. Their job is to get the party into office; their own election is assumed to be a secondary goal.

Clearly, representative politicians will attempt to establish themselves as knowledgeable in the various fields in which they offer themselves to the community for election: health, housing, taxes, foreign policy, or whatever.   They may be elected—or defeated—based on the positions they express. The parliamentary slate is promoted by politicians who may know the stance, but little of the content, and who may care less about what the platform elements propose.

If, as in Britain, a labor party relies heavily on trade union support, it needs to pay particular attention to the leadership of its trade union constituents. However, trade union policy formation is similarly oriented. The implications for the health field are powerful. In the United States, health legislation and detailed implementation (like legislation in most other areas) is the result of a host of political forces: The health position of any number of Representatives and Senators, the impact of the public on their political positions, and interest group pressures on the public and, more directly, on the legislators.   The party position must take second place to these considerations. Despite Democratic party commitment to national health insurance for over 30 years, no comprehensive health insurance bill has come close to passage in the U.S. Congress.

Because of this multiplicity of forces at work on the U.S. political scene, operational details, monitoring, and modification if any, tend to be less *professional* (bureaucratic) than the political decisions in parliamentary democracies. They are also more likely to be influenced by interest groups in a representative democracy. Other factors enter into this perhaps too-pat analysis, of course, since history also plays a role. Patients—the public—in Britain, tend to be much more accepting of government's role in the health services, much more likely to accept bureaucratic decision making.[1] British and European experience with cholera in the 19th century fostered health department formation and greater public reliance on and trust in governmental health services. A respected professional health bureaucracy is a very old phenomenon in Britain.

During the 19th century, immigration and population mobility frustrated local health activities in the United States while constitutional barriers obstructed national health action. Consequently, no influential national health service in which the citizenry could have confidence was ever constructed.

Other historical factors that promote or obstruct events or decisions dilute the potential of comparative analysis. Despite similar needs and resources, it may be impossible to achieve in one country a desired change that took place in another—a change that took place because of the conjunction of certain political and social factors. Britain's excursion into the National Health Insurance program in 1911 facilitated entering into the National Health Service in 1948. Canada, geographically close to the United States but culturally related to both the United States and Britain, adopted its National Health Insurance program a decade ago. It is not unlikely that Canadian social attitudes—toward welfare and social services, for example—derive more from British attitudes than American social attitudes do, possibly because the U.S. freed itself from British domination in 1776 and Canada did not cease to be a colony until about 100 years later. Of course, Canada is also a parliamentary democracy.

The distrust of government that was characteristic of the immigrant waves plus population mobility and the open American frontier also contributed to the delay in formation of all kinds of government welfare services. Education may have been the exception only because it was a local function from the start. Independence of character is a personal trait still widely admired in the United States. Ten years ago, a television film on hunger and malnutrition in America showed poor families who were eligible for food stamps, food distribution, and cash allowances, but who refused to register for the programs and acknowledge their dependency.

These comments are not made to extol, defend, or criticize American or European social values and attitudes. But it is important to keep these distinctions in mind when considering comparative practices.

Other, more technical factors, must also enter into the comparative considerations. What a doctor is and how doctors are trained, what a nurse is and how they are trained, must be clarified before manpower figures can be compared. Basic social structuring, unemployment levels, minimum income guarantees, family allowances, housing, educational attainment, and other social factors will influence health as much as or perhaps more than the health system itself.

This review of child health programs is aimed at describing and analyzing the health system, particularly as it applies to children, in several European countries. From the description and analysis, conclusions and recommendations for improvement of the child health system in the United States may be drawn. In general, the analysis attempted to establish:

1. whether universal entitlement to medical care reached children in a sufficiently comprehensive way; and
2. whether preventive services for children needed special attention in any case.

Some questions could not be answered because there was little basis for comparison. It was not possible to tell exactly how important child and family allowances are in promoting or maintaining health in children, since all European countries have similar, but varied, programs. Since public health levels vary, allowances alone are clearly insufficient to guarantee the health of children.

For nearly all children in European systems (children of migrant "guest" workers excepted in some countries, and children of the rich in others) access to curative medical services is a universal benefit as part of the health insurance or health service system. It is in the different assigned roles of preventive services that one tends to see the largest variations.

Observations

Two child health programs in Europe were selected for comparison and study: Scotland and Holland. Scotland offered the following useful benchmarks:

- A long-standing official program of child health and medical care services within a national health service offering universal comprehensive entitlement to medical care
- Designated systems of case finding and treatment of handicapping conditions in young children as well as a specific school health service
- Clearly identifiable child health workers—pediatricians, health visitors, public health physicians ("child health officers")—along with general practice child medical care responsibilities
- Traditionally superior leadership in public health planning and administration
- For the investigator—reports, circulars, and documentation in the English language!

Furthermore, in recent years, a number of private, professional, and official publications had appeared, indicating dissatisfaction with the performance of the Scottish National Health Service as it affected children particularly, with discussions reflecting opposing interests and proposals for change, modification and improvement. Various committees with official standing had published critical commentaries and recommendations.[2] With the aid of a WHO team, an analytic approach had been taken to establish performance criteria and improve managerial efficiency[3] and, of course, a number of professionals, in and out of the government service, had published critical and reform essays.[4]

All in all, it seemed a particularly appropriate time to review the child health system in Scotland to assess what the participants saw as their difficulties and their opportunities for change and improvement, and then to reflect on the applicability of these findings to the United States. Since England and Wales had also expressed some dissatisfaction with the status quo in their child health services and had created a committee to review, report on, and recommend improvements of those services,[5] an unusual opportunity was available to make even broader comparisons.

The Setting

Scotland is the large northern section of Britain, mountainous and more sparsely settled (with a population of 5 million) than the southern section, consisting of England and Wales (with 45 million). Scotland has shared one sovereignty with England since the "union of the crowns" in 1603, but it retains considerable national identity and many of its own institutions. It has worked out special arrangements for the conduct of its own affairs, a process that has accelerated with the increasing nationalist mood of its people and the concomitant discovery of North Sea oil. It is a lovely scenic area, with many lakes and islands to the northeast and west. However, it is currently severely depressed, even more so than England and Wales, with almost twice as many unemployed proportionately. It has always been a relatively poor country, with a gross national product and per capita income significantly less than Britain's as a whole. Housing is in acute, short supply (Scotland has the lowest rate of home ownership in Europe) and the concentrated population in the south of Scotland suffers the worst, or at least as bad as the worst, housing situation in Britain. Only inner London and Liverpool may have greater density per room or fewer indoor plumbing facilities.

In the Glasgow area called Clydeside, 37.3 percent of the population live in households crowded to more than 1.5 people per room; 13.5 percent of the households do not have exclusive use of basic amenities (hot water, bath, inside WC).[6]

Most of the population is concentrated in the south; 2.6 million people (half the population) live in the Strathclyde region, one of the nine administrative regions of Scotland. The city of Glasgow, within the Strathclyde conurbation, has a population of over a million people, and a 25 percent unemployment rate.[7] Glasgow has its previous important industrial position to thank in part for its present extraordinarily difficult economic situation, since for many years Clydeside was the seat of extensive British industrial production —shipbuilding, steelmaking, and other heavy industry. Immigration, especially from Ireland, just before the depression set in, has left Clydeside with its markedly high unemployment, young families with many children among the unemployed. Clydeside has the highest population of young people (under age 14) in the British Isles—13 percent.

North Sea oil, recently discovered and beginning to be exported, may be the economic solution for the impoverished territory. Much political and economic controversy has been stirred up and a strong strain of Scottish nationalism reinforced by the discovery. It is unlikely that much effect upon the health services will result, except as more funds become available.

THE SCOTTISH NATIONAL HEALTH SERVICE

The Scottish National Health Service is similar in its operations, though not entirely identical, to the national health service in England and Wales. The differences were small in the days before reorganization (1948-1974) and are characterized today chiefly by the fewer number of levels in the administrative hierarchy. This is probably a function of the smaller population and more scattered distribution.

The Scots have eliminated the Regional Authority and operate through 15 Area Health Authorities in the nine administrative regions. Both England and Scotland delegate responsibilities to District Management Teams from the area (District Executive Groups in Scotland), but there is one less level of authority in Scotland. Abel-Smith points out the dangers of interpolating too many levels of authority and responsibility. "A multi-tier organization plan may make sense on paper, but the more tiers there are, the greater the number of points at which pressure can be applied to veto progressive or experimental policies."[8]

District Management Teams vary in their responsibilities in Scotland inasmuch as the 53 administrative districts may vary in population from 10,000 to nearly a million (greater Glasgow).

In the reorganized British National Health Service, the purpose was to integrate what had be a tripartite health service consisting of general practitioners, hospitals and consultants, and local authority public health services, each separately funded and administrated. Through this reorganization, of course, existing resources could be reallocated and better liaison could be established with the simultaneously reorganized administrative structure of local government and the personal social services function.[9] The reorganization was the climax of long-standing professional dissatisfaction with the fragmented health services, a managerial solution deriving from bipartisan attraction to the developing industrial management theory. "... the reorganization of the NHS ... is going to allow, for the first time, a synoptic view of health services at each administrative level. In other words, it will in the future be possible to look at needs, whatever they may be; to look at resources; and from there to try to move on to arrive at rational priorities and make logical decisions."[10] So spoke a high-ranking, distinguished medical civil servant.

Not everyone was quite so sanguine. Another distinguished physician, a professor at the London School of Hygiene, denounced the reorganization as "The Fabian Curse," saying that nothing can or will work if there is too much "managing," if the system is too highly engineered.[11] Rudolph Klein saw it as a deliberate effort to separate the responsibilities of management from consumer control.[12] Barbara Castle, Minister of State (Department of Health and Social Security), who inherited the reorganization structure when the Labour government took over, complained that they couldn't "re-reorganize" but had to make the best of it. She denounced the "semblance of democracy" and counselled living with it until it could be reshaped; until it could be a "more radical democratization [by]... elected regional government."[13]

This long-awaited, long-desired, clearly not-so-happy eventuality did simplify the administration of medical care services in Britain. Central responsibility for the Scottish NHS was lodged in the secretary of state for Scotland, who would be advised by the Scottish Health Planning Council. This council consists of members representing each of the 15 area health boards and each of the universities with medical faculties, with a chairman and other members appointed by the secretary, including six members from the Scottish Home and Health Department. The elimination of intermediate regional health boards meant that area health boards were funded directly by the central department. What had been the Scottish Health Department continued, in effect, to be a "headquarters" for health services and served as staff to the planning council. Day-to-day operations were delegated to district executive groups except for areas with relatively small populations. For services to be provided most economically and efficiently on a national scale (e.g., information, statistics, blood banking), the Common Services Agency was established under the control of the Planning Council.

To represent the interests of various professional groups, local and national consultative committees were appointed by the Planning Council. For specific planning and program development, ad hoc Program Groups (e.g., child health, mental retardation) are appointed by the Planning Council. These Program Groups are multidisciplinary as a rule and not categorically professional. To represent the interests of the public, each Area Health Board and District Executive Group has a Local Health Council, appointed by the health boards, to review and report on health services in their areas.

An important safeguard, for patients and others, lies in the appointment of a health commissioner for Scotland, an ombudsman to investigate complaints regarding health services. While some areas, such as contracts, are out of the ombudsman's purview, failures of services (other than purely clinical) are his (or hers) to investigate.[14] (It may be of some interest to malpractice students that there were 40 complaints lodged against general practitioners in 1974!)

The administrative machinery of the health boards is responsible for the smooth operation of general practice and of hospital, child health, school health, maternity, and public health services. The Area Health Board is headed by an Area Executive Group, including the Chief Administrative Medical Officer (CAMO). Area Health Boards have a committee structure similar to that of the National Planning Council.

General practice, which involves over 50 percent of practicing physicians, is still largely in offices, although general practitioners moving to health centers and group practice is increasing. The GP group relates to the Area Health Board through a committee.

Budgeting is a central function. For Scotland, the overall British budget is determinative. But within Scotland, the finance officer, aided by the Advisory Working Party on Revenue Resource Allocation, decides on the Area Health Board budgets using a formula that takes into consideration population, special needs, and the like. Areas make policy decisions and provide services within these budgetary limits. The National Council can suggest, urge, and provide data supporting a particular policy or priorty, but it cannot *command*. To prod local agencies into adopting a suggested course, or alter priorities, some financial incentives should be available to the council. This is virtually impossible. Decisions on such additions have to be made with the consent of *all* area administrative officers, who make up the area's "Advisory Group for New Development in Health Care," and who agree that the added funds will provide information or demonstration of national significance. The sum available for this purpose is, however, so small as to be an insignificant budgetary factor. There is now considerable discussion about the formula for allocation of funds, and the government is making an authoritative demand to reconsider allocation based on need.[15]

Child Health Services

Before the reorganization in 1974, prenatal and child health clinics were the responsibility of the Local Authorities Health Services, and school health the responsibility of the Educational Services. In fact, the same type of physician served in both areas, as "child health officer." Since reorganization, the Area Health Board has the former local authority responsibilities: providing and supervising health visitation, midwifery, child preventive services, immunizations, health center facilities, ambulance services, and school medical and dental services.

Theoretically, the integration of services implied much more in the way of supervision from pediatric consultants (in the hospitals), and to a very limited degree, this has taken place. But for the moment, the former child health officers still carry out their former duties, under a different paymaster (the Area Health Board rather than the local authority) and under a new supervisor (Community Medicine Specialist of the Area Health Board rather than a Medical Officer of Health and a senior school medical officer of the educational authority).

The trend toward more of these services in the general practitioner's office seems to be accelerating, with fewer pregnant women and well preschool children being seen in public clinics.

Background Information on the Child Health Services (1974)

Of Scotland's population of just over 5 million people, nearly 400,000 are children under age 5 and nearly a million between the ages of 5 and 14. Compared with the United States (18 percent of the population in these age groups) Scotland's 25 percent represents a much larger burden of responsibility. However, in infant mortality rates, Scotland's average of 19 per 1,000 live births is well behind the United States' rate of 16.7. But of course there is variation in Scotland, as in the United States, geographically and by social classes: as much as 26.8 for black children in the United States and as much as 20.3 in Glasgow.

Nearly 99 percent of Scottish babies are delivered in hospitals; a little less than half the pregnant women in Scotland attended the public clinics for prenatal care, while only a fraction (less than 10 percent) attended the postpartum clinics. A quarter of the children under 5 attended official child health centers. In short, prenatal and postnatal care and well-baby services are largely outside the public service facet of the National Health Service and are cared for by the private physician, if at all.

An important source of information about the health status of children, as well as an important entry to medical care and attention for many handicapped children or children with physical, mental or emotional defects, is the physical examination given the children. Of the 80,000 children entering (all examined) 50 percent showed defects of one kind or another. Over 13 percent of these were visual defects and 1 percent hearing defects. On leaving school, another compulsory examination point for all school children, the 69,000 children examined showed 45 percent with defects. Since the recordkeeping does not indicate: (a) if the defect existed previously; (b) was previously known; or (c) had been corrected, the information is almost useless. But it does show that the case-finding mechanism is effective.

An important characteristic of the value of a preventive service system is the immunization status of children, and not just what it is at school entry. After all, the various childhood diseases can attack anytime between birth and school entry. For children to be immunized the day before admission to school in order to comply with regulations would hardly be evidence of effectiveness of a preventive program. In Scotland, although the data are incomplete, it would appear that 50 percent of children one year old had been immunized against the usual diphtheria-pertussis-tetanus, 60 percent against polio and 30 percent had completed measles vaccination.[16]

So far as the manpower available for child health services is concerned, there were:

2,765 general practitioners (whole time equivalents)
   51 pediatricians (whole time equivalents)
1,700 consultants (whole time equivalents)
  106 community medicine specialists
  201 child health officers
1,573 hospital based midwives
   98 community based midwives
  905 health visitors

The health visitors made nearly 1 million home visits and saw over 350,000 preschool children at home; 36,000 school children at home.

The total cost of the health services in Scotland in 1974 was £446 million ($800 million or a bit less at the rate of exchange of that time.) This comes to $154 per person. (In the United States that year, expenditure nationally came to $495.)[17]

Social Services

Two points should be particularly noted regarding social services available to children in Scotland and in Britain generally. One is that social concern has been explicitly expressed in legislation since the middle of the 19th century. There is a positive, legislated social policy regarding children. For example, Lord Shaftesbury's "Apprentices Act" is based on the premise that the state has a responsibility to children.[18] The most recent "Children Act," following the specifics prescribed in the controversial Children and Young Persons Act of 1969, carries on the tradition of national concern and responsibility.[19] Protection of the child and concern for the child, expressed in law, is a clear social policy. Family and children's allowances provide an economic platform for this concern and policy.[20] Some brief descriptive material may be helpful in visualizing the extent and depth of this application of social policy.

In 1975, some 13,000 Scottish families were receiving long-term social support, 4,000 short-term. Long-term support was more than 50 percent higher than in 1970, when 8,000 families were receiving such support, a fact which spotlights the effect of the economic depression.

Maternity and child health services have been available to all, without charge, since 1918. Family allowances (for all children after the first child) have been available since 1946, and 4.5 million families with children under school-leaving age (or older, if still in school) receive modest weekly stipends. There is a maternity benefit and paid maternity leave for working women. There are no charges for prescription medicines for children and pregnant women or for the aged, disabled war pensioners, or those receiving supplementary welfare benefits.

Social service authorities support an urban program, including a "rights action group" that provides a grievance channel for poor families and supports voluntary agency efforts in the community. A special court-related hearing committee can, in the case of neglected children, impose compulsory care measures on parents and the community.

An important element of social action is the strength of the reorganized social services as independent authorities. Social workers may be associated with health or education authorities to help them carry out their objectives, but the basic policies and social goals are set within the social service professional arena. This creates conflict, of course, and demands effective channels of liaison, not all of which are currently in place or fully operative. It does, however give free professional rein to social workers and theoretically, at least, allows for more professional services and attention to children.

SOME PROBLEMS IN THE CHILD HEALTH SYSTEM

The chief medical officer of Scotland, in pointing out the anticipated changes and developments in the health service reorganization, wrote, "... though there have been great improvements in child health within Scotland, the country's position in the international 'league table' of vital statistics has dropped relative to other comparable countries. And within Scotland analysis of health statistics shows that children from poor socio-economic groups have a much worse health record than their better-off peers, and that some areas are considerably less favored than others."[21] In later expansion of these remarks, he notes:

... in the last 20 years England and Wales have slipped from fifth to eighth place and Scotland from eighth to twelfth in the ranking of countries by infant mortality. The rate of Social Classes IV and V is still higher than for Social Class I and the gap has not been reduced in recent years. Striking regional differences exist within Scotland in infant mortality ... immunization rates in Scotland leave much room for improvement .... there are regional variations in the provision of certain services, for example, health visiting, and there is also evidence that handicapped children do not always receive the services they require .... attendance at Local Authority Child Health Clinics remains poor .... the overall use made of preventive services is less than it ought to be ...[22]

It appears, from documentation supplied by the British Department of Health and Social Security, that the same sort of criticism might be directed at child health services in England.

The indicators of need tell a different and more disturbing story. Although infant mortality has been reduced, the improvement is far less rapid than in other developed countries. While it is not possible to infer any trends from statistics about the abuse and neglect of children by adults, there is no mistaking the increase in public concern about it.... handicapped children are one of today's chief problems in child health.[23]

Comparing Scotland against England, one finds that only Liverpool has a worse infant mortality rate than the Glasgow region, which has the worst record in Scotland. Industrial cities in England and Wales (Leeds, Manchester, and Birmingham), while doing more poorly than the rest of England, are in far better shape than Scotland as a whole.[24] Official statistics show that only half the Scottish children born in 1973 had completed immunization against diphtheria, tetanus, and pertussis as compared to 80 percent in previous years.

Examination of specific reports reveals a wide variation within Scotland and raises surprising questions about the "equity" presumed to exist under the National Health Service. Infant mortality varies from 17 to 27 per 1,000 live births in different area health authorities; polio immunization rates range from 100 percent to 55 percent. Resources figures are equally lopsided: per 1,000 population, one area will have as few as 10 beds, another 29, and general practitioners per 100,000 population vary from a high of 92 to a low of 43, with an average of 55.[25] Of course, in England there is also great variation among the health regions in infant mortality and immunizations, but in every respect, England's average resource/population ratio is *lower* than Scotland's. For example, England spends £5.2/person compared with Scotland's £6. There are 55 GPs per 100,000 people in Scotland, whereas England has 46 GPs per 100,000.[26] This requires some explanation.

When the National Health Service went into operation in 1948, it was with the guarantee that no area would receive less than it was currently spending from whatever source and that future increments would be distributed *equally*. Scotland entered into the National Health Service with many more beds proportionately than England, an inheritance from wartime emergency construction and with relatively more physicians. Since then, several thousand hospital beds have been eliminated (from 65,000 to 62,000) and the ensuing lesser costs have perpetuated the Scottish funding and manpower advantage. The population of Scotland has decreased proportionately as well. Scotland's greater poverty, unemployment, and housing shortage may offset this advantage by creating a greater need for medical care, but the fact of the differential remains. The problems seem to be inherent in the system, with deficiencies in both the Scottish and English child health services. Scotland, however, remains more disadvantaged despite a relatively greater supply of resources.

Studying the Deficiencies

There is no way of determining whether and to what extent children suffer a greater disadvantage than adults in the National Health Service. Some difficulties may be of long standing, since in studies made before the reorganization, deficiencies in the preschool and health service screening examinations and assessment were evident. Lowdon and Walker report that more than half the defects found at school entry had not been found previously, and only 8 out of

24 children with cardiac defects were previously known.[27] In Sweden, on the other hand, Wagner reports that only 2 out of 15 cardiac conditions discovered in a mandated examination of 4-year-olds were *not* known.[28] Furthermore, in the English study, there was no follow-up on 27 percent of the defect cases; all of the Swedish cases were followed up on. It is unfortunately true, however, that data on the health of school children are too inadequately reported and insufficient in detail to allow accurate estimates of the efficacy of school health examinations.

In a wide-ranging discussion of child health needs and medical care system deficiencies, Alfred White Franklin presents some data, inconclusive but persuasive, that large numbers of children at school-leaving examinations were found to have untreated defects, particularly refractive errors and hearing loss.[29] We can conclude, on this evidence, that a gap in the child health services does exist, probably because of lack of mandatory examinations between birth and school entry or little follow-up between the school-entry and school-leaving examinations. (School health service reporting does not indicate how many defects found are treated, and if not, why.) This tends to undermine the purpose and value of the school health service, for, as Franklin notes, "The aim of the school health service at its inception in 1907 was to insure that school children would not be prevented from securing the benefits of education by reason of ill-health or defect. It was hoped, too, that the detection of existing disease in its early stages would lead to more effective treatment."[30]

While these data on school children were from English sources, they could apply to Scotland as well. So, despite the lack of unassailable and altogether convincing evidence, there is reason to believe that the child health services do fail to reach all the children they should and that some children are more affected by this than others.

Percent Gross National Product Spent on Health[31]

	1968	1974
United Kingdom	4.6	5.7
Sweden	6.0	7.0
United States	6.5	7.7

Comparative Health Personnel Growth

	Doctors/10,000 population		Nurses/10,000 population	
	1960	1970	1960	1970
UK				
England	10.5	12.7	20.8	30.7
Scotland	11.8	15.6	22.0	35.5
Sweden	9.5	13.9	28.6	40.7
USA	13.4	15.4	27.9	37.3

Economics as Explanation

In the literature and in discussions with many professionals and officials in Scotland and England, several kinds of explanation were generally offered—combinations of the same explanations usually, but with different emphasis. Britain's economic strain was an inevitable explanatory introduction. Where individuals or groups did have clear positive proposals for remedy, they would explain that tight financial straits in Britain obstructed action, an excellent excuse for not having undertaken what was necessary. However, an examination of data on the United Kingdom's long-term financial investment in health and the growth of resources generally tends to weaken this argument. Money alone, or the lack of sufficiently increased expenditures, can hardly be the reason. True, Britain did (and does) spend a smaller proportion of its gross national product on health than most other countries in its economic bracket, but the increases have been comparable. As a matter of fact, Britain's percentage increase has been greater than both the United States' and Sweden's. Between 1973 and 1974, while Sweden actually reduced public expenditures for health services, and the U.S. public expenditure went up 6 percent, the UK public expenditures for the health services rose 20 percent. Sivard shows the United Kingdom spending the equivalent of $160 per person for health (1974 figures) while Sweden and the United States were spending about $500 per person.[32] This difference, however, is due more to British health workers' lower salaries than to lesser resources. Furthermore, the numbers of physicians, nurses, and other health workers in Britain did not, as a result of inflation, decline in comparison to these other countries and, as a matter of fact, kept pace.[33] The economic situation, then, cannot be used as an excuse for the deficiencies.

The failure of the so-called welfare state to eliminate gross poverty or to provide more equitable access to social services must receive at least part of the blame for the more obvious deficiencies. Social scientists continue to point out the lag in income and benefits for the lower socio-economic groups and the impact this must have on their health needs and the extent to which they take advantage of health services. As Field points out in *Unequal Britain*, "Women in the lower social classes. . .were less likely to have had an early examination after being pregnant. . . ."[34] Townsend, a constant critic of Britain's inadequate efforts to combat poverty, makes the point that social policy determines the improvement (or lack of it) of health indices and points to the decline of the use of milk in lower income families following the abolition of specially priced cheap milk for welfare recipients and older school children.[35] Crossman, the first Secretary of State for Social Services, speaking in 1971, said, ". . . (it is) apparent that those living in some parts of the country run a greater risk of mortality than others. Broadly speaking, the urban areas of declining employment, a high degree of overcrowding, low standards of accommodation and low wages are those with high mortality rates."[36]

In a 1971 survey, Field found 60 families, with 200 children, in various parts of the country, 70 percent of whom had incomes below the poverty line. Fifteen percent met all of the seven "undesirable criteria"—missing school for lack of suitable clothes or shoes, never having a cooked breakfast, going all day without a cooked meal, inadequate footwear for rainy weather, never having a holiday, going to bed early for lack of fuel, and buying only second-hand clothes.[37] Franklin quotes the United Nations Declaration of the Rights of the Child, published on November 20, 1959: "As long as social and economic pressures are thoughtlessly mobilized against family life, the health of children will suffer."[38]

The British have lagged behind most of Europe in reducing the proportion of the population that lives in poverty. Despite extensive welfare commitments, benefits are meager, and, as the title of an important article states, "Poverty Prevails." There is some irony in the fact that the United States, particularly the more conservative political elements, have held up Britain as the epitome of the welfare state, the bogey with which to frighten entrepreneurial Americans away from socialism. The irony is that what may be the unfortunate consequence of *insufficient* social welfare action is held out as the result of the overabundant largesse of a prodigal state.[39]

Unlike its European counterpart, Holland, which, by providing food, shelter, and medical and social assistance, strives to put families with children on a financial footing with similar-income families without children, Britain has taken only tentative steps in this direction.   "Disadvantaged," the Field article quoted previously states, is easily defined: "a large family, low *per capita* income, inferior housing with overcrowding, father employed irregularly, poor physical care of the children, and erratic contact with the statutory health and welfare services." Such disadvantage is not restricted to one social class—even some Class I professional families may fit the pattern.   But "cot deaths" (the British name for the Sudden Infant Death Syndrome) are four times as frequent among the lower as among the upper socioeconomic groups. In children age 1 to 14, over a five-year period, the total death rate was twice as high among the lowest social class as among the highest. Neville Butler, a distinguished pediatrician and student of social medicine, claims that the closest correlation can be found between poor housing and poor health care of children.[40]

But poverty cannot explain everything, nor can poor housing. The Wynns, persistent critics of British apathy toward child health services, point out that Finland, although a very poor country, is fanatical about following up on children, "sending out teams of pediatric community nurses—if necessary on skis" to ensure that children get the care they need—*all* children, without regard to social class or income.[41] When benefits are means tested, those who suffer most are those families just above the poverty line, those who are not eligible for supplementary benefits and are unable to obtain all that is needed on their earnings. Poor Finland has less than half the perinatal mortality of relatively well-off Manchester. More investment in health visitors and a better sorting out of priorities for those health visitors is one important answer. Another is a greater financial investment in benefits for families with children.[42]

Professional Explanations

Professional explanations tended to be of two kinds: criticisms of the system and critical views of the kinds of families who failed to use the service. The latter kind of explanation might be grouped under the heading of "Blaming the Victim." Poverty and unemployment, along with the failure of the social and economic system to provide satisfactory economic support can certainly create an indifferent attitude toward health and a family setting in which health matters are neglected. Lack of adequate housing, schooling, and social support services exaggerates this effect. If the concept of "the vulnerable family" is added to this destructive mixture, the result is a fairly clear-cut social group wholly outside the mainstream of family behavior patterns. The vulnerable family is one already stricken with one or more physical, emotional, or social injuries. Manciaux and Deschamps include in their definition a variety of factors, some, of course, much more damaging than others:

- single parent families
- only child
- large families
- incompetent family (retarded parent or parents, lack of schooling, or neglected children)
- illness, acute or chronic; handicapped parent or child
- mental illness, alcoholism, or family conflict
- poverty
- poor housing
- lack of local social services.[43]

John Smith, a senior advisor in social work to the secretary of state of Scotland, pointed out that *all* families are potentially vulnerable, that vulnerability is simply the result of an accumulation of unresolvable problems. Where money, housing, social support, and health services can be made available, the impact of illness, parental retardation, or neglect can be mitigated. The concept is not too different from the psychiatric opinion that all soldiers are subject to combat fatigue. It is all a matter of the degree and duration of stress.

Poverty, a system defect, may well have powerful influences that the best health system cannot correct. But "disadvantaged," the label that is almost synonymous with "vulnerable" or "multiproblem," while including poverty, is not always marked by poverty. Disadvantaged families are distinguished by a lower proportion of vaccinated children, fewer visits for preventive services, and, not surprisingly, a lower intake of means-tested benefits.[44]

For many professional observers, the situation in the Strathclyde area is a case in point. Unemployment is the heaviest there; large families and poor housing are common. However, in Dundee, where unemployment and poverty are roughly equal to that of the Glasgow region, the public health statistics are dramatically different. When Glasgow's infant mortality rate was 27 per 1,000 live births, Dundee's was 19. Immigrant families do less well than native families, since an additional stress factor is at work.

To the "urban complaint" must be added what the professionals criticize as the failure of the health service system to respond appropriately to needs. The Scottish and English documents responding officially to the query about the inadequacies of the child health system react similarly to the challenge. In 1973, Scotland proposed:

- to provide pediatric advice before birth and supervision in the neonatal period and to ensure follow-up of high risk infants . . .
- a feedback on handicapped children . . .
- a diagnostic service for the identification and evaluation of a child's total disability . . .
- genetic counselling . . .
- to keep the child health service under constant review . . .
- a plan for deployment of pediatricians . . . consultative services in district centers . . . use of junior hospital physicians . . .
- redefining the general practitioner's role in primary and continuing care . . .
- paying more attention to school health and routine medical examinations . . .
- making contact with families who do not make use of services[45]

The comparable English document, several years later, is more detailed, but roams in the same areas.[46] These matters have been noted for years. In 1967, the "Sheldon Report" noted, ". . . we are in no doubt about the continuing need for a preventive service to safeguard the health of children . . ."[47]

There can be no quarrel with the professional judgment that calls forth these recommendations. However, there is grave doubt as to the possibility of their fulfillment. Budget decisions have been made for the next three years that tend to eliminate the possibility of any extensive educational effort to increase the supply of health visitors, for example, or to employ more. The English Department of Health and Social Security document on priorities in 1976 proposed a 6 percent increase of expenditures for ". . . extension of health visiting services to allow for improvements in monitoring child health and welfare and support of mothers."[48] How this will be done, when the document itself notes that a *doubling* of health visitor numbers would be required, is unclear.

In Scotland, the annual increase is smaller and while "more positive development of health services for families in areas of multiple deprivation" is envisioned, it is "the projected reduction in the child population" that is expected to make it possible "not only to maintain the present range and standard of services but also to make worthwhile improvements without any increase in revenue expenditures. . . ."[49] This is hardly what the earlier Sheldon Report had in mind when it proposed "major changes, and if they are to be fulfilled, major efforts will have to be directed."[50]

Examination of other aspects of the proposals for change and improvement in child health services give rise to other doubts.

The year of study, 1976, was too soon after this radical reorganization of administrative units, social service activities, and the National Health Service itself, to provide a stable framework for analysis. In the health service, certainly, not all parts of the system had picked up the pace or achieved smooth operational momentum. The children's health service had undergone even more severe strain and administrative and professional changes than other parts of the system. The full effects of these transformations on the children's health services had not been fully anticipated, and a full counterpoise to the resulting imbalance was not yet decided upon, let alone in place. Redeployment of the child health service and augmentation of the preventive services have moved very slowly. The problems were clearly more difficult than envisioned and the obstacles more obdurate. In brief, the preventive aspects of the children's health services may have suffered more than other parts of the health service.

Where local authority clinics had existed and cared for preschool children, in the reorganization, clinics were no longer the responsibility of local authorities. Medical officers of health were eliminated from local authority control and clinics became the responsibility of the area health boards and community medicine specialists within the boards. The priorities of the boards and the qualifications of the community medicine specialists and *their* priorities affected the quality and even continuation of these services.[51]

The former "child health officers" who had served in these clinics, with no clear career line in the new organizational structures since they were not consultants (as the Community Medicine Specialists and pediatricians were) or general practitioners, had no claim to a salary line, promotion, status, distinction awards, or titles. They were in limbo—although still needed and employed on contract or by some other maneuver. Most saw their choice as either to become general practitioners (the younger ones) or to retire (the older ones). Becoming a consultant was pretty much out of the question, since training was not easy to enter, and job openings, even after training, scarce.

School health services suffered similarly since the child health officers had been the staff there as well. The educational authority no longer controlled this service and the community medicine specialist, as mentioned, while responsible, might not put the same priorities on the service that the medical officer of health once did.[52]

For a long time, "integration" had been the watchword of public health administration. All of the general practitioners' problems were going to be solved by elevating their status and giving them more responsibility, especially supervision of preventive services: prenatal care, child health, and school health services. This meshed with the managerial philosophy so prevalent in our time: avoid duplication, fragmentation; don't divide the child (or any patient) into professional pieces—unite prevention and cure, eliminate clinics, and put the child into the general practitioner's office for preventive services as well as medical care.[53]

Now that reorganization had confirmed this by urging and energizing general practitioners to take over the preventive responsibilities, the administrative reduction of pressures to use clinics or even continue them, reinforced the "integration." The difficulty, of course, was that general practitioners had too little knowledge of well-baby care or well-child preventive needs and little interest in these matters. They were not specifically dedicated to well-child and preventive services as the child health officers in the clinics had been. Those officers were forbidden to treat sick children or order medication but were restricted to preventive and health educational activities.

The "social handicaps" are usually the ones the doctors have not been trained to recognize or expected to look for, those previously enumerated characteristics of the vulnerable family: "poverty, inadequate housing, those parents hindered by chronic physical or mental illness or instability in their personal relationships . . . severe disturbance or permanent disruption of family life . . . particularly important when considering the needs of immigrant families. Just as some children are born with physical defects, others are born with social defects and doctors must learn to recognize social symptoms and use social remedies . . ."[54]

Evidence to confirm the suspicion that more than good intentions will be required to involve the general practitioners seriously in prevention comes from a 1974 study. Three different health centers in which the team of general practitioner, midwife, health visitor, and district nurse had been assembled were reviewed for effectiveness. "As might be expected, the doctors' and district nurses' main interests lay in curative work . . . the health visitors were interested chiefly in primary prevention, health education and the social aspects of community work." And further, "But because the priorities of general practice were clearly seen by the health visitors to focus on treating illness, they seemed to consider that their own work was not considered important . . ." So far as "team" work or coordination was concerned, "In few teams did health visitors appear to make attempts to discuss openly these differences . . . In most cases their contacts with colleagues were hurried . . . Because of status differentials, health visitors possibly felt unable to engage in argument with doctors and because of the pressures to maintain harmonious relationships they preferred to avoid controversy." And finally, "There were indications that health visitors were extending their services to age groups older than young children with whom they had traditionally been associated."[55]

Many critics of the earlier child health system, before reorganization, had some harsh things to say about the child health officers. They had had insufficient pediatric training, of course. Some were retired from practice or military service. But the bulk were women physicians, and it is hard not to see traditional sexism in the criticisms of their activities or the lack of concern for their future when the National Health Service was reorganized. During my visit I heard men frequently comment about "pin money doctors," implying that the female child health officers had no real interest in medicine generally or in preventive services and school health particularly, and that they served in their underpaid, noncareer job, for "pin money," to buy luxuries or additional clothes or furniture beyond their husbands' putatively adequate earnings.

Women's increasing concern about, and more aggressive attitudes toward, social barriers that formerly kept them relatively weak and submissive, as well as underpaid, unpromoted, and subordinate to men in their careers could play a very definite role in the solution of the problem. On the one hand, something like an intermediate physician, not a general practitioner and not a consultant, is clearly needed and may well be needed for a long time—perhaps permanently—in the National Health Service. The push to use general practitioners may falter. However, the women who made up such a large part of the child health officer cadre were not aggressive and did not try to make a career of their jobs as the general practitioners or specialists did. If the women see a challenge and opportunity in this job and find they can get fulfillment from it, perhaps they will shake up the presently complacent, patronizing male planners, compelling them to give status to the job and certainly to recruit for and staff the service with less submissive types.

Something has to be said, too, about the somewhat condescending attitude of the pediatric consultants or, for that matter, any sort of specialist physician. They do consider themselves a cut above the ordinary practitioner, better trained and brainier. They do not want to be seen doing the same things as the lesser breeds, or in the same places. Their locus is the hospital and they want patients brought there. They prefer sick children with complex conditions. Providing comprehensive care is hardly their watchword. The Scottish and English planners may have in mind that the consultants will become "community paediatricians," but it will be a hard recommendation to enforce.

Health visitors, the backbone of the preventive child health system, were also to be transferred to the general practitioner's office at an accelerated rate as part of the reorganization. This had been discussed and decided years before as part of the move toward "integration" of health services, "team practice," and the elevation of general practitioner status and effectiveness. It is logical to visualize team practice and hard to argue that health visiting and medical practice should remain separate. The coordination was really inevitable after the assignment of local authority health responsibility to the area health authorities.

But the health visitor then becomes subject to the general practitioner's priorities, which, as mentioned above, give much less importance to the preventive role. Since older people are much more in need of home services, the general practitioner is glad to use the health visitor for increasing services to the aged at home. This relieves the general practitioner of some onerous duties and provides the aged with needed care, but it is another source of deprivation of preventive services to children. Unfortunately, the health visitors did not resist this transformation of role and seemed only too willing to go along with it.

Both prenatal visits and attendance at child health centers dropped more precipitously than the birth rate in Scotland in a 10-year period (1965-1974 and 1961-1973).[56] While no records of kinds of visits performed from the general practitioner's office are available for comparison, other evidence indicates that the slack in lost clinic visits is not being taken up by the general practitioner.[57]

Kingsley Whitmore, at one time responsible for health services in the Ministry of Education and Science, was crisply realistic in an interview on the effects of this process. The general practitioner is not geared to "population responsibility," knows little and cares less about preventive services for children. He estimates that 25 percent of inner city children need special attention to eliminate physical and emotional handicaps, attention that only a health visitor is capable of responding to, with home visits and conferences with mothers and preschoolers. The less time health visitors can spend with this group, the greater the risk of a population of handicapped school children and, eventually, handicapped adults.

In Whitmore's view, more health visitors with geographic responsibilities would go far toward resolving the problem. In the long run, social rehabilitation, more family allowance, and general practitioners better trained in pediatrics will help. But we needn't and can't wait for the long run.

When society assumes responsibility, as it does with the promulgation of laws for child health services, then parents are relieved of responsibility, and it becomes doubly important that society discharge its responsibility effectively. And parents need to be involved in carrying out needed care, because professionals alone cannot be relied upon to respond wholly to the needs of clients or to make the most effective use of resources. By temperament, professionals see problems in professional and not in personal terms.

Finally, another good and useful move with unfortunate side effects is the strong push to bring general practitioners together in health centers for a form of general practitioner group practice. This activity has had some considerable success in Scotland. By latest figures, there are 75 in operation serving approximately 20 percent of the population (963,000 people) with twice that many planned.[58] Health centers offer great opportunities for improving quality of services and patient care and introducing flexibility into general practitioner practice, allowing modest specialization and perhaps eventually some concentration on pediatric preventive services, as in the Scottish Model Health Center at Livingston.[59] Meanwhile, this has not been a widespread phenomenon, and at work again are the factors that reduce attention to children: the general practitioner's lack of interest in and training for child care and health visitor redirection to care of the aged. In addition, general practitioners are no longer in the neighborhood or as easily available as they once were, so patients increasingly use hospital emergency rooms for nonemergency services.

Shortages of health visitors, specifically to give services to children, will continue, and although some addition will be allowed, it does not augur well for the future.[60] But the concentration on the role of the general practitioner and the future role of the child health officer and the pediatrician in some choreographed arrangement for child care give reason to hope. A number of solutions are being debated. Among the consultant physicians, the emphasis is on the hospital, of course. The four major chiefs of service in the teaching hospitals visualize somewhat different, though not too dissimilar, solutions along these lines:

- The pediatric consultants (hospital physicians) would see all sick children and take responsibility for all assessment centers. (These are multidisciplinary units to which children are referred after screening for physical, mental, or social evaluation and treatment.)
- The general practitioner will do the screening and give primary care to sick children.
- As more general practitioners cluster into groups in health centers, some sorting out of specialty interests will take place, and some general practitioners will "concentrate" on (rather than "specialize" in) children. Some problems may arise about income; for example, the smaller panel size may not provide sufficient capitation money to the doctors who take a specialized panel of this kind, but this presumably can be worked out.
- Medical schools will increase pediatric teaching, and all graduates will be expected to spend two or three years in postgraduate work (residency) before entering practice. This will include child health service training.
- The registrars (residents) will play a part in child health work at the hospital (assessment) and in the group practices in the district (screening).

- Both general practitioners and residents will take part in the school health services.
- The former child health officers will not be needed and can be phased out, i.e., they can retire, become general practitioners, or be elevated to consultant status.
- One professor (Mitchell, at Dundee) envisions the development of a totally new kind of consultant, on a par with the community medicine specialist, concentrating on educational medicine, a specialty cognate with occupational medicine. He sees this specialty as a study of the child in the context of the school, involving knowledge of learning difficulties, the psychology of teaching, and health aspects of the school itself. This, of course, would be an addition to, not a substitute for, the above strategies.

Not all the professional groups agree on this scenario. The consultants tend to resist sharing pediatric responsibility with the general practitioners, and some designers prefer to keep the child health officers, with a true career line, in place.[61]

Crossman, first Secretary of State of the combined Department of Health and Social Security, also pointed out why it was likely that the pediatricians (consultants) would obstruct any mixing of the general practitioner and the consultant role. He said, "consultants are the most powerful autocrats in the world . . . What chance is there of a shift of money to the communities' services . . . ? They know nothing of what goes on outside hospitals and resent having to visit them . . . It is a marvelous service for the excitingly ill . . ."[62]

It will not be an easy solution.

It must not be concluded that the reorganization *caused* difficulties in the child health service or was responsible for what seems to be a decline in the effectiveness of the child and school health programs. The factors discussed, that in my mind played key roles in the development—the movement of the health visitor out of the public health center and into the general practitioner's office and the extreme reliance on the general practitioner altogether as the source of preventive services for children—long predates the reorganization. They are as a matter of fact, essential principles of British medical practice theory. The 1967 Sheldon Report, in its recommendations, states: "Eventually the child health service will . . . become part of a family health service provided by the family doctor in a family health center." It describes the varied forms of this practice:

"Some general practitioners, working on their own will give special sessions to running a child health service . . ." and goes on to say that "development of a group practice needs to be fostered." It calls for the "attachment of health visitors to the practice of the doctor concerned" and notes that" an increasing share in the preventive health services for children is being taken by general practitioners" a statement as hard to support as to refute since no data were provided. The same report adds a little hurriedly toward the end that "there is evidence that many general practitioners are unable to find the necessary time for preventive work."[63]

Whatever the theory, there is little doubt that the lesser success of the Scottish (and British) child health services generally, as compared with some other European countries, must be laid at the door of the child health care system. Poverty, unemployment, a depressed economy, financial starvation of the health service, and increasing numbers of vulnerable families certainly have had an important negative influence. The fact that family and children's allowances in Britain are lower than in other European countries has also played a part. But pushing the children into general practitioners' offices, where prevention and pediatric attention are a minimal concern, and pushing the health visitors into general practitioners' offices, where they inevitably must turn to work other than child care, are more important causes. Less prenatal and well-baby care in clinics hasn't been accompanied by increased prenatal and well-baby care in doctors' offices, and the decline in health visitors' home visits to preschool children is greater than can be accounted for by a decline in population.

These factors plus the confusion inherent in the reorganization have had their unfortunate impact. The relegation of the medical officer of health to the wings, as a community medical specialist with multiple responsibilities but no authority, was the crowning blow. Children had lost a significant sponsor and, consequently, priority concern status.

Jekel, in his own reaction to the reorganization of the British National Health Service, notes, "An important lesson for our country would seem to be that *preventive* care for children and adults is not assured when primary care is made accessible."[64] And Ann Cartwright, in her study of general practitioners, commented that they are alienated from the idea of prevention which is time consuming and neither professionally nor financially rewarding. [65]

The ambiguity in the general practitioner's role is the central difficulty in the problem of child health services and in the possible solutions. The GP may be deeply concerned with giving needed and appropriate primary care, but that does not include all the preventive services that constitute good child health care.

POLITICS OF CHILD HEALTH

Most puzzling to an American observer with some experience in the intricacy of health policy formation in the United States is the absence of any but professional (official, really) contribution to British policy making. Some of the basis for elected politicians' lack of interest or, at any rate, participation, may be the factors discussed earlier: the views of government members and party officials toward policy and political positions in a parliamentary form of government. This would help explain the dominance of professional officials, but it would not wholly explain the lack of public contribution to policy making, nor the weakness of the professional organizations in influencing health policies. A political scientist writes, "[the] British Labour Party ... [has] been able in recent decades to reform both health finances and health delivery system over the opposition of the leadership of medical associations. . . [yet] traditions of party discipline immunized legislative majorities against medical lobbying efforts." He adds, "A factor contributing to the lesser attraction and cohesion of the British Medical Association was the sharper division of interests between specialists and hospital based doctors on the one hand and general practitioners on the other."[66]

The political party in power cannot replace civil servants when the government changes, so one cannot accuse the Department of Health and Social Services of "politics" in their public policy positions. Still, it is interesting that the Labour Party document propounding the party position on health, published in 1977, echoes the administrative strategy of the department. It blesses the Court Report and calls attention to the fact that infant mortality rates are not keeping down to the low levels of Scandinavian countries and that the class differences in infant mortality have not narrowed. But the priorities are with the aged.[67]

Child health rarely receives even that much political party attention in the United States. In Britain, however, a public constituency for children, if not for child health, does exist. And perhaps the fact that the political party mentions child health is an evidence of the power of that constituency. In an amusing sidelight on the visibility of that children's constituency, the (Child Poverty Action Group), a minor scandal of the sort usually reserved in this country for national incidents of the Daniel Ellsberg or Daniel Schorr type, erupted when Frank Field, director of the Child Poverty Action Group, released extensive secret cabinet minutes to the press. Of course, the information concerned a cabinet decision not to increase children's benefits, but the prime minister had to address Parliament and put Scotland Yard (the Serious Crimes Squad!) on the trail of consultants and junior ministers and other such traitorous types to try to locate the leak. [68]

An exception to the singular lack of specific interest in health system organization by political parties is the Scottish National Party. This group, promoting a separate Scottish state, established a health policy committee and endorsed a number of straightforward actions to improve health, health services, and medical care in Scotland. To be sure, the majority of recommendations did not differ markedly from official professional recommendations in Scotland, but it is significant that the *party* adopted a health policy position.[69]

The professional group, the pediatric consultants, being only a handful, might be expected to wield little influence, or else to wield it only through the official matrix of consultant groups and advisory committees. But one would expect to find discussion and controversy among the physician groups who a) are in contact with children and see the defects of the system and b) are bound to be affected by whatever changes take place in system organization, pay arrangements, and the status of various groups or career lines.

Examination of the files of pediatrics publications offers some evidence of the weakness of this particular interest group's participation in policy making. There is no British journal exactly equivalent to the American journal *Pediatrics*, but the *Archives of Diseases in Childhood* comes closest.   Over the past five years, only one *Archives* article appeared that might have been called "community pediatrics" and two that touched on social pediatrics; they concerned the health status and treatment of immigrant children. In 1969, the *British Journal of Medical Education* published a series of articles on pediatric practice. The *British Medical Journal* in 1973 began to publish periodic news notes relating to the Court committee, looking forward to recommendations about pediatric practice. The journal *Developmental Medicine and Child Neurology* did substantially better, possibly because the contributors were closer to the effects of the medical care system imbalance as it touched children. Since the publication of the Court Report, there has been lively discussion and controversy, but largely over its recommendation about the doctor's role. *Developmental Medicine and Child Neurology,* beginning in 1975, published at least one article in each issue, sometimes only an editorial, relating to the need for reconsideration of the system, the participants (doctors, health visitors, and public health professionals), and the social attitudes toward the health rights of children. *Lancet,* a journal born in controversy and politically orientated from its beginnings in the early 19th century, was the exception and carried frequent articles on social pediatrics, the doctor's role, and suggestions for the reorganization of the service, both in editorials and signed articles.

One is tempted to wonder if the apparent lack of concern on the part of the professionals responsible for child care was the reason for their being barred from policy making participation. Or perhaps the social failure to recognize them and give them a participant role caused the physicians to fail to occupy themselves with studies and plans for the improvement of the system.

So far as the reason for public dissociation from policy making, one can only speculate. The Reorganization Act specifically provides for community health councils (local health councils in Scotland),[70] but except for London, they are virtually inactive. I interviewed the chairman and secretary of one such local health council and found that they met infrequently, had not demonstrated much concern yet for serious grievances (e.g., long waiting time in the doctor's office), and were concerned that physicians might not be paid enough! (American physicians fearful of nationalized medicine, take note.) True, their responsibility is not yet clear, and the Scottish experience is an early one. But at the moment, public participation seems minimal.

Political and academic spokesmen for the public are not happy with the health council structure. Barbara Castle feels the council idea was "tacked on" and was not intended to provide an appropriate grievance mechanism.[71] Other writers are more critical. Rudolf Klein, of the Center for Study of Social Policy, has written extensively on the British National Health Service's lack of democratic form. He writes bitterly, ". . . Parliamentary control is largely mythical . . .," (the bureaucracy runs the show with no check from government.) He notes, that "participation is high only if it involves access to extra resources ... linked to local self-interest ..." Why attend meetings if you can't correct the situation? As he observes, "the first law of participation, [is that] participation will increase in direct proportion to the resources at stake."[72]

Klein has also analyzed the effects of reorganization in disestablishing the previous informal structure of consumer representation. The area health authorities, *appointed* by the secretary, will provide a handful of public members (five or six) where the previous regional hospital boards and local hospital management committees had recruited literally hundreds of local people on a volunteer basis.[73] He goes on to analyze the class composition of representative community health councils to show that social class I and II are over-represented. He makes the same sort of analysis to show that the older age groups (50 percent of the population is over 55) hold 71 percent of the seats.[74] This makes a mockery of the intent ("The councils will . . . have strong roots in community and should be in a good position to represent the 'consumer' and the community as a whole. . . ."[75]) and leads to the kind of criticism that appeared in the *London Times* last November under the headline "Health Council Chairman Goes": "I have been chairman for two and a half years but I do not think the council has done anything to help anyone get better or quicker hospital treatment."[76]

Unlike in the United States where the general public, trade unions, elected officials and interest groups, comprised of both teaching and practicing professionals, actively try to influence health planning, in Britain only civil servants formulate policy.

CONCLUSION: LESSONS FOR THE UNITED STATES

The Scottish Health Service, promising comprehensive, universal entitlement to health services, obviously served the people well in ways they wanted and needed. Mortality and morbidity rates are well within the limits of acceptability for a high economic level, industrialized Western community. Patients—the consumers— are apparently quite satisfied with the service in view of the low level of complaints or other evidence of dissatisfaction.

However, there was clear evidence of insufficiency in service to children: relatively high infant mortality and infectious disease mortality rates, unnecessarily low immunization rates, and some undiscovered and untreated handicapping conditions.

It is too easy to lay the blame at the feet of the reorganization of the British National Health Service, which essentially accompanied, but did not cause, the intensification of health needs. In the Scottish experience, at least, the faltering economy exacerbated a variety of social ills, increasing the numbers of vulnerable or disadvantaged families and intensifying their distress. Since this problem is one that must be dealt with in the context of a comprehensive medical care system based on equity and universal entitlement, the confusion of the reorganization has not been helpful. That medical care system has survived, though staggering, under the massive blows of long-standing insufficient investment, misguided professional attacks, continuing academic neglect, and the ill-conceived (or at least ill-timed) administrative response that accompanies a radical reorganization of political regions, social services, and educational and health administrative systems.

Children's health services have fared least well within this congeries of calamitous events. Elimination of local administrative oversight has not been accompanied by effective planning, programming, or oversight from the new area health authorities or the new community medicine specialists. Putting health visitors in doctors' offices has been good for old people and bad for children. Giving responsibility for preventive services for children to the general practitioners has reduced the provision of those services.

Within the framework of universal entitlement to medical care, something more needs to be done to assure children of the preventive services they desperately need in order to grow to healthy, competent adulthood.

The Scottish program[77] and the Court Report for England[78] respond reasonably adequately to the specified needs:

- many more child health visitors (a marvelous designation!) with specific responsibilities for preventive services to children
- a special category of general practitioner with an interest in and training for care of children
- a consulting community pediatrician, a new type of specialist, who will work not in hospitals principally, but in community health centers to advise and supervise the general practitioners
- district "handicap" teams, working out of local hospitals to review and follow up on children who are screened and suspected to have physical, mental, or emotional defects

What is proposed is an *integrated* service, one that follows the child and has the child as its focus from before birth, through preschool and school years, and into adolescence.

We might say, that despite universal entitlement, many of the same kinds of children—poor and disadvantaged—who did not get care in the United States (where there is no universal entitlement) did not get care in Scotland, and the available data confirmed this. The situation isn't quite as bad—there is greater equity in access to care, obviously. But the preventive services are not all they could be.

The explanations offered were not too different from the explanations provided in the United States: familial neglect, poverty, vulnerable families unreached because of system defects, health personnel shortages, and the failure of outreach.

The solutions proposed were not too different either: "management by objective"— targeting the poor or vulnerable for specific care; changing the attitudes of physicians, especially general practitioners and pediatricians; increasing the numbers or availability of nurses; establishing priorities for care to focus on those in greater need.

Overall, the effects of poverty could not be ignored. A great deal more could be expected if the social system would provide more money to families to change their attitudes of hopeless desperation and to provide better housing and better schools. In other words, social justice, not charity, is as necessary as health and medical care systems improvement.

The poverty of the health system was also an important, if not overriding, factor. It is difficult to expect more to be done without more money. "The real cause of the present malaise in the National Health Service is that the Service is having to adjust itself to economic stringencies and new social attitudes..."[79]

When measuring the performance of the Scottish National Health Service in the area of child health care against America's haphazard medical care system, two questions emerge:

1. Is universal entitlement—a national health service— really the answer to the tormenting question of why health care for America's children is so poor?
2. Are a preventive system and greater social contributions necessary to perfect a child care program?

REFERENCES

1. R. Klein and J. Lewis, *The Politics of Consumer Representation* (London: Center for Studies in Social Policy, 1976). Klein pointed this out and mentioned an international income study in which the author concluded that it was most advantageous to be a physician in the United States, an academic in Germany, and a civil servant in Great Britain. "The best and brightest go where the rewards are greatest." His judgment, not mine.

2. Scottish Home and Health Department, *Toward an Integrated Child Health Service* (Edinburgh: HMSO, 1973); also, *The Health Service in Scotland: The Way Ahead* (Edinburgh: HMSO, 1976).

3. Scottish Home and Health Department, *The Child Health Services: A Systematic Planning Approach,* mimeographed (Edinburgh: HMSO, 1974).

4. Roy Mapes and Richard Dajda, "Children and the General Practitioner," in *Sociology of the National Health Service,* Margaret Stacey, ed., Sociological Review Monograph #22, University of Keele, March 1976.

5. "Court Committee on Paediatric Health Services," *British Medical Journal 4* (December 22, 1973): 748. A similar comment appeared in "Question Time," *Lancet 1* (June 23, 1973): 1,458.

6. Data provided by the Department of the Environment and the Scottish Development Department.

7. Data from Central Office of Information, *Scotland* (London: HMSO, 1974) or Scottish Information Office, *Scotland in Profile* (Edinburgh: HMSO, 1976).

8. Quoted in A. Yerby, *Community Medicine in England and Scotland* (Washington, D.C.: Government Printing Office, 1976), HEW pub. no. (NIH) 76-1061.

9. Fuller descriptions of the actual operation of the British National Health Service today in England and in Scotland can be found in a number of books and articles. There is Ruth Levitt, *The Reorganised National Health Service* (London: Croom-Helm, 1976); T.E. Chester, *Organization for Change: The British National Health Service* (Paris: OECD, 1975); G. MacLachlan, *The British National Health Service: Policy Trends* (Paris: OECD, 1975); and Scottish Home and Health Department, *The Health Services in Scotland: The Way Ahead* (Edinburgh: HMSO, 1976).

10. J. J. A. Reid, "Epilogue," in *Positions, Movements and Directions in Health Services Research,* ed. G. MacLachlan (Oxford: Oxford University Press, 1974). Dr. Reid is now chief medical officer for Scotland.

11. Personal communication, Professor J. N. Morris.

12. Department of Health and Social Security, *Democracy in the National Health Service* (London: HMSO, 1974). Rudolf Klein, then with the Center for Studies in Social Policy, described reorganization as "..a curious hybrid between 19th century Fabianism and 20th century managerialism."

13. Barbara Castle, *National Health Service Revisited* (London: Fabian Society, 1976).

14. Central Information Office, *Health Services in Britain* (London: HMSO, 1974).

15. Department of Health and Social Security, *Sharing Resources for Health in England* (London: HMSO, 1976). For another view, there is *Whose Priorities?* (London: Radical Statistics Health Group, 1976), in response to DHSS, *Priorities for Health and Personal Social Services in England* (London: HMSO, 1976), as well as the more measured and more conservative dissent in M.H. Cooper, *Rationing Health Care* (London: Croom-Helm, 1975).

16. Scottish Home and Health Department, *Scottish Health Statistics* (Edinburgh: HMSO, 1975).

17. Ibid. (for Scottish data). U.S. Data from U.S. Department of Health, Education, and Welfare, *Health—United States, 1976-1977* (Hyattsville, Md.: HEW, HRA, 1977), HEW pub. no. (HRA) 77-1232.

18. *Statutes at Large*, UK 14 and 15 Victoria, 1851, Chapter XI.

19. H. K. Bevan, *Laws Relating to Children* (London: Butterworth, 1973).

20. Scottish Home and Health Department, *Social Work Services in the Scottish Health Service* (Edinburgh: HMSO, 1976). See also Central Office of Information, *Social Services in Britain* (London: HMSO, 1976). Some observations were made directly in conversations with Beti Jones, chief social work advisor to the Scottish Office.

21. Scottish Home and Health Department, *Toward an Integrated Child Health Service*, p. 1.

22. Ibid. pp. 8-11.

23. Department of Health and Social Security, *Priorities for Health and Personal Social Services*, p. 62.

24. Department of Health and Social Security, *Prevention and Health: Everybody's Business* (London: HMSO, 1976), Figure 4.3, p. 48.

25. Scottish Home and Health Department, *Scottish Health Statistics 1975*.

26. Scottish Home and Health Department, *Health Services in Scotland, Report for 1975* (Edinburgh: HMSO, 1976); Treasury, *Public Expenditures to 1979-80* (London: HMSO, 1976); Scottish Office, *Accounts 1974-75* (Edinburgh, HMSO, 1976).

27. G. M. Lowdon and J. H. Walker, "The School Health Service and the School Doctor," pp. 45-85 in *Bridging in Health*, ed. G. MacLachlan (Oxford, Oxford University Press, 1975).

28. M. Wagner, *Sweden's Health Screening Program for Four Year Old Children* (Washington, D.C.: Government Printing Office, 1975), HEW pub. no. (ADM) 76-282.

29. A. W. Franklin, *Widening Horizons Of Child Health* (Lancaster: MTP, 1976), Tables 8.1 and 8.3.

30. Ibid., p. 65.

31. R. Maxwell, *Health Care: A Growing Dilemma*, 2nd ed. (New York: McKinsey & Co., 1975).

32. R. L. Sivard, *World Military and Social Expenditures 1977* (Virginia: WMSE Publications, 1977).

33. Maxwell, *Health Care*.

34. Frank Field, *Unequal Britain* (London: Arrow Books, 1975).

35. P. Townsend, *Sociology and Social Policy* (Harmondsworth: Penguin, 1975), pp. 326 and 327.

36. D. Boswell, "The National Health Service," in *Health: Decision Making in Britain* (Bletchley: Open University Press, 1972) p. 97. R. H. S. Crossman, the first secretary of state for social services, in the same article (p. 88) from a speech he made to the Fabian Society after he left office, is quoted as saying that the continuing inequities were the direct responsibility of the professional oligarchy controlling the National Health Service. In his colorful way he attacked "the most perfect example of a self-perpetuating oligarchy since the Persians' rule by Satraps. . . . " and he added, "It is a marvelous health service for those that are excitingly ill, not desperately ill—you mustn't die boringly for the consultants. . . . "

37. Frank Field, *Poverty: The Facts* (London: Child Poverty Action Group, 1975), p. 39.

38. Franklin, *Widening Horizons*, p. 249.

39. See Shari Steiner, *The Female Factor* (New York: Putnam, 1977) pp. 30-48 for an extended treatment of the lack of concern for women, in what she calls the "vaunted welfare state." Steiner reviews the situation of women in several European countries and puts the U.K. fairly low on the scale of concern. For example, the employer in Britain does not have to allow a pregnant woman to continue to work, pay her a maternity benefit, or save a job for her when she returns. Because she feels babies of normal weight have a better chance for survival at home (an opinion not generally shared by obstetricians, however) she is critical of the National Health Service for not fostering home childbirth service. From her interviews and observations, she believes 9 out of 10 women would prefer to have every baby except the first at home. See also J.M. Gandy, "Scottish Governmental Reorganizations and Human Service Delivery by Teams," in *Meeting Human Needs: Additional Perspectives*, ed. D. Thursz and J.L. Vigilante (Beverly Hills: Sage, 1976), Chapter 2.

40. Field, *Poverty: The Facts*, p. 39.

41. Comment by Margaret and Arthur Wynn, authors of *The Protection of Maternity and Infancy: A Study of the Services for Pregnant Women and Young Children in Finland* (London: Council for Children's Welfare, 1974); and "Report of a Study Group on Pediatricians and the Health of Children," mimeographed, Moor Park College, 26th to 29th April, 1976.

42. Barbara Evans, "Poverty Prevails," *World Medicine*, July 14, 1976, pp. 61-67.

43. M. Manciaux and J.P. Deschamps, "Les Familles Vulnérables," *Médicine Sociale et Préventive* 19(1974):79-83.

44. Evans, "Poverty Prevails."

45. Scottish Home and Health Department, *Toward an Integrated Child Health Service*, pp. 5-16.

46. Committee on Child Health Services, *Fit For the Future* (London: HMSO, 1976), known as the "Court Report," after the chairman, Professor S.D.M. Court.

47. Central Health Services Council, *Report of a Subcommittee of the Standing Medical Advisory Committee on Child Welfare Centres* (London: HMSO, 1967), known as the "Sheldon Report," after the chairman, Sir Wilfred Sheldon.

48. Department of Health and Social Security, *Priorities*, p. 62.

49. Scottish Home and Health Department, *The Way Ahead*, pp. 16-18.

50. Central Health Services Council, *"Sheldon Report."*

51. Scottish Home and Health Department, *Toward an Integrated Child Health Service*.

52. Yerby, *Community Medicine*, p. 54. ". . . reorganization often meant assignment of a medical officer to a narrow categorical program area in a new location and with a change from an executive role to a staff or advisory capacity."

53. See, among others, European Office of WHO, *Problems of Children of School Age: Report of a Working Group* (Copenhagen: WHO, 1976); and other papers referred to above: *"Sheldon Report," "Court Report,"* and *Toward an Integrated Child Health Service*.

54. Donald Court and Anthony Jackson, ed., *Paediatrics in the Seventies* (Oxford: Oxford University Press, 1972), p. 7.

55. M. Gilmore, N. Bruce, and M. Hunt, *The Work of the Nursing Team in General Practice* (London: Whitefriars Press, 1974), p. 154.

56. E.J. Thompson and C. Lewis, ed., *Social Trends No. 6 1975* (London: HMSO, 1975), Table 2.24, p. 73.

57. Personal communication from Dr. George Forwell, CAMO, Greater Glasgow Health Board. Professor Hutchinson, professor of pediatrics at Glasgow University, points out that before reorganization, only 47 percent of children who appeared in emergency rooms came self-referred, while in 1974, 87 percent. Further, over 50 percent of children at school entry have handicaps previously undiscovered.

58. Scottish Home and Health Department, *Health Services for Scotland.*

59. Central Office of Information, *Scotland*, p. 69.

60. Attaching the health visitor to the *center* rather than to an individual general practitioner may serve to modify the impact on children's services, allowing the health visitors the lead in determining priorities and visiting objectives. If the health visitors can establish clear priorities, with major emphasis on the vulnerable families, those truly needy in preventive terms, it may be that more health visitors may not be needed and, in addition, a much more satisfactory job done. One Community Medicine Specialist in Glasgow put it this way: "they [the health visitors] need to be alerted to those falling by the wayside. Right now, we'll get a card that reads 'moved', or 'door is shut, no answer.' It means they feel they're not welcome; they're not invited in for a cup of tea, as they used to be. Those are the families that need them the most!" It appears that the whole system needs alerting to this, not just the health visitors.

61. J.A. Davis and F.N. Bamford, "The Community Pediatrician in an Integrated Child Health Service." *Archives of Diseases of Childhood*, 50 (January 1975): pp. 1-3.

62. Boswell, *Decision Making in Britain*, p. 88.

63. Central Health Services Council, *"Sheldon Report."*

64. James Jekel, "Maternal and Child Health Services Under the Reorganization of the British National Health Service." mimeographed. Presented at the Annual Meeting of the American Public Health Association, October 23, 1976. Available from the author, Yale University Department of Epidemiology and Public Health.

65. Ann Cartwright, *Patients and Their Doctors* (London: Routledge and Kegan Paul, 1967).

66. A.J. Heidenheimer in *Comparative Public Policy*, ed. A.J. Heidenheimer, H. Heclo, and C.T. Adams (London: St Martins Press, 1976), p. 24.

67. Labour Party, *The Right To Health*, "Labour's Plan for the National Health Service" (London, July 1977), pp. 20-22 and 43.

68. "Yard Unable to Identify Social Benefits Leak" *London Times*, 18 November 1976.

69. Scottish National Party, "Health Policy Committee Report"

70. Scottish Home and Health Department, *The National Health Service and the Community in Scotland* (Edinburgh: HMSO, 1974).

71. Castle, *National Health Service Revisited.*

72. R. Klein, quoted in S. Hatch, *Towards Participation in Local Services* (London: Fabian Society, 1973), p. 9.

73. Klein and Lewis, *Politics of Consumer Representation*, p. 11.

74. Ibid., p. 61.

75. Scottish Home and Health Department, *The National Health Service and the Community.*

76. *London Times*, 12 November 1976.

77. Scottish Home and Health Department, *Toward an Integrated Child Health Service.*
78. Committee on Child Health Services, *"Court Report."*
79. Castle, *National Health Service Revisited.*

Chapter 9

Holland

THE SETTING

Holland (the Netherlands), a small country in northern Europe, is the most densely populated country in the world with 326 inhabitants per square kilometer. In 1974, thirteen and a half million people lived in the Netherlands, 27 percent of the population under fourteen years of age; two and a half million were school children, one million toddlers, two hundred thousand under one year of age.

The largest city is Rotterdam, with a population of just over a million.[1] Confined as they are in a tiny territory, a large part of which has actually been "made" out of drowned land by judicious diking and draining by the shrewd, industrious, imaginative people, the Dutch early learned the lesson of mutual interdependence.

Their history unfolds the complex and fascinating story of a brave people committed from the earliest known times to democratic forms and local self-government. John Motley, in his inordinately detailed and splendidly embellished account, *The Rise of the Dutch Republic*,[2] expresses his unstinting admiration of this worthy people at the beginning of the 16th century:

> three millions of people, the most industrious, the most prosperous, perhaps the most intelligent under the sun. Their cattle ... are the finest in Europe, their agricultural products of more ... value then if nature had made their land to overflow with wine and oil. Their navigators are the boldest, their mercantile marine the most powerful, their merchants the most enterprising in the world. The Flemish skill in the

mechanical and the fine arts is unrivaled. Their national industry was untiring; their prosperity unexampled; their love of liberty indomitable; their pugnacity proverbial.

He speaks of this people with great respect and describes a nation marked "by one prevailing characteristic, one master passion—the love of liberty, the instinct of self-government."[3] The remarkable qualities that the Dutch people display in modern times —resolute and resilient, freedom loving and respectful of the freedom and liberty of others—is a heritage of the bloody times that marked the formation of the Dutch Republic.

It is a country even today sharply divided along religious lines. Although Christianity found a foothold in a Netherlands in early Roman times, this was not a province very dutiful to papal authority. As Motley writes, "Heresy was a plant of early growth in the Netherlands."[4] The suppression of Protestant heretics of one kind or another persisted for four hundred years, culminating in such severe persecution by the Inquisition under the Catholic kings of Spain, that one result was the revolutionary uprising to establish the republic. However, despite a significant Protestant minority, Catholicism remains the dominant religion of Holland, providing us perhaps with one key to an understanding of the forces allowing the maintenance of that balance that marks the Dutch people today.

An important aspect of the Dutch response to the social needs of individuals is the maintenance of pluralism. The encouragement of separatism as a useful response to social needs may very well be a result of the historic forces that make it necessary for people of differing opinions, differing backgrounds, and differing religions, to construct a common life in the compressed space given to them. The strengthening of pluralism has, however, historically been a natural concomitant of Dutch life. A critical element of this pluralism is that it is inclusive rather than exclusive, welcoming new and added models rather than resisting and attempting to fuse heretical and dissident ideas into the status quo.

Other countries tend to restrict their pluralism to traditional patterns and reject unfamiliar models. The Dutch seem to seek them out and encourage differences. Even the amalgamation of previously independent lines, as, for example, among the various Cross societies to be discussed later, the fusion is carried out with respect for the continuity of individual concerns—of the individual organizations and of the individual members of those organizations as well—and the separate nature of the included elements is maintained.

The Dutch have long taken the sophisticated view that the responsibilities of government are merely extensions of already assumed social obligations and not inroads into private ones. In other words, "law follows custom" or, as we sometimes say ironically in the United States, "The Supreme Court follows the election returns." In Holland there is none of the argument and conflict that still goes on in our own country about whether there should be public support for day care, children's allowances, and school health services, court support for children in broken families, or battered wives and treatment of abused, neglected, and battered children. The reason is simple. Before the government will concern itself with these matters, the private sector will already have undertaken measures to cope with these issues on fairly extensive bases. Government action follows, and is supplementary or complementary to an already committed social decision. Private initiative had banned child labor fifty years before a law banning child labor was passed. "The measures taken by government frequently link up with what has already been achieved by the social forces themselves."[5] A half century before the passage of the Housing Act, private housing associations had already been founded and were improving housing conditions for working people. But, "private first, when private fails, public steps in."[6]

The history of the Netherlands offers us some background on the origin of this kind of social sentiment: the respect for individual opinions and liberty of thought on the one hand and, on the other, continuing sentiment favoring equity and protection for individual citizens demonstrated by common action. The legislation that follows voluntary action is for the purpose of equity; it assists the voluntary action and is not intended to compel or to impose unwelcome restrictions on the citizens. It is not unlikely that the pressures of population within the small national area, coupled with oppression by foreign rulers, played some part in this, but economic history also played a part. When Belgium and Holland were one, Antwerp, now the chief port city of Belgium, was the major seaport of the Low Countries. For a hundred years it was the chief port of Europe and the commercial capital of the world. The Low Countries grew wealthy as the silks and spices of Asia and then the gold and fascinating, heretofore unknown produce of the New World were hauled across the docks of Antwerp. Marvelous finished goods of the Low Countries flowed out and the traders and shopkeepers grew wealthy.[7] The wealth and interdependence of these bourgeois leaders gave them a stolidity and stability that eliminated any need to be persecutors or oppressors.

In speaking of William of Orange, who successfully led the revolt against Spanish Rule, Motley writes, "Sincerely and deliberately himself a convert to the Reform Church, he was ready to extend freedom of worship to Catholics on the one hand and to Anabaptists on the other, for no man ever felt more keenly than he, that the reformer who becomes in his turn a bigot is doubly odious."[8] This is not the place for an extensive review or analysis of the fascinating historic events that have contributed to the attitudes, and eventually programs, of the people of modern Holland. Nevertheless, it is important that these historic matters be kept in mind as the nature of the child health program is described and analyzed, particularly as one attempts to move from appreciation of the humane and beneficial aspects of the Dutch medical care system to a consideration of what might become useful models for our own country. While the differences in history alone may not be sufficient to create a barrier to acceptance, the attitudes and habits of mind that are the result of those different histories may well be insurmountable obstacles.

HEALTH AND WELFARE SERVICES

Social Benefits

Almost all European countries offer a wide variety of social services that represent a basic platform upon which health services are built. These include special attention to the pregnant woman —maternity leave with or without pay, a maternity allowance that in some countries is translated into a layette for the child instead of money, home help services for the mother if the child is delivered at home, and varying periods of paid leave from work (up to seven months in Sweden) after the child is born.

For each child almost all the countries in Europe provide a children's allowance on top of a family allowance. In general, the health services pay for, or provide, medical care required by the pregnant woman, midwifery, and the medical services required by the child, both preventive and curative. To this, many countries add a rent allowance for families with large numbers of children to allow them to provide better housing for themselves, recognizing how difficult it is for a paycheck to stretch across the housing needs of families with large numbers of children. In Sweden, where this concept of fairness is emphasized, it is recognized that childless individuals or couples, and families with children can be expected to live at the same level only if there is family support, and they feel there should not be a penalty attached to having children. In Denmark, rent subsidies for low-income families amount to the entire cost of rental if the family has six children.

In 1972 when the average weekly wage of a Dutch male industrial worker with two children under sixteen was 315 florins ($125), he received an additional 9 percent of his wages—27 florins ($11)—as a children's allowance.[9]

Children are protected in other ways by the social structure. For example, in Finland, when the parents are not living together, and one of them is obliged to pay the other a child support allowance, the state is permitted to pay "prepayment maintenance" to ensure that the parent with the child will have adequate funds to support the child. The state then collects from the parent who owes the money.[10]

Holland stands very close to the top in providing most of these support structures for child care. In public expenditures for education and health, Holland spent well over 10 percent of the gross national product, surpassing most other European countries, whose expenditures were 10 percent or below.[11] In brief, European society attempts to compensate for whatever deficiencies the economic situation may impose on the family, so that all children may have an unrestricted opportunity to develop their own potential. In addition to the economic and social efforts for balance and equity, the law is heavily committed to the children's cause. Single parents, under an extra burden, are compensated with additional funds from the state treasury for mother's helpers to assure that the child will not be overlooked. In the schools, health examinations, health assessment, and preventive services include the search for handicaps, for which treatment is assured. Meals are provided and nutrition is guaranteed. All of these efforts are aimed at compensating possible deficiencies in the home.

One major difference between American and Dutch social settings that may have an important influence on this area of intensive child care and child concern is the surprisingly small number of Dutch married women in the labor force—3 percent as compared with 25 percent or more in other countries.

The implication of this figure for debates about child care in the United States cannot be overlooked. Dutch society has little need for day care centers when that society provides liberal and extensive incentives for mothers to remain at home and look after their own children. The school's influence on health care will be powerfully supplemented by the fact that a nurse visiting will probably find a parent at home and there will be few if any "key" children. What further implication this may have for the feminist struggle toward equity in employment and social advancement is beyond the scope of this book, but there can be little doubt that that too would be reflected in the relation of families to children and child health.

Health Services

Health and medical care services in Holland represent a curious patchwork of many disparate elements. As Professor Kronendonk, director of the Institute of Tropical Hygiene, commented cheerfully, "Health services in Holland are the best organized chaos in the world! We prefer it that way. Personal individual *curative* approach; community approach to preventive care."[13] Public health services include *all* preventive services and environmental control services as well as the research activities in the National Institute of Public Health and Hygiene. The director-general of public health is responsible also for the supervision of other health aspects, without direct administrative control: social security medical care services, hospital care, out-patient care, mental health care, pharmaceutical preparation, and food product purity. There is a health council to provide scientific advice and guidance. In addition, the Ministry of Health has an Inspectorate General whose task is to investigate public health conditions and indicate means of improving them, reporting on the implementation of the acts and decrees concerning health and medical service in the Netherlands. The Inspectorate General reports directly to the minister and operates through seven district inspectors who have staff for looking into all the matters relating to physical health, mental health, environmental health, pharmaceuticals, food licensing, and veterinary affairs.[14]

Parallel with the official governmental role is a private health role, chiefly in the field of preventive medicine and heavily concerned with maternal and child health. As a matter of fact, the great majority of official preventive service is delegated to private agencies while continuing to be supervised by the official health services. The private agencies are the Cross societies, their number and variety deriving historically from Dutch efforts to maintain separate and equal religious programs in every area of life. This unusual Dutch social "denominational separation," "verzuiling" (columnization) in Dutch, will also be discussed in some detail later.

The medical care system admits certain shortcomings. A serious lack of vital data on functioning obstructs any self-correcting mechanism to reward for good care or penalize for bad care. Corollary with this is inadequate regulation and practically no liaison with other health care elements such as the educational, research, or the preventive sectors. Recommendations for improvements sound oddly like American proclamations: cost benefit analysis of new services, specialties, and equipment before introduction; reduction in the number of specialists' referrals; treatment of "social" conditions as medical; more data and a better coordination of records; better education of physicians; cheaper and more effective techniques; education of patients; social reforms; and, particularly important, more government leadership in designing data collection and assisting in the linkage of the general practitioner, the specialist, the hospital, and sick fund data.[15]

Medical Insurance

Medical care is provided through a variety of insurance programs, some compulsory and some voluntary. For all those in paid employment and earning less than a fixed amount, compulsory insurance against the cost of medical care is provided. About 70 percent of the population is covered, the cost met equally by employer and employee contributions. This insurance covers the services of general practitioners, either at their offices or in the patients' homes, specialists' services (including those of an obstetrician or midwives), medications, a full year's hospitalization, and nursing and treatment in a sanatorium. In addition, there is another insurance fund, to which the employer alone contributes and which the government subsidizes with tax funds, that provides for long-term care in mental hospitals and other institutions for mental or chronic illness. Everyone is entitled to these services. Old people and pensioners have their insurance paid for either in part or wholly by the government through participation in the compulsory health insurance scheme. The rest of the population (over-income, or privately employed), although voluntarily insured, under the latest law has access to the same sick funds and the same coverage as those covered in the compulsory plan.

Under the sick fund insurance, the general practitioner, who receives a fixed amount per patient, is permitted private practice as well, but is discouraged from taking too many capitation patients by a sharp reduction in the capitation allowance for any patients over 1,800. The specialist is customarily paid on a fee-for-service basis. Both the general practitioner with paying patients and the specialist charge according to a negotiated fee schedule. Patients never see a bill and do not have to pay at the point of service. The physician's income is totally provided through the insurance organizations. Capitation fee and fee-for-service scales are negotiated annually between the insurance organizations and the doctors' organization.

While there are the usual complaints of overutilization and unnecessary hospitalization as well as unnecessary specialist referrals, the system seems to be satisfactory to both doctors and patients. At various levels of control in the insurance funds there is representation of the trade unions, hospital administration, physicians, the patients themselves and the government. There is an umbrella organization of the 70 or so sick funds, and while there is competition for new accounts among them, charges, reimbursements, and benefits are obviously the same.

Van Langendonck makes the point that the general government insurance for long-term care and chronic illness, which covers 100 percent of the population, may be the reason why there has been no impetus in the Netherlands to insure larger numbers against the ordinary costs of medical care. While less than 80 percent of the Dutch population has general health care insurance, France and Belgium, for example, have almost 100 percent coverage, and a national health system covers the whole population in Britain.[16] Yet, while Holland operates under an insurance system in which the patients pay something on the order of 30 percent of medical care costs if they are not under the compulsory full-cost coverage, families that must purchase voluntary insurance do not pay for children under age 16.[17]

Preventive Services

The jewel in the crown of the health service is the emphasis on prevention. On the preventive side, public health in Holland consists of wide-ranging national requirements supervised and controlled at the local level by municipal authorities who are chiefly concerned with *health* care. In addition, there is a surprisingly strong and interestingly different private sector element which is involved in the delivery of preventive services, sometimes independently, and some-times in association with municipal authorities.

The system pays for preventive services and for broad ambula-tory psychotherapeutic help. It also supports neighborhood health centers, which take the place of private physicians' offices in 30 or 40 locations. These are well received and may eventually replace the doctor's office as ordinary primary care units.[18] Federal expenditures for public health services (excluding medical care paid for out of sickness insurance) come to 1.4 percent of the gross national income in 1972 (most recent data). Of the total $3.3 billion (translated into American money) that was spent in Holland for all medical and health care, about 25 percent went for preventive services and 40 percent for medical care. Of the amount paid for all preventive care—of mothers and children, school children, preventive services for those working in factories, boarding out of children and so forth—the federal government paid 25 percent. Obstetrical care, maternity aid, preventive care for mothers and children, and pre-ventive services for school children and for older students came to something under 3 percent of the overall cost of health and medical care.[19]

The official—municipal—authority in most urban areas operates prenatal and well-baby clinics and supervises the school health services consisting of 144 school health centers staffed by full-time physicians who are responsible for all the school children in Holland. District School Health authorities have the responsibility in rural areas, but both district and municipal authorities operate under the supervision of provincial health authorities who in turn are respon-sible to the chief medical officer of public health. While there is cooperation with the Cross societies at all levels, only in one province (Limburg, with a population of one million) do the Cross societies actually operate the school health services.

While parents are permitted to select their own physician for school health services, nearly 100 percent choose the school doctor. Examination of the school child, except for adolescents, is done in the presence of the mother when possible. School doctors are specially trained in the Netherlands Institute for Preventive Medicine in Leiden and receive three full years of training—one in the school ("child and school health") and two in the field—and are recognized specialists in social medicine after completion of that course. How-ever, fewer than half the present school doctors have had that training.[20]

Perhaps about 2 percent of the children in Holland with handicapping conditions may not come under the umbrella of care because they are neglected by their parents or they fall through the net of nursing and health care services. However, unlike the United States, it is not likely that all of these will fall in the category of minority or migrant children. Special efforts are made with outreach services to make sure that the children of migrant workers ("guest workers" is the polite term), for example, and migrants now represent one seventh of the population, are not overlooked. The children from the former colonies in Indonesia and Surinam receive identical care with other children in the community. In certain circumstances, according to the columnization system in Holland, such care may be provided in their own clinics, staffed with their own nurses and physicians.

The director-general of health services spoke of how carefully district nurses follow up on the children for whom they are responsible. They visit homes periodically, and they make sure to visit when a child misses a scheduled examination, assessment, or immunization to discuss with the family the cause and what can be done to remedy it. When possible, the nurse gives immunizations or examinations in the home. The director-general himself is responsible for 2,600 children—the children of migratory families, the so-called canal children, and gypsy children. He notifies district nurses in areas where these migrant children are to be found at the specific times they are to be examined or immunized to make sure that they get the necessary visit.

Maternal Care

In 1971, sixty percent of the births in the Netherlands were at home, the majority attended by midwives. The Dutch have also created a special person called a maternity aid, who receives 15 months' training and looks after the mother at home after the child is born. The norms for maternal care under Dutch preventive services, whether in a municipal health department or in a Cross organization, are carefully spelled out. They are designed to offer the maximum protection for mother and child consistent with modern medical philosophy while satisfying the family's need and desire when births take place outside the hospital. Many hospital deliveries are also performed by midwives, although specialists are beginning to take over more maternal care. These specialists, however, seem to be taking practice away from the general practitioners rather than from the midwives.

While data for specific years are not available, a rough comparability for the period 1973-1975 can be established. There were 373 obstetrical specialists in Holland during that period, 862 practicing midwives, and 4,800 general practitioners. Of the nearly 90,000 babies born in hospitals, 80 percent were delivered by obstetricians (in most instances with the assistance of midwives), 15 percent by midwives alone, and only 5 percent by general practitioners. However, of the approximately 90,000 babies born at home, 53 percent were delivered by midwives and 47 percent by general practitioners. In all, midwives appear to participate in the delivery of about 35 percent of all babies born in Holland.

Home deliveries take place not only in small rural communities. Nearly 11,000, or one-third of all the births in large cities, took place at home, while 78,000, or 50 percent of the births in smaller communities or rural areas, took place at home. Even in large cities, half the children were born with the assistance of midwives.[21]

The care with which the Dutch maternity service observes the pregnant woman, reducing the possible risks in home deliveries, is indicated in a table in the 1976 report from the Ministry of Health on obstetrical services.[22] In that year, when 90,000 babies were born in the home, only 571 pregnant women had to be hospitalized—fewer than 1 percent—which is a fairly good indication of how careful the selection process is, as well as the relatively low danger level of home delivery in Holland.

Home deliveries are facilitated because of the existence of an active and enterprising Home Help Organization. This again is a private organization, some 50 years old, which has had its most remarkable growth since World War II. Well over half of the deliveries, all those that take place at home, are attended by a maternity home helper. To a considerable extent, the services are paid for under the maternity option of the sickness benefit fund, and the government subsidizes the organization as it does other voluntary health organizations. The growth of this service has not only benefited the women who delivered at home, but has also made it possible for women to be discharged earlier from the hospital, within a few hours or, at the very most, after a few days' confinement. The maternity home helper provides care for the mother and child for ten days after confinement. In cases where a midwife is not present, but a general practitioner is performing the home delivery, the maternity home helper assists the physician.[23] The effectiveness of the Dutch maternal and infant care system is reflected in its infant mortality rate. In 1972 WHO reported the Netherlands' rate among the lowest in Europe: Sweden 11.1, Finland 11.3, and the Netherlands 11.5 per 1,000 live births.[24]

The Dutch Cross Society

The private nonprofit organizations which play such an important role in the Netherlands' health services and which employ 3,800 nurses in almost 2,000 branches are called Cross organizations. Over 3 million families are members (nearly 10 million people). At the present time, there is a union of Cross societies that operates in provincial groups under governmental supervision but is not controlled by government. These Cross organizations began in the late 19th century in response to the agitation by the then inspector general of public health, for private, self-help organizations to combat typhoid epidemics. He did not believe that these patients should be in hospitals, but that they needed nursing at home. The Cross organization was developed to provide for home care for these typhoid patients.

White Cross in North Holland was the first such organization. Green Cross followed soon after, and the White-Yellow and Orange-Green came into being in this century. In the rural areas, where these organizations are strongest, the official district nurses are attached to them. The local Cross organizations at one time had only limited responsibility for nursing in the home, but their responsibilities have since been widened to include preventive care, care of tuberculosis patients, maternal and child health care, mental health care, and education on and treatment of venereal disease and cancer.

Local chapters are chartered as corporations and are in fact autonomous, electing their own boards and deciding on policies such as coordination with other agencies or with local health departments. Their responsibilities are modest, and more specialized services are provided through a variety of consultants employed by the next echelon—the provincial Cross organizations. All these are under the umbrella of the National Cross Society, with headquarters in Utrecht.[25]

The largest of the societies today is the Green Cross (nondenominational) with the White-Yellow (Roman Catholic) and the Orange-Green (Protestant) evenly matched just behind it. As mentioned earlier, the bulk of membership is in the rural areas.[26]

The Cross organizations charge a modest membership fee. Their budget is "topped off" by government in the form of grants. The budget of the Cross organization includes nurses' salaries, physicians' consultation fees, and whatever transportation and equipment are required for the preventive services. The income from dues and whatever fees are charged to patients not eligible for the services are subtracted and the government pays the difference. The grants may be subjected to qualifying conditions to guarantee that the subsidies are spent as effectively as possible. The authorities try not to interfere with the independent operation of these nonprofit organizations, but it does set conditions on the use of these funds. It is estimated that 25 percent of the Cross organization budget derives from dues; 15 percent from charges; 35 percent from the state; 5 percent from the province; and 20 percent from the municipality—which means that 60 percent is basically tax funds.

Professional Training

Medical education is quite similar to that in the United States and hardly needs elaboration. The difference is in the relatively smaller number of specialists who are trained and available, and the subsequent greater reliance upon and confidence in family doctors or general practitioners. There is also a category of "social medicine" practitioners, some with training at the Netherlands Institute of Preventive Medicine, who act as consultants to the Cross societies and health departments. In effect, they act as intermediaries, rather than as consultants in our sense, between the general practitioners, school doctors (some of whom are themselves social medicine specialists), and the hospital specialists.

Following graduation from a nursing school, Cross nurses used to go through 10 months' training, which was largely an apprenticeship, following the working nurse in an on-the-job experience. Recently, the training was expanded to 22 months and now includes academic or scientific training, including physiology, psychology, sociology, and theology. Also included is a social medicine component, which includes psychiatry, social problems of families, children, and the aged, and methods of home care. Following this, 6 of the 22 months are spent in the field as before, 1 month of which is an elective.[27]

Among professional administrators and especially in the official health departments, there is some expression of dissatisfaction with the Crosses. ("The Cross we bear," an anonymous administrator proclaims.) Some local groups are tiny, some small communities have to put up with a number of very small Cross units for the sake of "denominational separation." It is increasingly difficult to staff small organizations, and they tend to be less cost-effective. Nevertheless, despite disparaging comments of anonymous commentators— "Verzuiling is out-of-date; time to intergrate!"— the coalition of the Crosses is being accomplished in discreet and relatively painless ways, allowing the organizations to continue to be the employers, if not the directors, of the nurses and doctors in the preventive services, to continue to operate within the framework of the combined official agencies.

CHILD HEALTH CARE

As pointed out earlier, while the Cross societies take a very large share of responsibility for the preventive services for mothers and children, gradually, and especially in the large cities, the municipal services are absorbing the activities, providing services to all the mothers and children in the municipality while utilizing the Cross nurses and doctors for the work. Amsterdam is the model of such absorption.

Because government has been assigned and has assumed so much responsibility for assuring Dutch citizens that they will receive prompt, necessary medical care of good quality, local health departments have elaborate supervisory and control mechanisms as well as operational systems for the delivery of services within the Office of the Director of Health Services. In Amsterdam, for example, an assistant medical director provides liaison with interacting departments, to give added leverage and support to the Department of Child Hygiene. Social welfare work is carried out by nurse social workers, one of whom is assigned in various districts of the city. The nurse social workers take responsibility for detailing domestic help, family welfare workers, and hot meals, including meals-on-wheels. Within the framework of public assistance they investigate the necessity for financial support in cases where there may be extra expenses for special diets, appliances, or other medically indicated materials. Rehabilitation is a part of this activity, and physically handicapped children who require such rehabilitation services or accessories, such as wheelchairs and carriages, obtain them through this associated service.

The mental hygiene needs of the children, along with those of other citizens, are provided for within the framework of community services. The health officer's job is to prevent people with psychiatric problems from entering institutions and to provide the maximum in the way of suitable supervised ambulatory care, so that patients are looked after in their own surroundings wherever possible. It is only when patients have no homes or can no longer be accepted or tolerated by relatives that patients are sent to nursing homes associated with the provincial and psychiatric hospitals. Institutionalization in an asylum or long-term psychiatric hospital is a last resort. Amsterdam is divided into districts, in each of which a psychiatrist, assisted by one or two nurses with social work training, can examine patients, make diagnoses, and prescribe treatment and supervision by the family doctor in an effort to keep the patient in the community.[28]

The Youth Health Care Division

The Youth Health Care Division of the Amsterdam Public Health Service, is responsible for safeguarding and improving the health, growth, and development of the young people living in Amsterdam from birth to 18 years of age. At present, the division is responsible for about 150,000 children. The staff includes 53 general practitioners, some of whom are specialists in "social medicine" (which in Holland has come to mean youth health care), 3 pediatricians, 3 ear-nose-and-throat specialists (including 1 speech therapist), 2 gynecologists (obstetricians), an oral surgeon, a plastic surgeon, a dentist, 89 qualified public health nurses, and 8 district nurses without public health qualifications. In addition, there are 19 speech therapists, 16 remedial gymnastics teachers, 2 obstetricians, a social worker, a specialist in teaching, and a teaching specialist for adults.

The work of the division comprises prenatal care, the care of infants, toddlers (preschool children), school children and adolescents. All the division services are free. The vast majority of the work is prophylactic. A child who needs any treatment other than speech therapy, remedial gymnastics or delousing is usually referred to the family doctor. Health education is an important part of all the division's activities. Most of the medical and nursing staff work in teams concentrating on babies and nursery school children, or nursery school and primary school children. The teams run 27 clinics in Amsterdam. The usual district teams are composed of a general practitioner and two nurses. As a rule, the children are examined at the clinics, although some, particularly secondary school pupils and those at special schools, are examined at school. In addition to teams working in the clinics, there are special teams to inspect day nurseries, to work in institutions for the aftercare of asthma patients, and to carry out hearing tests. Children are vaccinated at the clinic against diphtheria, whooping cough, tetanus, poliomyelitis, measles, and German measles. However, since children may be vaccinated by their family doctors, pediatricians, in independent Cross societies or in private schools, the division operates a central vaccinations registry. There is a computerized vaccination record system which is linked with the population registry and a national vaccination registry. Over 90 percent of the children are immunized.

For prenatal care, two gynecologists, two obstetricians and a teacher of prenatal gymnastics work with the team. Private obstetricians may refer expectant mothers to the panel for examination and advice. The panel has a laboratory and gives courses in prenatal and postnatal gymnastics, the latter for a small fee. General practitioners, midwives, or obstetricians can refer patients there.

The 8,000 babies born annually in Amsterdam can all come under the care of the municipal service, and in 1976 the parents of more than 86 percent took advantage of this. Most of the remaining 14 percent were checked by their family doctors or pediatricians. Introductions to the clinic are made by nurses who pay registration visits to all families in their districts. The visits take place between the seventh and eleventh day after each birth, at which time a blood sample is taken for detection of phenylketonuria. The Registry of Births, Deaths, and Marriages notifies the clinics of each new birth. For each newborn child, the municipal computer center makes out a sticker that is attached to the health file and kept up to date until the child reaches the age of 18. Another sticker goes to the vaccination registry. Clinics are notified of any change of address. The health files of children who are not being observed by the baby-care clinic are kept in case the child visits the center.

If the family with an infant moves into a district, a nurse will visit the newcomers. Most clinics have several hundred babies under their care. They are brought for the first time when they are two weeks old and then at three weeks, five weeks, and seven weeks. After that, they are brought once a month, so that in the first year a child makes ten to twelve visits. Teams are advised on the child's physical, mental, and social well-being. Special attention is paid to the main features of family life that affect children in their first years, the so-called "first environment." For older children, the "second" and "third" environment, that is, school and leisure time, are also considered. Routine vaccinations are given during consultation and the hearing of all babies nine to ten months old is tested. The mothers whose babies are not under the care of the clinics are also called for this test. If a defect shows up twice during the checks, the child is referred to the municipal audiological center for a detailed check.

In 1976, 78 percent of the children of nursery school age in Amsterdam were under the division's care. From the age of one, a child is eligible for the toddlers' clinics. Each clinic reserves one to two half-days a week during which consultations for nursery school age children are held by appointment. This first consultation usually takes place when the child is about fifteen months old. Each clinic cares for about 400 to 800 nursery school children. The nurse also sees the children at home. Those children who have not been under surveillance for infant care are visited by the nurse and registered in the health care system. Extra visits are paid to the homes of high-risk families (i.e., those in which there is a possibility of cruelty to children) where necessary. Psychiatrically trained social workers may be consulted or referrals arranged if necessary. Toddlers visit the clinics at intervals ranging from three to six months. If they go on to nursery school at the age of four or five, their health care is taken over by the school health service. If not, they stay with the clinic until they enter primary school.

At many clinics, nursery school and primary school teachers give courses in the care of these toddlers for parents. Day care centers are inspected according to the regulations of the municipality on criteria for management, composition, and hygiene. The centers must comply with these bylaws to be eligible for grants. The license and grant can be withdrawn if they do not comply.

School Health Services

Nearly all the pupils in nursery, primary, and state-run secondary schools, as well as most of the pupils in private schools, come under school health care systems. Schools for mentally retarded children are looked after by the special psychiatric office. Medical supervision of the schools for slow learners, children with behavioral disorders, and severely maladjusted children is provided by the Institute of Child Therapy, by referral from the municipal health service.

Each of the city clinics sets up several half-days a week for the state-run and private primary schools. The medical practitioner and the nurse again collaborate. General health checks are carried out on the youngest nursery school pupils and pupils in the first and fifth or sixth classes of the primary schools. Children in the intermediate grades who may be expected to need special attention, such as those who have repeated a year or children with a high risk background, are given special interval checks. There are also special consultation hours for children called up by the school doctor or children whose parents request a checkup. The periodic medical examinations are combined with a physical fitness test for sports.

The nurses make inspections of the primary schools to see that there are no children with contagious diseases. They check for head lice and arrange for delousing if necessary. They also train children in hygiene and inspect the toilets and washrooms. If necessary, nurses will visit the children's homes for background information on domestic conditions. Hearing and visual acuity are tested and speech defects are treated. Posture and physical coordination are treated by physiotherapists and with gymnastic exercises. Five- to nine-year-old school children are given booster inoculations against diphtheria, tetanus, and polio. One of the unusual features of the Dutch school health system is the so-called "health colony" to which children can be transferred if their physical condition requires special attention. As in the American "Fresh Air Camps," the children are given outdoor experiences, a nourishing diet and supervision regarding exercise, sleep, and so on, while school work continues.

School dental services are part of the preventive program for all children in nursery and primary grades. A shortage of dentists has interfered with extension of dental services to all secondary school children. Social insurance, however, covers the cost of fillings for adults and children not cared for in school.[29] There is a close cooperation between the school system and the youth psychiatric service. Children with learning difficulties are referred by teachers and receive guidance from social workers or psychiatrists. Teachers may be invited to participate in discussions about the children's needs. In the special schools, pediatricians or general practitioners collaborate with the specialized school nurses to provide necessary care for the physically handicapped, the mentally handicapped, the deaf, and delicate children.

Secondary school health care is not organized along the same district lines as primary school care, and the coverage is not so complete. Care for secondary school children is dispensed by seven teams that operate from centers in the town. In these age groups, the teams will deal largely with psychosocial problems and give advice on matters such as nutrition, contraception, and drugs. There is some deficiency in adolescent care services.

Municipal health service and the preventive services of the Cross organization are linked with the family court, social service agencies and community board of guardians. The family doctor is a critical person to whom the Cross agency, municipal agency, and school doctor report. If there is a problem with a child and the health service cannot seem to get cooperation or assistance from the family, and the child's health is being neglected, a social worker can be appointed by the court to be a "guardian" for the health of the child. Before this can be accomplished, however, a "medical referee" must be appointed to discuss the matter with the family doctor and health service nurse to ensure that the protective action is necessary and in the best interest of the child.

Judge Johanna Hudig, the first woman judge in the family court, estimates that about 25 percent of Dutch children need help of one kind or another—physical, emotional, or social. This figure is not too different from estimates provided in other countries, in the Wagners' study of Denmark and in Whitmore's study of Britain. The main difference is that Hudig estimates that less than 5 percent of these fail to obtain needed support.[30]

While Holland certainly has one of the more efficient, comprehensive child health care systems in the world, the implications of one recent trend—"child power"—should be noted. Children over 14 can now make application to a social agency or board of guardians for relief from an intolerable situation at home or in school. Children under supervision and out of their homes are now demanding the right to pick their own schools and their own doctors and to have a union to deal with the social agencies and the medical organization. This may reflect individuals' growing restlessness with the state's role in their lives. The increasing supervision and bureaucratization, although a result of the society's care and concern, are, nevertheless, creating resentment and beginning to be seen as intrusions, excess "hovering," and too-obvious evidences of control.

HISTORY OF MEDICAL CARE DEVELOPMENT

It may be useful to look at the development of medical care in its present form from a historic standpoint in order better to understand both the successful operation of the Dutch medical care system (successful and amazingly effective despite its complex and seemingly chaotic form of organization, financing, legal base, and reimbursement mechanism) as well as the potential applicability of aspects of the Dutch medical care system to the United States.

The first health legislation in the Netherlands dates to 1818, when local medical committees comprising at least four physicians were authorized to supervise practice and medical education outside the universities. These local committees had epidemiological and law enforcement responsibilities that were considered necessary and desirable at the time.[31]

The idea of prevention did not enter the Dutch medical system earlier than in other parts of Europe, but the structure for the development of a preventive service was laid down earlier because the municipalities began to take responsibility for medical care for the poor early in the 19th century. The first purely preventive baby clinic was established in The Hague in 1901. Compulsory vaccination and the appointment of school doctors in all local communities came into effect about the same time.

The preventive services were further strengthened, paradoxically enough, by the failure to obtain a unified sick fund act after World War I. Promotion of the preventive services became more and more the responsibility of the private societies, the Cross organizations, with the government fostering this promotion by grants and aids. This system not only permitted the government to pay a fixed percentage of the costs of those cases for which it had direct obligation, but also allowed the government to help make up the operational deficit of these private agencies providing care to those not necessarily charges of the central government. Dutch pluralism gave priority to the private and religious organizations but required that the support be equivalent for all organizations that met the government's rules and regulations.

After World War II, more extensive sociomedical legislation was passed, maintaining the balance between strong municipal health departments and firm financial support for private organizations. It did not cure "the famous crazy quilt of Dutch preventive medical organization," it merely strengthened the role of prevention that continues to exercise a primary role in Dutch medical matters.[32]

Despite the large role and quite evident successes of prevention and child care in the Dutch medical system, some criticisms are leveled at its complexity. Querido writes, "The way in which preventive medicine developed in the Netherlands is in itself a serious obstacle to an integrated system of overall medical care.[33] He points out that the gap between preventive and curative services resulting from differences in payment sources creates serious problems for the doctor, although perhaps not so much for the patient. Since preventive care is financed by grants and only partly by direct action by local authorities, and curative care is in the hands of the family physician and is paid for by social insurance, absurdities exist. For example, "the sick fund does not pay for immunization against diphtheria; but it does pay hospital costs if the non-immunized child contracts diphtheria."[34] General practitioners who give well-baby care in their sick fund practices will not be paid for it. Also from a quality standpoint, this separation of preventive and curative services raises questions about the lack of a data base, coordination, and evaluation and, of course, makes planning almost impossible.

"Freedom of Denominational Choice"

Before discussing some of the legal bases for the protection of children in the Netherlands, it may be well to discuss the "peculiar institution" which is the basis of Dutch pluralism and a reflection of their devotion to liberty, independence, and individual rights—"verzuiling" —which literally means "columnization." The multiplication of the Cross organizations was a typically Dutch response in this mode, reflecting consideration for religious and denominational differences. "Verzuiling" is so closely interwoven with the other aspects of the Dutch social system that its application has to be appreciated if the workings of the system are to be understood. Johan Goudsblom in his book, *Dutch Society*, comments on this phenomenon: "at the age of six the population is already divided into three separate blocs. . . ." (secular, Protestant, Catholic) and "one may receive the most extensive university education without ever leaving one's own bloc." Furthermore, "Political parties, trade unions, mass media, leisure associations, health and welfare organizations, all follow this principle. . ."[35]

In the 16th century, when the Spaniards were driven out and the Dutch people came to govern themselves, that governance had to take control of a sharply divided country, split principally along religious lines—40 percent Roman Catholic, another 40 percent Protestant, and the rest with no strong religious affiliation or perhaps even strongly antireligious. If the country was to survive, these ordinarily antagonistic and sometimes aggressively hostile elements had to be reconciled. In his book *The Politics of Accommodation: Pluralism and Democracy in the Netherlands*, Arend Lijphart writes that a society with a multiplicity of units will generally achieve a more viable national form if it is "crosscut" with clusters of these different groups working together at common tasks. He also argues that large cleavages or group separations present the danger of civil war between hostile subcultures. Nevertheless, this is the social structure that the Dutch have chosen—parallel rather than crosscutting—an overlapping solution.[36]

He goes on to point out that the religious divisions have geographic locations. The Roman Catholic population is clustered in the south, the emphatically Protestant (Calvinist) population is in the southwest and center, while the so-called secular group, which includes some of the less strenuously religious Protestants, is concentrated in the west and north. There is also a striking class difference in the Netherlands, a strong antipathy between the middle and lower classes, possibly because the bourgeois middle classes took power right from the start with the founding of the republic. While in most European countries, and in the United States, objective economic inequalities have decreased significantly since World War II, this is much less evident in the Netherlands, where 5 percent of the population has 24 percent of the income. "[I]t is therefore more accurate to speak of two separate secular blocs: a Liberal bloc, consisting of the secular upper middle and middle classes, and a Socialist bloc, consisting of the secular lower middle and lower classes.[37] In voting, the Catholic political parties obtain 30 percent of the vote, the Socialists 30 percent, and the Liberals 10 percent.[38]

Labor unions reflect this four-way split as do the media. Newspapers are divided in accordance with religious and class differences; radio and television "programming is in the hands of private organizations with large dues-paying memberships,"[39] so the programs share time in proportion to their membership. If one examines the voluntary associations, in which there is no restriction on membership and no demand that an individual applying for membership belong to a certain religious group, one finds 77 percent of the Catholics belong to Catholic organizations, and only 20 percent to other organizations. In the rigidly Protestant group, 74 percent belong to similar religious groups, while only 19 percent belong to other groups. Among the moderately religious, only 30 percent belong to religious voluntary associations and 56 percent to general groups, and of those who profess no religion, 86 percent belong to the general groupings.[40]

In education, 28 percent of the schools are public, 43 percent Catholic, 27 percent Protestant, and 2 percent associated with other private organizations. Even though nine of the twelve universities are public, the extracurricular life is not integrated. Most student clubs are organized on a bloc basis, and in an ironically amusing way, the textbooks continue social and class bias. In the Calvinist textbooks, "innocent people were tortured and murdered" during the Inquisition by those the Catholic texts refer to as "wise and pious bishops."[41]

What may explain the Dutch cohesion as a country despite the persistence of the blocs is that "class composition of each bloc is virtually identical to the class composition of the population as a whole."[42] What also may play a part in keeping Holland from splitting along bloc lines is the common language, which saves them from the fate of Belgium, and the denominational equality, which seems to be saving them from the fate of Northern Ireland.

As Lijphart has observed, "Dutch politics is the politics of accomodation." This accomodation is institutionalized in the Social and Economic Council, which really runs the country. It represents all the disparate interests, and any governing cabinet must seek its advice. "The political consensus does not have to be comprehensive or strong. It must include, as a minimum, the commitment to maintain the system...." It is to the commitment to equity and to the maintenance of the political structure that one can attribute the survival of Holland and the Dutch "verzuiling."

Committed to liberty, independence, and equity, Dutch citizens respect their neighbors, attend their churches, vote their consciences, read the newspapers that represent their viewpoints, and are content to let their neighbors do the same.[43]

One more point. It would be a mistake to consider this mature political approach an oddity of Dutch character, not transferable to other scenes. Lijphart writes, "national character analysis is more of a hindrance than a help. It obscures the fact that the Dutch are by no means unique in exhibiting these subjective qualities, ... minimum requirements for the politics of accommodation are not unusually difficult demands."[44]

As a consequence of the columnization process, the preventive health services that children require are provided through Cross organizations that are denominationally related. The White Cross, the first of the private voluntary health agencies, had its origins in 1875 at the solicitation of the then inspector general of health services in Holland who was desperately seeking a way to involve the private sector in dealing with the epidemics that periodically ravaged the country and with which the health department by itself was unable to cope. This White Cross organization was essentially a product of the secular or mildly religious grouping in the north. The others followed, the Roman Catholic grouping in the south not developing its own Cross organization until the early part of the 20th century.

Even now, the Dutch consider maintenance of this "separate and equal" approach suitable to new problems. For instance, the Dutch relinquished colonial control of its South American colony, Surinam, a few years ago. Some Surinamese, who represent a racial type of mixed black, white, and Indian, chose to become citizens and remain in the Netherlands. Perhaps 100,000 or so reside principally in the two large cities, Amsterdam and Rotterdam. The Dutch have succeeded in training the Surinamese physicians, nurses, and social workers who work in Surinamese clinics to provide the services required by the Surinamese, although Surinamese are quite welcome to attend other clinics. The same sort of arrangement has been made for a much larger group of immigrants, the Eurasians, some 300,000 of whom moved from Java and other Indonesian islands after the nationalist struggle ended Dutch colonial rule there in the late 1940s. While the hundred-odd thousand Surinamese represent almost a third of the population of that former Dutch colony, and while there is some discrimination against them (as much as Dutch can discriminate!), there is hardly any discrimination against the Indonesian Asian group who have successfully been integrated into Dutch society.

The Moluccans, another group of immigrants numbering less than 50,000, arrived at the same time as the Eurasians. They did not seek to become assimilated into Dutch society but insisted on retaining their own identity, aspiring to return to their homeland, islands which they claim the Indonesians treacherously and illegally occupy. The denominational equity that seems to have worked so well with varying elements of the Dutch population and even with large numbers of immigrants of different races, colors and beliefs has begun to falter with the more recent immigrants, the Moluccans and, to a lesser extent, the Surinamese.

A newspaper report titled "Racial problems seen as growing in the Netherlands" quotes a Professor Koppen as saying, "The Dutch self-image was always that of a very tolerant people. We always said, 'Those foolish Americans and those foolish South Africans, they can't cope with race. We can, of course, cope with all that.' Then when the influx came, all kinds of prejudice started to appear. You can now hear racist jokes here of the same kind you hear in America. The same things are said of the Surinamese that are said of the American negroes: 'they are oversexed, they are stupid, they are lazy.'"[45] Nevertheless, while the famed Dutch tolerance may not be completely successful, in terms of delivery of preventive services to children, there is no question but that the separateness and the denomination-al approach have been highly successful in assuring that all children receive the preventive services they are entitled to.

THE DUTCH DEFINITION OF CHILD ABUSE

We should start by pointing out that failing to bring a child for a necessary examination or failing to provide necessary treatment for a child who has been diagnosed by a physician, is considered neglect, and even child abuse. So is failing to supply glasses or hearing aids, as well as specific evidence of child abuse as reported by the child, a teacher, or a neighbor. In these instances, a new form of remedy and a specific program is in operation in many parts of the Netherlands.

In the Netherlands, it is not compulsory to report child abuse ("nonaccidental injury" to children), but when it occurs, Dutch civil law provides for placing the child "under supervision." This means limiting the authority of the parents by appointing a counselor, a so-called family guardian. While this family guardian is generally a social worker employed by a private agency, the measure is imposed by the family court and may last for as long as one year if the minor is threatened by moral or physical danger. On the presentation of additional evidence, the measure can be continued until the minor reaches majority.[46]

An experimental program providing for a "medical ombuds-man," which is in place in a large part of Holland, operates in the following manner. A physician, nurse or neighbor reports to a social agency a suspicion of child abuse. There are nine "medical referees" jointly appointed by the minister of public health and the minister of justice from among respected local physicians. This is not a full-time job, but the referee has an office and is assisted by a social worker and a clerk. When the suggestion or suspicion of child abuse is reported, the referee consults with the family physician and a district nurse to get whatever evidence possible. The referee does not provide treatment or participate in the treatment, but is a consultant. If there is abuse, this is reported to the court, which will appoint a guardian for the purpose of carrying out whatever is necessary to protect the child.[47]

If a school doctor reports to the family doctor that the child's health is neglected, the same procedure can be followed and a social worker appointed to be a guardian for the child's health.

CONCLUSION: THE STRUCTURE OF SOCIAL AND HEALTH SERVICES

The Netherlands is small, densely populated, industrially and technologically advanced, and highly urbanized, with a sharply divided class structure. Many of the ills of civilization certainly are present here. However, the history of the Netherlands has encouraged the development and maintenance of a system of closed denominational groups, one Roman Catholic, two variations of Protestant, and a nondenominational grouping that resembles in attitudes and values the less strenuously religious Protestant group. Class distinctions exist in and among these religious groupings and a large number of private health, education, and social welfare agencies attempt to cope with much of the social and health needs of the Dutch people in accordance with the principle of denominational separation. This approach has been largely successful in the past. Although it makes for a very varied patchwork arrangement, the aim of equity seems to have been accomplished.

In the health field, this patchwork is exaggerated because of the added fragmentation of health and medical care elements. Preventive services are provided both on an official and private basis. Medical care financing is the function of sickness insurance funds, which are compulsory for some, and the voluntary insurance funds. There is a very well funded official health agency that not only supervises the sickness insurance funds, but also provides a great many health services, supplementing and in many instances duplicating services that are performed by the private agencies. Monitoring and supervising the health services is carried out through an added branch of the ministry.[48]

Part of the effect of this complex system is that the Dutch people spend more out of pocket than most Europeans do under either health insurance or a national health service. However, the system seems to work to the satisfaction of both patients and doctors. The family doctors who are paid by capitation can also have some private practice and apparently achieve a satisfactory income, as do the specialists who are paid fee for service, with the fees negotiated and arranged in advance. The salaried physicians are also apparently satisfied with their income since salaries approximate what physicians earn in private practice.

As one sorts out the tax funds that go to various services, one might keep in mind that 20 percent of the Dutch taxpayers' money goes to keep the water out! One needs to be constantly reminded that most of the land upon which the Dutch live has been recaptured from the sea by ditching and diking, and a good deal of money has to be spent to keep it that way. Despite this vast expenditure, social services do not suffer.

As in Britain, the public health and social medicine people are very concerned over the separation of prevention and cure. Querido, professor of social medicine in Amsterdam, points out that there is a "deep chasm between preventive and curative care resulting from differences in their respective financial systems ...." He points out a paradox as a characteristic defect: "If a general practitioner wishes

Table 9-1   Sources of Health Services Funding (1971)

(%)

	General Revenues	Social Security	Out of Pocket
U.S.A.	38.5	—	61.5
France	7	60	33
Sweden	85	8	7
U.K.	85	8	7
Netherlands	22	44	35

Source: R. Maxwell, *Health Care: The Growing Dilemma*, 2nd ed. (New York: McKinsey & Co., 1975).

to supervise babies in his sick fund practice, he will not be paid for his work . . . . he can work on a part-time basis in the clinic of a Cross society, but there he will probably see no babies from his own practice."[49]

Nevertheless, where the effort has been made to bring the family doctor into the preventive service, the lack of cooperation from the doctors tends to frustrate the project. Querido points out that in order to involve physicians, "immunization associations" were established right after World War II to allow parents to take their children to their own physicians. The Cross society provided the immunization materials, and the municipality, from its child health budget, paid the doctor a fee. Says Querido, "The project has been only partially successful; it is very difficult to gather data from the physicians."[50]

SYSTEM SHORTCOMINGS

We have mentioned some of the problems in passing.

- The "crazy quilt" makes it difficult to collect data or to evaluate or estimate quality. It also makes it difficult to exercise sufficient controls over expenditures.
- There are some social problems stemming from columnization.
- Medical costs are rising because of the increase in the supply of specialists and the significant influence of the insurance system on increased demand for specialists' care.[51]
- There is growing criticism of the community's lack of participation in decision making with regard to the insurance, hospitalization, or delivery system.[52]
- The system costs too much and 5 percent of the total working population works in the health system.[53]
- Medical education is criticized, as it is in our own country, for failing to respond to social needs.
- Economists and administrators within the system are critical of some bureaucratic conflicts that appear from time to time because of the independence of so many units—the preventive and curative system and the social work and legal agencies.

Goudsblom sees the defects as corollary to the virtues. "The social and cultural environment they [the Dutch] live in is, in many ways, the result of rational deliberations. The highly effective (if not altogether efficient) system of health organizations which has gradually been built up is a manifest example of how rationalization has pervaded Dutch society—and altered—in this case prolonged—people's lives." He goes on to point out how this has resulted in increased bureaucratization. "Between 1900 and 1950 [civil servants] increased more than eight-fold, while the total Dutch working population approximately doubled." This bureaucratization has facilitated the centralization, and it is centralization that he sees as the major obstacle to innovation and participation.

Gouldsblom makes a number of other points, but I must say that since so many of the problems seem to be similar to the problems we face, I am more hopeful that what is successful in the Dutch system may be more readily seen by Americans as relevant to our situation.[54]

SUMMARY

One major, important difference between Holland and the United States, in regard to child health services at any rate, is the presence in the Netherlands of a large and influential child advocacy group. Not only is there the Society Against Cruelty to Children, but there are official advocacy bodies like the Council for Child Protection and the Bureau for Life and Family Difficulties.

In addition, the family court assumes responsibility for the child, since, as Judge Hudig puts it, "civil child law is based on the principle that the government as *parens patriae* has to look after the welfare of those in need of help and contains restrictions as to the parental authority in case the parents fail to do their duty as educators.[55]

Private initiative in child advocacy and in child care in the community is represented by the Society for Family Guardianship. This organization, through its referees, selects guardians or refers guardianship cases to the courts. The official agency is the Council for Child Protection.[56] Every court region has a child protection council. This council is appointed by the Crown and has a professional secretary, a lawyer who is director of the executive office. The office employs social workers who carry out the investigations. Neither these official nor unofficial child protection bodies is legally bound to consider parents' rights as overriding.

In every step along the way we have seen how, in both law and social custom, health care is considered a primary responsibility of the state toward the child. Every child is given an opportunity to be born healthy. Even before the child is born, there is maternity leave and maternity allowances. Medical care during pregnancy is a right. The woman's wish concerning the location and type of birth is respected, but few risks are taken. Midwives and doctors cooperate to educate mothers and families to an appropriate response to pregnancy. The Dutch infant mortality rate is among the lowest in the world, and while more than half of the babies are born at home, because of careful screening and supervision, very few risky childbirths are at home and very few untoward occurrences are recorded. The state provides an allowance to the family to be sure that children are properly nourished and housed. There are special clinics for care and supervision of infants. For toddlers, there are clinics for immunization and examination. Midwives must report births so that a record is made of every child born. Nurses must visit. The family is sought out—there is no waiting for the parents to report for examination, for assessment of problems, or for immunization. Families that fail to provide proper care and medical attention for their children are pursued as if they were guilty of child neglect or abuse and are so treated. Children, by law, must receive the medical care, medical supervision, and health service to which they are entitled. School health services likewise offer protection, examination, and care.

In the intertwining of health, medical care, social services, and legal protection, the whole society and the state devote considerable effort and expense toward the healthy development of every child.

REFERENCES

1. Central Bureau of Statistics, *Compendium of Health Statistics of the Netherlands* (The Hague: Ministry of Public Health and the Environment, 1974).

2. John L. Motley, *The Rise of the Dutch Republic* (New York: Dutton Everyman Library, 1906), vol. 1, p. 89.

3. Ibid., pp.89-91.

4. Ibid. p. 69.

5. Ministry of Public Health and the Environment, *Health Services and Public Health in the Netherlands* (The Hague: Ministry of Public Health, 1975), p. 4.

6. Personal communication, Dr. J. L. Doek.

7. Motley, *The Rise of the Dutch Republic*, vol.1, pp.82-83.

8. Ibid., vol. 3, p. 450.

9. Central Bureau of Statistics, *Compendium. p. 53.*

10. J. Lindgren, in "Working Papers for the Arden House Conference on Family Policy," mimeographed (New York: Columbia University School of Social Work, 1977).

11. R. L. Sivard, *World Military and Social Expenditures, 1977* (Leesburg, Virginia: WMSE Press, 1977).

12. J. Goudsblom, Dutch Society (New York: Random House, 1968), p. 49.

13. Personal communication.

14. Ministry of Public Health, *Public Health in the Netherlands.*

15. Personal communication from Professor Aakster, Dutch economist.

16. J. van Langendonck, *Prelude to Harmony on a Community Theme: Health Care Insurance in the E.E.C. and Britain* (Oxford: Oxford University Press, 1975).

17. European Institute for Social Security, *Evolution and Financing of the Cost of Medical Care* (Leuven: Aurelia, 1972), p. 391.

18. A. Querido, *The Development of Sociomedical Care in the Netherlands* (London: Routledge and Kegan Paul, 1968).

19. Central Bureau of Statistics Compendium, Chapter 13.

20. J. H. de Haas, *The School Child in the Netherlands* (The Hague: Ministry of Social Affairs and Public Health, 1963).

21. Central Bureau of Statistics, *Compendium* and *Health Services in Europe,* (Copenhagen: WHO European Office, 1975).

22. Ministry of Public Health and Environment, *Statistische Gegevens over verloskundige zorg 1960-1974* [Obstetrical data 1960-1974] (Leidschendam: 1976).

23. H. P. Verbrugge, *Kraamzorg bij Huisbevallingen* [*Maternity home help and home deliveries*] (Groningen: Wolters-Noordhoff NV, 1968), p. 83. "...a normal delivery should preferably take place at home, whereas in the case of high risk groups, the doctor or midwife who makes the prenatal examinations should advise the expectant mother to have her baby in a well-equipped hospital." Dr. Siderius, director-general of health services, said to me casually, in discussing the suitability of the home for childbirth, "and of course there are no bad homes."

24. *Health Services in Europe* (Copenhagen: WHO Europe Office, 1975).

25. Personal communication, Dr. H. Verbrugge.

26. Ministry of Foreign Affairs, *The Kingdom of the Netherlands* (The Hague: Ministry of Foreign Affairs, 1971).

27. Personal communication, Dr. H. Verbrugge.

28. Communication from Dr. C. P. J. LeNobel, head, Department of Youth Health Care, Municipal Health Service, Amsterdam in a letter dated September 15, 1977.

29. Communication from Dr. J. W. L. Phaff, director of maternal and child health, National Health Service.

30. Judge Johanna Hudig in a personal communication. For Denmark, see Marsden Wagner and Mary Wagner, *The Danish National Child Care System* (Boulder: Westview Press, 1976); for England, M. Rutter, J. Tizard, and K. Whitmore, *Education, Health and Behaviour* (London: Longman, 1970).

31. This and the following paragraphs derived from Querido, *Sociomedical Care in the Netherlands.*

32. Ibid pp. 98-100.

33. Ibid p. 101.

34. Ibid.

35. Goudsblom, *Dutch Society,* p. 55.

36. Arend Lijphart, *The Politics of Accommodation* (Berkeley: University of California Press, 1968), p. 15.

37. Ibid., p. 23.

38. Ibid., p. 36.

39. Ibid., p. 40.

40. Ibid., p. 52.

41. Ibid., p. 52.

42. Ibid., p. 90.

43. Ibid., p. 103.

44. Ibid., p. 207.

45. *New York Times*, 5 June 1977.

46. Judge Johanna Hudig, "Civil Aspects of Child Law," Address delivered before the Council of Europe, October 11, 1976, mimeographed.

47. Ministry of Public Health and Environment, "The Dutch System of Medical Referees for Child Abuse," mimeographed (The Hague: Ministry of Public Health, undated).

48. Ministry of Public Health and the Environment, *Public Health in the Netherlands*.

49. Querido, *Sociomedical Care in the Netherlands*, p. 92.

50. Ibid., p. 102.

51. J. van der Gaag et al., "Aggregated Dynamic Demand Equation for Specialists, Specialistic-Outpatient Medical Care" (Economic Institute, Leiden University), mimeographed, Report 76.07, April 1976.

52. J. B. Stolte, "Democratization in the Hospital," *Hospital and Health Services Review*, October 1976, pp. 348-353. This is a report on the paper presented to the European Conference on Hospitals, April 1976.

53. W. Peterson, project leader, "Final Report of the Case Study, Netherlands: Restructuring of the Netherlands Health Care Delivery System," mimeographed (Paris: OECD, 1975). Cost and overabundance of manpower are ascribed to lack of cost control and to fragmentation of the system. There is over-use of hospitals, overuse of technology, insufficient organization of in- and out-patient services, and is lack of citizen participation in development of health care. Sounds like home!

54. Goudsblom, *Dutch Society*, pp. 23 and 24.

55. Hudig, "Civil Aspects of Child Law."

56. M. Rood de Boer, *Child Care in the Netherlands 3rd ed.* (The Hague: National Federation for Child Welfare, 1971).

Chapter 10

Some Random Observations on Other European Child Health Systems

This volume is not intended to be an inclusive study of all European health services. The purpose of the study was to review situations in which children were entitled by law to all the health and medical care that every other citizen was entitled to, and to determine if improved child health care resulted from increasing the preventive services and removing the barriers that contribute to the neglect of child health in the United States, where there is no universal health service. At the same time, the study examined situations in which, in addition to comprehensive and universal medical care services, special programs were aimed at children, to determine if such programs made any difference in the outcome. The two nations compared in detail were Scotland, in which the contribution to the care of children derived largely from the universal comprehensive health service, and Holland, where, despite a patchwork of medical care eligibility, all children were entitled to medical care and where there was an extensive preventive health service for children under both official and private auspices. The Dutch system seemed to provide more and was more successful than the Scottish system in reaching most children. As pointed out in the earlier discussions, there were many other reasons that might have contributed to this difference, not the least of which is the relative wealth of Holland as compared to Scotland. However, it was clear that the organized approach and outreach in the Netherlands service was fundamentally responsible for the system's reaching every child, and that it was not lack of funds that could be wholly blamed for the failure of the Scottish system to reach every child with preventive services.

In Scandinavian countries, Denmark, Sweden, and Finland, for example, as well as in some other countries, many of the positive elements of the Dutch system exist also. It might be well to summarize these rather than to discuss each country in detail, so as to emphasize particularly the different ways in which these countries approach the same problems and the factors that contribute to their success (or failure) in meeting child health needs. In the countries with the most successful programs, the elements that were considered basic to the value and success of the Dutch system are present. However, emphases vary.

In Denmark, for example, the chief responsibility for preventive services to the child is left to the family physician. There are outreach services, visiting nurses, and extensive reporting of the findings, but basically, the family physicians are responsible. They are the ones who provide the immunizations, examine the child, and make the reports.

The major difference between Sweden and Holland is that the Swedish system is much more hierarchic and less "patchwork." There is little if any private sector involvement, and the examinations, treatment, and supervision are all carried out through the official agencies. However, an interesting distinction between Sweden and the other countries is that the *funding* of the services is local; therefore, there is local county control of the official agency responses. In both these countries, Denmark and Sweden, nearly all the children are seen, nearly all the children are immunized, and nearly all the handicaps are found and treated.

If this last statement seems somewhat exaggerated, it is supported by Wagner's report on the large-scale study of the effectiveness of preschool examinations in Sweden. In one county, all the children who reached age four were reexamined by two groups of physicians to determine a) whether any of the illnesses or handicapping conditions among them had gone undiscovered or if discovered, untreated, and b) whether the nurses' examinations (which take the place of physicians' examinations at various times in the first four years of life) were as useful in the discovery of these handicapping conditions as the physicians' examinations.

It turned out that, with few exceptions, all the handicapping conditions had been found *prior* to this examination at age four, and had been treated. Furthermore the nurses had made no mistakes, that is, had not skipped or missed diagnoses. It appeared from the

Swedish and the Danish experiences, that in a specifically designated child health program, results are pretty much as in Holland, even though there are significant differences in operation. In one case (Sweden) the program is totally under official auspices; in the other (Denmark) preventive services are carried out almost entirely by family physicians. The key seemed to be in the special nature of concern for child health.[1]

Two other countries, Finland and France, have been remarkably successful in recent years in improving child health services, and this is reflected in the statistics on infant mortality, immunizations, and the handicapped children reached. Both differ from the Dutch operational model, though not significantly, as they do from Denmark and Sweden, but both have specific child health programs in addition to medical care insurance systems.

Finland has a special child health program locally controlled as in Sweden, but federally financed. France has a federally funded special child health program, but the local control is not as strong as in these other countries, because the responsibility is delegated to *départements*, which are larger and less independent than the counties in Sweden or communes in Finland.

Nevertheless, all these share that important aspect of the Dutch program—extraordinary reliance upon specially trained child health nurses. Denmark, with emphasis on the family doctor, is different, although nurses do play a large role in Danish health services for children, through home visitation and follow-up. It is safe to say that the reviewed countries with the most successful programs gave special emphasis to child health and relied extensively upon nurses. Beyond social support and universal medical care entitlement, special attention to children is the common thread that runs through the health and medical care services of these countries.

Tables 9-1 and 9-2, found at the end of this Chapter, summarize the comparisons of health policies and expenditures among some European countries and the United States.

FINLAND

In Finland, an area ten times the size of the Netherlands, live less than five million people. Finland's birth and death rates, while a bit higher, are roughly comparable to the Netherlands'—12.7 for the birth rate and 9.6 for the death rate. Infant mortality also is

practically identical—11.3 in 1972.   Other public health statistics—life expectancy, and causes of disease and mortality—are just
about the same. Medical care services have been decentralized so that
the national health service, the Directorate of Health, supervises but
does not operate, provincial health services. Within the provinces, a
commune, or a group of communes, provides health services through a
health council that represents the consumers. The health council
bears responsibility for both personal and environmental health
services and operates on a five-year plan approved by the provincial
directorate of health. The local councils receive funds from the
central government and report to the provincial departments.
Ambulatory care can be provided in the communal health center
along with preventive services.   When private physician care is
provided, the health insurance scheme reimburses the private practitioner according to a fixed fee schedule. Hospitals are also regional-
ized around groups of communes, and a small daily fee is charged,
with the bulk of the hospitals' budgets subsidized by the state.

Payment for services differs a bit from the system in other
European countries, but not too much.   Until only recently, the
patient paid a small fee to the doctor for curative services and
nothing at all for preventive services. The doctor is now reimbursed
by the national sickness insurance fund, supported in part by the
national and in part by the local government. The patient still pays a
modest daily charge for hospital care. Physicians in the health
centers are salaried, as are hospital physicians.

Preventive services for children, which include the entire range
of maternal and child health care, are part of the local health center
activity. These services are all free. Their use is not compulsory, and
private doctors may be consulted if the family chooses. Public health
nurse-midwives provide prenatal care and assist at most of the
births, almost all of which are performed in hospitals. Preschool
children are examined at the health center, or at home by the public
health nurse. School health services are carried out by the commune
through full-time physicians and nurses.[2]

The child and maternal health service began in Finland in the
1920s, as a private effort, with the creation of "health houses," which
have now become maternity and child welfare clinics under official
auspices. The private organization responsible for the health houses,
the Mannerheim League, also trained nurses and midwives, with an
emphasis on their role in the education of mothers and fathers. Other

private agencies also set the stage for the present Finnish health services. One was the Central Union for Child Welfare, which took responsibility for handicapped children; another was the Population and Family Welfare League, which undertook to train homemakers and to provide housing projects, garden cities, and family planning education and services. Today these private organizations are concerning themselves with drug abuse among school children, organization of day care centers, and health education for adults. There is still a very strong link between private and official organizations in their common efforts to promote health and foster preventive services.

Preventive services cover 100 percent of the mothers and children. "A Finnish perinatal mortality survey in 1963 ... showed the same strong association between perinatal casualties and the failure of pregnant women to cooperate with the preventive services." In 1968, 90 percent of pregnant women made their first prenatal contact with the health service before the fourth month of pregnancy. Over 99 percent of all pregnant women were registered before delivery.[3]

Maternity Services

A notable aspect of Finnish maternity services is the extraordinary emphasis on hospital delivery of babies. This emphasis seems to be greater than in other European countries. The Finns argue for a variety of reasons for centralization of deliveries in large hospitals. One is to provide the expensive equipment necessary, second is to be able to take care of frail babies, third is that the shortage of doctors and obstetricians makes it necessary to concentrate and centralize this meager resource. Some of these arguments are a little thin. There really isn't any shortage of physicians. However, since general practitioners are involved only in the maternal health centers, it may be that there are too few obstetricians.

Yet, as the Wynns point out, "The difficulties of achieving 100 percent hospital delivery in Finland are substantial. The distance from home to hospital may be over 100 miles or even 200 miles in Lapland. In the north it is dark throughout the 24 hours in winter, temperatures are low, and the snow is deep." (Yet in 1972 there were only two births in Finnish Lapland not in hospitals!) So, "Finland is also concentrating all deliveries in large central hospitals and is eliminating maternity beds progressively from smaller district hospitals which are used mainly by adult and elderly patients."[4] It is their feeling that even under the best prenatal care arrangements, professional anticipation of difficult deliveries is not wholly reliable. "Centralization of delivery in fully-equipped hospitals is the only way of insuring coverage of all unexpectedly difficult deliveries. Total coverage of the risk cases is again seen to be a part of the prevention philosophy."[5] This is a dramatic contrast to the Dutch approach, in which 50 percent of the babies are born at home, and yet the Dutch infant mortality and the Finnish infant mortality are identical. The proportion of mothers who are seen in pregnancy is the same and the proportion of midwife deliveries is the same, so it is hard to believe the hospital makes that much difference.

It is also true that Finnish obstetrical practice may vary considerably from American or other Western European obstetrical practice in regard to the use of chemicals to induce labor, the use of anesthesia in delivery, the use of forceps, and other mechanical and technological approaches that characterize "advanced" obstetrical practice. Fetal monitoring, for example, seems to increase Caesarian section rates. On the other hand, the Wynns point out, the use of forceps in delivery has almost disappeared in Finland. In 1971, forceps were used only on 30 occasions in over 61,000 births, in the whole of the country. In one major hospital forceps have not been used for several years. Accepted techniques include "vacuum extraction."[6]

The maternity care system, which covers the entire group of pregnant women systematically and is scrupulously attentive to the special needs of high-risk women, deserves the major share of the credit for the admirably low infant mortality rate. The Wynns compare the situation in Glasgow, in which more than 10 percent of the home confinements booked in that city (54 out of 495) were actually previously classified as high risk and should have been hospital rather than home delivery cases. Furthermore, 106 cases delivered at home had been booked for hospital delivery and didn't reach the hospital in time, a reflection on the system. In addition, 78 cases had never been seen in prenatal clinics and were emergency home confinements.[7]

In 1972 Finland had 5,500 physicians, 1,250 midwives, and 21,000 nurses, as well as 7,500 children's nurses. Unlike in other Scandinavian countries, in Finland midwifery is nurse-midwifery.

The Health Delivery System

"The Finns believe that health care is a natural right of the citizen and that society has an obligation to organize needed health services."[8] "Among the generally accepted moral concepts of Finnish society, social justice has a very central position. One of the elements of this concept is 'distributional justice,' which relates to equitable distribution of social benefits and resources.[9] Finland tends to provide these services through regional decentralized programs. The aim is to form small, manageable units where responsibility and accountability can be easily recognized. The focus is the patient. Primary services are delivered directly in a commune or a small unit within a commune, but more specialized services can be provided by combining neighboring communes.

There are 475 of these local authorities or communes, roughly one for each 10,000 people. However, the size varies. For example, the city of Helsinki is a commune with about 500,000 inhabitants. The communes have taxing authority and collect on the basis of income. Because they have the taxing authority, they also have much greater administrative authority than such a small unit would ordinarily be expected to have. The national government subsidizes health services, roughly 50 percent of cost, but the communes prepare their own budgets, supply all the necessary information, and are accountable for the nature of the services delivered.

Such a communal tax base and health service system provides for actual consumer control. The health councils are elected locally by proportional representation. Health service grievances can thus become political campaign fodder. Physicians are not members of local health boards unless they are elected. Practitioners employed by the local commune health centers are on salary; other physicians are in private practice. Even salaried hospital specialists, for example, may engage in part-time private practice, but all physicians' charges are regulated, and there is a scale for reimbursement. There are no charges for maternity costs or child care.

There are 211 health boards that have primary care units. The health centers look after ten to fifteen thousand inhabitants in an urban area. (In Helsinki, many more.) However, there are 922 maternal and child health centers, many of which obviously are located outside the health centers and independent of them. In the maternal and child health centers, one public health nurse-midwife is considered sufficient to take care of about 100 mothers. Over 90 percent of the population uses this free, voluntary service. The mothers visit the center nearly 20 times during pregnancy. The nurse-midwife sees the woman during each of her visits and is the main agent for supervision of the pregnancy. A physician is called in only when the midwife thinks it is necessary. This nurse-midwife initiates any necessary liaison with social agencies and also visits in the home. She teaches nutrition and exercises and assists in delivery of about half the babies in the hospital. The nurse-midwife also takes care of all postpartum visits. (Over three home visits are usually made postpartum.) [10]

Two ancillary social and health services, the Homemakers and the Home Helps, look after young children at home while the mother is in the hospital, and the helper stays with the mother after she returns from the hospital. Homemakers have a training of 22 months that includes domestic work, cooking and nutrition, child care, child development, and social policy. Home helps have a training of 200 hours, and are mostly older married women who help with the housekeeping and shopping. [11]

The child is registered by the midwife in a local child health clinic and followed from birth to age seven; after that, the school health services take over. While the health center service is voluntary, nearly 100 percent of the children under the age one are looked after there. [12]

The Infant and Preschool Child Care

Over 90 percent of the children born in Finland are registered in the community child health centers before they are one month old. On the average, they are seen about once a month during the first year of life. Each clinic has a schedule of developmental tests to check on the possibility of handicapping conditions not discovered in the initial examination. In addition, nurses visit the home for the purpose of health education and education in child care, in addition to immunization services.

The average child is seen by a doctor only twice before the age of twelve months. The remaining examinations are by the nurse. After the age of one year, the children are seen at least once a year for a developmental examination until they go to school. On the average, preschool children are seen in a clinic at least twice a year, although policy dictates only once. It seems that the average Finnish child is examined by someone in the health services nearly 18 times after the midwife's postnatal visits until the child goes to school at seven. Records are meticulously kept and follow the child from the health center to the school. In addition, the mother is given a book in which to keep a record of findings and treatments.[13]

Nurse services in the clinic as well as home visiting outreach play important roles in seeing to it that needed preventive services are obtained. Family planning services, for example, can be, and are, brought to the home and are part of the health education responsibilities of the nurse in the home. Immunizations can also be brought to the home if the parents do not bring the child to the clinic. In the United States in 1973, 60.4 percent of children age one to four years were vaccinated against polio (down from 84.1 percent in 1963), 61.2 percent of all children were immunized against measles, and 55.6 percent against rubella. In Finland, over 98 percent of the children under six are protected by such immunizations.[14]

> The main means of insuring that pregnant women and young children do not escape the net of the preventive services is visiting by midwives and health visitors.... The view was expressed repeatedly in Finland that home visiting by midwives and health visitors was basic to the achievement of their low perinatal and infant mortality rates. The average number of home visits per pregnant women in Finland was 4.3.

> The Finnish midwives and health visitors have the time and the duty not to confine discussions with pregnant women or mothers to medical detail, but to discuss family, economic and social problems where other services may be called in to help.[15]

Costs and Expenditures

Social and health expenditures in Finland are relatively modest compared with other Scandinavian countries and with the United States, because Finland is a poor country. The liberal social policy is reflected in the social emphasis in the small budget and the corollary limited investment in arms and military expenditures.

Finland's gross national product per capita is 50 percent less than the United States, Sweden or Denmark, half that of Switzerland, but somewhat higher than that of the United Kingdom. Yet Finland spends more public monies per capita for health than the United States and, per capita, only 15 percent of what the United States spends on arms.[16] Comparing Finland with other Scandinavian countries, 1970 data show that Finland spends less and demands less in individual taxes to carry out its programs.

Social Commitment

Social aspects of child care include maternity allowances (which includes a layette), maternity leave (reimbursement for 174 working days), and guarantee of return to job. As in other Scandinavian countries, there is a liberal abortion policy permitting abortion on demand. The maternity allowance is geared to the mother's income, if she is working (higher wages, less allowance); if she is not married or has other children under 16 years of age (and therefore needs home help), the maternity allowance is increased.

Maternity grants are paid only if the applicant has seen a doctor or midwife or has registered in a maternal health center for examination and advice within the first four months of pregnancy. The

Table 10-1   Social and Health Expenditures as % of GNP

	Total	Health
Denmark	23	7.3
Sweden	19.6	8.3
Finland	18	5

Source: Association for University Programs in Health Administration, "Health and Health Services in Finland," mimeographed (Washington, D.C.: AUPHA, 1975), Table 14, p. 42.

Table 10-2   Proportion of Health Care Costs Borne by

	Employer	Insured	Local government	National government
Denmark	4%	14%	16%	66%
Sweden	24%	13%	30%	33%
Finland	41%	9%	19%	31%

Source: Association for University Programs in Health Administration, "Health and Health Services in Finland," mimeographed (Washington, D.C.: AUPHA, 1975), Figure 6, p. 44.

maternity allowance is paid to insured working women in installments before and after childbirth and is determined when the mother appears for medical examination.[17]

Regardless of how much time a woman takes off as a result of pregnancy, the total benefits may amount to as much as 40 percent of the previous year's pay. If the mother is the sole or principal earner in the family, she will get more than this. Most women take off a third of the time before and two thirds after giving birth, and the benefits are paid accordingly.

The children's allowance is paid to the mother or other adult in the family for each child under 16, graded according to the number of children, with an extra sum paid for all children under age three. On the average, the government grant amounts to about 10 percent of what it costs to take care of a child per year. Large families are eligible for a means-tested housing subsidy, and there is a non-means-tested grant for every family with a severely handicapped child.

One unusual and important aspect of the Finnish support system for children, which underlines and emphasizes the concern for the child, is "prepayment maintenance." In this situation, as mentioned earlier, if one parent is dependent upon another for child support, the state is permitted to pay the requisite amount to that parent and then collect it from the parent who owes it. This is logical and often necessary when a parent is delinquent or when litigation is involved, and it prevents the payment delays usually caused by long, drawnout court processes.[18]

One gets the impression that the social commitment in Europe generally, as exhibited in Finland, is facilitated by public pressure from women. With the exception of Holland, there are proportionately many more working women in Europe than in the United States. There also are many more women in the Parliaments than in the Congress of the United States. The agitation for legislation and more public spending for social purposes that women initiate and promote strengthens the arguments of the professionals in the push for and the public support of child care services in Europe.

Summary

In summary, Finland, rather small in population, relatively poor in national income and resources, devotes a major portion of its wealth to social benefits aimed at the protection of children and the family. But it is not the social benefits and elaborate child health system alone that should receive credit for the success of the program. As one American pediatrician writes, "It will be noted that none of the ingredients are unique; they are all present in most advanced countries. Where Finland differs is in its *commitment* to insure full coverage and full use of the country's available resources." (emphasis added)[19] As a result, "Finland has become one of the world leaders in maternal and child health . . . not as a consequence of an exceptionally high standard of living comparable to that, say, of Sweden."[20] The commitment is carried out in ways that foster and facilitate the full capabilities of the services and program. Accountability and local involvement are emphasized.

The Finnish system delegates administrative responsibility for the operation of the maternal and child health services to the commune and makes the provincial governments responsible for record keeping since supervision is an important and powerful antidote to bureaucratization of a system. One can see that this kind of official hierarchic arrangement could very easily become an impersonal bureaucracy, but sufficient high quality staff and delegation of authority, accompanied by the obligation for reporting, results in good preventive services with a personal flavor and an unobtrusive bureaucracy. The commune's accountability to the province for fiscal matters and to the local health council (an elected body) for performance, means that the consumer plays an active role in the operations and decision making.

Finally, reliance on a professional group, well-trained and interested in the whole range of preventive services, is the hallmark of the effectiveness of the child health services. As the director of the European office of the World Health Organization, Dr. Leo Kaprio, himself a Finn, says, "The health care system is only as good as the content and people who carry it out. In Finland there was no change in the medical care system, but the preventive services were assisted by putting the job into the nurses' hands, which had a tremendous effect on infant mortality and immunization."[21]

FRANCE

While there is really no need to examine every country's approach to child health programming, since the critical differential elements are visible in the three fairly extensive descriptions of the models of Scotland, Holland, and Finland, assessment of the impact of the critical elements in a few other countries may be useful. France, for example, has had large-scale social benefits for families and children for nearly half a century, yet began to exhibit leadership in the reduction of infant mortality and the discovery and treatment of handicapping conditions only within the last decade.

Following five years of study by a number of health task forces, a report "Pour Une Politique de la Santé" (Toward a Health Policy) was published in 1971.[22] Prior to that, legislative action had already been taken in an attempt to reduce the number of births of handicapped children, find those handicapped children who were born, and improve follow-up and treatment of these children. The emphasis of the legislation was principally on improving prenatal care. The largest budget increase, more than half the total budget increase for health in that "Sixth Plan" for 1971, was for that purpose. Other funds were made available to increase the numbers of chairs in obstetrics in medical schools, increase intensive care units for the newborn in teaching hospitals, improve record keeping, enforce safety standards in institutions, and to establish an immunization program against rubella.

Social Benefits

The improved prenatal care program was interesting because it included reorganization and consolidation of maternity and infancy care services into one ministerial department allowing for much more powerful leverage on the system. It also offered an unusually attractive incentive to prenatal care. A pregnant woman had to register with a clinic or physician before the fourth month of pregancy in order to receive *any* maternity grant, and since payment was divided into three parts, she had to visit at least twice more to obtain the *full* grant (more than $200).[23] A similar incentive was offered for eligibility for the children's allowance, and, again, more than early registration was needed to obtain the full allowance. The child had to be brought for examination at fixed intervals.

Whether the benefits or improved supervision are to receive the credit, infant mortality in France in 1975 was 13.6 per 1,000 live births, compared with 21.9 only ten years earlier.[24] The rate was close to those of the European leaders—Holland and Finland and the Scandinavian countries—and well below those of the United Kingdom, Belgium, and Germany, although ten years earlier France had ranked higher. In any case, the three critical elements—social benefits, comprehensive universal coverage by medical care services, and an independently focused preventive service available to all children—have been at work in France since 1970.

There is general approval of the approach. David and Lézine, in their study of the operation, recently wrote, "France has a very comprehensive system of child care including an elaborate system of financial allowances under the various funds of the social security system which provides a broad base of monetary support in addition to medical services."[25] Allowances paid to the mother, regardless of family income level, are not taxable.

The French spend much more proportionately on family benefits than any other European nation—4.1 percent compared with the United Kingdom's 1.7 percent, Netherlands' 3.1 percent, Germany's 2.2 percent.[26] Social benefits include, in addition to the maternity allowance noted, children's allowances that can come to more than a quarter of the family's total annual income, paid to the mother and not taxable; means-tested housing allowance along with public housing, eligibility for which is related to income; and a special allowance for families with handicapped children. The mother is entitled to a paid pregnancy leave of 14 weeks. If both parents in a low-income family work, there is a special allowance to facilitate child care. All single parents who work are entitled to the same allowance.

Systematic care is presumably guaranteed by the quasi-punitive ("incentive") measure whereby the substantial monetary allowance will not be paid without compliance with the examination schedules. The pregnant woman must make at least three visits and the child three—at one week, nine months, and two years.

Consolidation of supervision in the Ministry of Social Affairs (Public Health and Social Security) under a deputy director for maternal and child health in the Office of the Director-General of Health, means that nearly 85 percent of the necessary health expenditures are reviewed in one agency. However, the jurisdiction for oversight is delegated to the départements, through whom the funds are actually paid.[27] There is some question as to whether all the départements are equally energetic in carrying out their obligations in enforcing the laws concerning examinations and assessments.

There is also some question as to whether the very poor on welfare (who must use a special card, different from the regular card used in obtaining medical care) receive equal treatment and whether illiterate or foreign-speaking mothers and children (and there are many migrant workers with their families in France) receive equal treatment.[28] French bureaucracy is noteworthy for its intransigence and rigidities. If benefits are withheld for failure to comply with necessary legal registration, the child is punished more than the family. One does not see in France the same kind of outreach and follow-up on behalf of the child that is so noteworthy in Scandinavia and the Netherlands. Legal procedures safeguard the money more than they serve the child's interests.

But the fact that preventive services are paid for in the doctor's offices (as well as in clinics) through social security at 100 percent of cost, while for curative services for sick children the reimbursement is only 80 percent, tends to put a desirable financial value on prevention. The monetary stimulus is also an incentive for doctors to do more in the way of preventive services for children, just as the fact that a pregnant woman is entitled to four examinations without charge, and the doctor is paid for each of them, encourages the woman to take advantage of the opportunity and encourages the doctor to participate. Manciaux writes, "Law and conscience push the doctors and their associates to work in the same direction toward the prevention of disability through early care."[29] He could add money.

The Medical Care System

France has a population of about 52 million, which has shown very slow growth in the past 100 years despite a strongly pronatalist policy. The population plateau is generally attributed to the severe loss of young males in a century of wars. Health and welfare services are run at a district level by 90 départements. The program directors are rarely doctors. Health departments are a responsibility of the communes, of which there are 40,000, and these are generally run by the mayor. However, towns with more than 20,000 inhabitants must have a full-time health officer technically responsible to the medical inspector of the département.

Ninety-eight percent of the population is covered by health insurance through various schemes related to industry and place of employment. Patients pay the doctor, and are in return reimbursed by the social insurance fund. The fund is supported by employer and employee contributions, along with a tax subsidy to cover services for those unable to work.

Maternal and child health services are provided mainly through the general practitioners, but there is an active and growing public health program. There are 600 prenatal clinics, 8,000 infant welfare clinics, and 2,000 welfare clinics for preschool children. In the clinics, over 7,000 physicians are employed full or part time, along with 7,000 "assistant socials" (nurse/social workers) and 2,300 midwives. In addition, there are trained nurses, and puéricultrices as well as "mothercraft" assistants in these clinics.[30] Nearly all babies are born in hospitals. As mentioned earlier, infant mortality in 1975 was 13.6.[31]

The school health service is responsible for all children receiving preschool, elementary, and secondary education. Nearly 25 percent of children start going to school at age two, and by age five, over 90 percent of the children are in school. There are about 1,000 doctors (250 of whom are full time), more than 12,000 nurses, and 1,100 social workers in the school health system.[32]

There are four obligatory examinations or screenings prescribed for school children. The first is at three or four years of age as the child enters kindergarten—a follow-up on the three obligatory screenings of the infant and preschool child. The second is when the child enters primary school, at about six years of age, and the third is at ten or eleven. The last obligatory examination takes place when the child is 15 or 16 or leaves school.[33]

In 1974, expenditures for health represented 6 percent of the gross national product and 10 percent of the family budget; 68 percent of costs were included in social security. In all, costs averaged about $300 a person a year. At that same time, Britain was spending 4.9 percent of the gross national product, had just about as many doctors and hospital beds, but had a slightly higher infant mortality rate.[34] Later British budgets envisioned an accent on intensifying social action in favor of the family and providing more nurses and more social centers.

French analysis of the needs in child care and objective consideration of the costs of undertaking the expensive social actions that characterize their social policy should be of particular interest to us in the United States because the political decision was economically based. Following the task force reports ("Pour une Politique de la Santé") mentioned earlier, the Ministry of Social Affairs had its RCB (Rationalization des Choix Budgetaires, systems analysis teams assigned to each ministry) analyze the cost-benefits ratio of preventive services in eliminating or reducing handicaps against the eventual cost of treating handicapping conditions. At 1976 prices, for example, the total cost of reproductive casualties (i.e., still births, handicaps, congenital defects) in France, including cost to the government and family in actual expenditures plus loss of earnings, came to about $4 billion. Estimates in several countries, including the United States, seemed to indicate that something on the order of 30 percent of reproductive casualties could be prevented by proper prenatal care. It was on this basis that the added funds for prenatal care were provided and the effort undertaken to reorganize and make the maternity and infancy care system more effective.[35]

In short, the health services for children have a separate and independently funded and supervised pathway in the French government familiarly known as PMI, which stands for Protection Maternelle et Infantile (Protection of Mothers and Infants). PMI centers date from 1945, but have been stimulated and promoted more actively since 1971. It is intended that there be at least one center for each 10,000 children in every département. These centers offer immunizations, examinations, mental health services, consultation and advice, and home visitation. Diphtheria-tetanus immunization is compulsory, as is polio and tuberculosis vaccine. Compulsory smallpox vaccination has been eliminated, and measles, rubella, and whooping cough immunizations can be obtained from the center, but are not compulsory.

Mothers carry a "Carnet de Santé" (Health Record Book), which is a health record and also a ticket to the maternity allowance when properly inscribed. Children must have a "Carnet de Santé," also properly filled out, to guarantee children's allowance for the family. Private physicians as well as the clinic can fill out the forms. Considerable discussion is now going on in France about whether private physicians should be permitted to continue to provide preventive services since they tend not to keep records, and very little information can be obtained from them.[36]

The concern expressed socially for children in France can be seen also in the responsibilities that health agencies assume. The late Dr. Nathalie Masse, in her chapter on the PMI in the pediatrics textbook *Pédiatrie Sociale*, discusses at length the approach of center personnel to family life education and their encouragement of families to understand the system and the reasons behind the insistence upon examinations and immunizations. It is clear that, by reason of the complexity of French political structures, if there were not under-standing of and dedication to the child health goals, little could be accomplished. The complexity is formidable: separate administrative offices for social security and health services; separate funds for maternity and family allowances; separate paths for medical care and prevention; separate policy making by national and department officials; communal responsibility for public health; both private and public options for delivery of preventive services. The law has bound them together, but bureaucracy could easily keep them apart.[37]

Not every observer is entirely pleased with the success of the complicated funding/service design of the PMI. The immunization rates do not seem to have improved with the concentration of services. Dr. Rossignol, chief pediatrician of the Paris region for the Social Security office, said that only 55 percent of Parisian children are fully immunized.[38] Professor Bernard Pissarro pointed out that in his own studies, only 36 percent of children under two get through the PMI clinics. With evidence that another 46 percent go to private physicians, this means that nearly 20 percent of children are not seen.[39]

The confusions and inefficiencies that result from the complexity of the French child care system may not be too difficult to rectify. Dr. J. J. Hazemann, chief of the Central Medical-Social Bureau, Paris region, has developed a multiscreening center to review the physical status of preschool children—some previously examined and so certi-fied by practitioners, others initially examined in the multiphasic unit. As of 1975 he had examined 40,000 children, half of them not previously examined. About two-thirds of the anomalies found in those previously examined had been previously known. Aside from the fact that 8 percent of the 10-month-old infants are found to have a major handicap (a figure corresponding reasonably well with the British and American figures of 5 percent and 6 percent in other studies), the interesting finding in Hazemann's group was that 95 percent of his cohort of youngsters were brought back for follow-up on the succeeding required examinations. With a computer follow-up system he was able to reach the families with visiting nurses and assure that the children with defects and disabilities were not lost to the preventive program.[40]

The Wynns were impressed with the fact that in many instances parents are not aware of some defects, even serious visual defects, and screening is necessary to awaken parents to the potential dangers of the situation for the child's future. This, of course, implies not merely finding, but discussing and educating parents about the consequences and needed action. In other words, it is not simply a process—examination—but a process plus professional relationships that make the screening and examination at specific ages important. Parents must understand, someone must explain. If every child has a right to a minimum standard of health care, which the French Public Health Code proclaims, the nurse's role is crucial to achieving that goal.[41]

One other point is worth noting in connection with the design and effectiveness of the child care system in France. The professional dissatisfactions were noted, but here also we find that there is an interest group outside the medical profession, and outside the civil service, with a concern for children and the care they receive. Maternity and infant care and school health are also a concern of political parties. There are voluntary organizations concerned with the family, but none specifically with children. It appears that the most active and vocal protagonist on behalf of children is the French Communist Party. A Communist senator, Mme. Marie-Thérèse Goutmann, heads the Party Commission on Infancy. She has held a number of conferences on the deficiencies and needs in child health care, out of one of which came an excellent critical volume, *La Petite Enfance* (Infancy). The commission is critical of the failure of consolidation, of the separation of prevention and treatment, and of the separation of health and education in the schools. Mme. Goutmann is outspoken about the lack of sufficient medical personnel in the schools and blames it on the physicians' lack of interest in the preventive system and preoccupation with private practice. Her Senate speeches detail the lack of availability of medical care for the children of the poor and of the migrants, and the lack of doctors in specific school systems. A growing number of physicians attend or are associated with the health seminars held under the auspices of the Center for Marxist Studies and Research.[42]

Summary

France conferred social benefits on mothers and children in support of family health and welfare some time ago. Immediately after the Second World War, efforts were made to create an effective prenatal, infant, and preschool child health program, but the matter was left in the hands of private medical practitioners and on a voluntary basis. Cabinet-ordered studies in the late 1960s showed that many children were not being immunized and that important and damaging handicaps were not being sufficiently prevented, sought out, or treated. As a result, strong national legislative action was taken to consolidate the fragmented child care, preventive services, and curative services and to provide more funding for the prenatal and child health systems. The preventive services were given liberal financial incentives. Special child health nurses have been trained, and many more clinics opened and staffed. Nevertheless, achievement lags behind capability. Although PMI has accomplished much, because of the still-heavy reliance on private practitioners and bureaucratic obstruction to effective consolidation of health programs, much remains to be done.

As in the excellent Dutch and Finnish programs, nurses and midwives play a central role, and where they are free to perform without hindrance, the system is remarkably effective. Steiner writes, "the experts who give advice to the mother are midwives and nurses. . . ."[43] The French recognize this and are moving to enlarge and extend the pediatric nursing service. The Wynns write, "One central role of the community pediatric nurse has therefore always been to diagnose childish illness and to teach parents to recognize when a child is ill. . . . The French are achieving a high coverage with their periodic examinations. However, the French Inspector General in a distinguished review of preventive medicine in France expressed strong views on the need for more home visiting of families with young children. . . ."[44]

BELGIUM

Belgium has a population of about 10 million people, a tenth of whom live in the capital, Brussels. Infant mortality in 1971 was 19.6 per 1,000 live births. There is compulsory social insurance for all employed. The Ministry of Public Health supervises health activities; payment for cost of illness comes from the Ministry of Social Insurance.

In the medical care system there is free choice of physician, private practice, and reimbursements to the practitioners under fixed fee schedules. There are a certain number of comprehensive prepayment centers that cover a limited number of people. Hospitals tend to be voluntary or religious.[45]

The effectiveness of the Belgian system of medical care, both curative and preventive, can be discussed only in general terms. "It is impossible for us to analyse the total cost of medical care for the Belgian population between 1960 and 1970 because of the lack of sufficient statistical material."[46] So begins a chapter of the 1971 Belgian Report by the European Institute of Social Security.

Over 90 percent of the Belgian people are covered by one or another compulsory health insurance fund, and the other 10 percent voluntarily in the same funds. There is a single national organization that collects the money from employers and employees (Office National de Securité Social), but a variety of national sickness insurance companies deal with their individual membership, and payments and supervision are delegated to local mutual aid society affiliates. The complexity and pluralism make for competition, duplication, and variations in benefits. However, all basic medical care needs must be met as a minimum requirement of the law. A national institute (Institut National d'Assurance Maladie-Invalidité) with broad membership constituency determines policies, regulates the health insurance associations, negotiates salaries and fees with the health professions, offers a variety of advisory, consultative, and legal services, and distributes the monies obtained from the Office National de Securité Social.

Insurance indemnifies the covered person for 75 percent of the legally negotiated fee, whether for general practitioner or specialist, regardless of what the doctor charges. Welfare clients and the aged are reimbursed at 100 percent, but only of the negotiated fee. There is a small copayment charge for each day of hospitalization unless the patient is on a general ward service. Belgian patients have free choice of doctor, including specialists, to whom they may resort without prior general practitioner consultation. Patients are also reimbursed for medicines at different rates, depending on whether the medications are compounded, brand-named but in the official formulary, or unlisted proprietaries (for which there is no reimbursement). The health insurance system, despite its limitations, can include home nursing care, eye glasses, hearing aids, and preventive examinations or immunizations when given at a doctor's private office.[47]

Belgium has more than 17,000 physicians, greater proportionately than the number in Holland, unevenly distributed through the population, with the agricultural areas less well supplied. There are over 500 obstetricians, more than 3,000 midwives, and 1,200 maternal and child health nurses in the preventive services.[48]

Preventive Personal Health Service

These are principally furnished by a private health organization through its local organizations heavily supported by grants from the Ministry of Public Health.   The ONE (Oeuvre Nationale de l'Enfance), which was founded in 1919, has many of the characteristics of the Cross agencies in Holland.   Interestingly enough, the planning and administrative work is done principally by volunteer, middle-class women.   The ONE operates clinics for children and expectant mothers.   Prenatal care and routine preventive services for infants and toddlers are provided there.   Some clinics offer more comprehensive care.   Most infants are seen, at least once, but fewer children receive services in the preschool ages.   There are 350 prenatal clinics and over 1,000 infant welfare clinics, as well as 500 toddlers' (preschoolers') clinics.   Home visiting services are also provided by the nurses of the ONE.   Ninety percent of the funds for ONE come from the National Ministry of Health.[49]

Doctors are always in attendance and are paid a basic minimum per session plus a fee for each child or woman seen.   Usually these doctors are general practitioners, but occasionally they are pediatricians.   The reimbursement is arranged to compare with what doctors would receive for seeing children in their offices.   Pediatricians who work in the clinics are paid more than the general practitioners.   (The service is free to the patient in the clinic, but the patient must pay a part of the fee if the preventive service is performed in a doctor's private office.)   Of the 140,000 births in Belgium in 1972 (last statistical report available), the ONE has data on only 23,000.   Services seem to be declining as more people use the doctors' offices.[50]

While 80 percent of the newborns are seen in the ONE offices, older children tend to be seen, if at all, in the doctors' offices.   The births are reported to the local ONE council, and an ONE nurse makes a home visit, which then commonly results in an infant visit to the center.   Unlike Holland, most deliveries are in a hospital and by physicians, general practitioners usually.   The ONE clinics rigidly exclude medical care for sick children, and a sick child must be sent to the physician's office for care.   There is also simmering conflict over whether immunizations should continue to be done in the clinics or referred to the doctor's office.[51]

The Ministry of Health, through the Office of the Social Medicine, concerns itself with school health and services for the handicapped. These services are limited, constituting four examinations during the elementary school years (ages 6-12) and four times during the secondary school years (ages 12-18), for which general practitioners are hired and paid per examination. These examinations are usually carried out in the communal health center or on ONE premises. Handicapping conditions are referred to the family doctor. There is occasional nursing follow-up, but this is inconstant and depends on whether the commune employs a social worker or whether the insurance fund is one that provides home visiting of this kind.[52]

There are Cross societies in Belgium (Yellow and White), but they are exclusively home visiting and bedside care nursing agencies and do not engage in the extensive preventive activities of their Dutch counterparts.

Social Aspects

Keeping in mind the softness of the data, the contrast between Belgium and Holland is marked. It appears that Belgian social benefits are reasonably close to those of Holland and France. Medical care costs and family allowances come to about the same amount. Yet preventive services languish. Less attention is paid to children's needs in Belgium than in Holland. There are many more working women in Belgium than in Holland and day care centers are not entirely adequate in quantity and quality. ONE is heavily engaged in deploying day care centers, but is financially limited in how much it can do. While Belgium has almost as many migrant workers and itinerant gypsy communities as does Holland, no special effort is made, nor are clinic services specially provided for their care. They are expected to be looked after in the existing well-baby clinics and consultation centers.[53] Again, there is insufficient information on the effectiveness of the public health and preventive services in meeting their needs, so no firm judgment can be made.

Summary

It should be kept in mind that Belgium has many of the same problems that Holland has—a population sharply divided along religious and language lines. Belgium and Holland once made up one kingdom, the separation taking place only in 1830. The north of Belgium is Dutch-speaking, rural, conservative. The south is French-speaking, industrialized, and wealthy, with strong trade union and radical political activity. While the country is almost wholly Roman Catholic, there are pockets of Protestantism to add to the social conflict. Cultural differences have not been accommodated as they have been in Holland, in part because social classes are not equally distributed among the antagonistic groups. The southern, French-speaking section of Belgium had long been wealthy, and though the industry was largely destroyed during World War II, the aristocratic attitudes remained. Trade unionism from the French-speaking south has also brought radical industrial agitation, which was strongly resisted by the agrarian, politically conservative, Dutch-speaking north. The decay of the south following the war and the gradual loss of financial dominance (Flemish Antwerp is now the commercial leader) have led to conservative political domination of the country and to aggravation of cultural (and probably class) conflict. The health system reflects this basic conservatism.

Belgium has a separate child health preventive service, but it is hedged about by medical professional control and the nurses are not the principal figures in the preventive services. There are social benefits of importance to assure reasonably adequate financial support for the family. But again, the class and cultural conflicts interfere with social support to the family. As a result, the health and medical care system is less successful in maintaining good child health levels. Infant mortality rates and reduced immunization percentages among the children is evidence of this.

DENMARK

Denmark has a population of five million. In 1972, infant mortality rate was 12.2 per 1,000 live births. The administrative structure of the national health system is provided by the National Board of Health, a unit within the Ministry of the Interior that advises other ministries on medical and pharmaceutical matters. The National Board of Health is primarily a staff organization and carries out very few activities on its own. The board has mostly been concerned with planning, advisory, and consultative services. County and city councils run their own hospitals. The state-supported health insurance system finances medical care, which is supervised by the Ministry of Social Affairs.

Preventive Services

Preventive services—maternity care, for example—are the responsibility of the general practitioner. If it is a low risk pregnancy, the mother can be cared for by the general practitioner, or she can be cared for by a midwife during her prenatal period, or both. She can have seven to ten checkups paid for out of tax funds from the communes or municipalities that are directly responsible for these social and preventive services. Midwives are attached to either birth clinics in which prenatal care and deliveries are carried out, or to local hospitals.

If the family doctor or midwife decides that the patient is high risk, the case is referred to the local hospital where a supervising obstetrician manages the case. The low-risk woman can choose where she gives birth, and in almost all cases this is either the birth clinic or the hospital. All high-risk women deliver in the hospital. Childbirth is principally in the hands of midwives. All births are reported to local authorities, and there is a fine if a midwife fails to report a birth. A woman registering in this prenatal system receives a maternity allowance. If the pregnant woman is unmarried, she is eligible for other social assistance as well.

Preschool services from birth to school age include both home visitation and visits to the general practitioner. The health visitor who works for a communal agency, a nurse with pediatric as well as public health training, is expected to visit monthly during the baby's first year of life. The visitor offers not only the usual advice and guidance, immunizations if the doctors wishes, and counsel on feeding and child care, but may also take care of minor illnesses. If advisable, referrals are made to the family doctor. If the mother has a problem with her baby, she very often will call the health visitor, who is on call 24 hours a day, before she calls a physician. This visiting nurse is also expected to see to it that the child attends the doctor's office for well-child examinations.

The problem of Danish public health nurses who do visiting is that they are expected to combine responsibilities. Although some of them only do infant health visiting, others combine this with school nursing, and some combine both of these with home nursing. There are also registered nurses without training in public health who may be working in the field competing, to an extent, with public health nurses. So there is considerable flux and ferment in the system. Another problem is that 12 percent of the population does not receive nursing services because they live in townships where home visitation, which is not compulsory, is not provided.

Many people think that separation of prevention and cure also is a deficiency. The fragmentary nature of the Danish health system is a barrier to efficient care.

By the time a child is seven years old in Denmark, he may
have five separate health records: the midwife has a record of
his birth; the infant health visitor has her own record of her
visits to his home (kept in her own file for five years); the
family physician has his own record of treatment; the school
has a health record; and if the child has been hospitalized,
there is a record at the hospital. These five records represent
five separate health programs serving the one child. There is
a measure of communication among these programs—some
routine, some as needed, some mandatory, some voluntary.
The midwife always sends a report to the infant health
visitor; the hospital always sends a report to the family doctor
when a child is discharged. The mother may use the card on
which the infant health visitor and family doctor recorded
their observations and treatments when she is filling out a
report for the school health services. All such reports,
however, are merely attempts to bridge the separation of
these different services.[54]

There is a proposal in Parliament to combine infant health
visiting with school nursing and home nursing, to make it compulsory
in all municipalities, and to order the development of a priority
system for high-risk visiting (a needs test). More important would
be an increase in the number of public health nurses.

While no specific times are set for examination of children, they
are usually examined at regular intervals: 6 weeks, 3 months, and 10
months during the first year of life. The child is then examined at 15
months, at 2 years, and annually until entering school. Nurses have
been visiting monthly during this first year, but shortages of nurses
(and money) have compelled the communes to develop priorities for
home visiting, giving first consideration to those infants who are, for
physical, mental or social reasons, considered high-risk, which
significantly reduces visits to other children. Even so, over 90 percent
of the infants are fully immunized before their first birthday.

School health services take care of children from entrance until
school leaving. The school doctor examines the child four times: on
admission, the following year, in the fifth year of school, and at school
leaving. Vision and hearing are checked annually by the school
nurse.[55] The county is responsible through the county public health
officer who supervises the school health physician and a school health
nurse. The municipality pays for the school physicians and school

nurses, who are responsible for routine physical examinations. At these examinations, social as well as medical information is sought. The school nurse is expected to confer with the family doctor and the parents if there are social as well as medical problems. They must also consult with other necessary specialists as the occasion warrants.

Unfortunately, the Danes do not keep records of school health activity on a national basis, which makes it difficult to know whether all the work is being done and whether children do fall through the net. However, there is a very powerful child advocacy movement, and there are official agencies—Child and Youth Committees—attached to local municipalities and communes that look out for children. This makes it difficult for children to be abused or neglected without knowledge or intervention by the state. There are also extensive networks of private and public family care agencies to provide help if needed.

Social Action

The Child and Youth Committee is part of the city council. Although all the members of the committee may not be members of the council, one half must be. These committees have professional staff with professional consultants who work with the schools and with the various social agencies to protect the children. There is also an appeal line to the National Council on Children and Youth and, in rare instances, even to the Supreme Court.[56]

The Children's and Young Persons' Act of 1964 provides that, "The purpose of the child and youth welfare services shall be to insure that children and youth grow up under conditions promoting sound mental and physical development." The purpose of these committees, therefore, is as much health promotion as child protection. There are no juvenile courts in Denmark. These committees act to deal with child abuse and neglect as well as with social action in connection with children's misbehavior. The communes and municipalities maintain full-time staff of social workers and "family helpers" (who have less training than social workers) along with consultants to these Child and Youth Committees. As in Holland, neglect of children's health needs is considered child abuse.[57]

Child power is growing in Denmark as it is in Holland, and children can complain to the local authorities (Child and Youth Committees) themselves and have their parents brought up for questioning and examination. Welfare authorities are expected to recognize that their responsibilities are to the child, who has rights, just as the adults have rights.[58]

According to Danish social policy, it is the state's responsibility to share with parents the burden of child care and support. Children are the future and must be protected. The solutions to ordinary burdens—poverty and large families—are not too difficult. A substantial children's allowance (to age 16), annually adjusted according to the price index and tax free, along with a means-tested housing subsidy (15 percent of the rent cost for each child) can help with the ordinary burdens. Then there are extra-ordinary burdens. Single parents, invalids, or pensioners get a 50 percent higher children's allowance. A widow or a widower, and a mother of a child born out of wedlock where the father cannot be made liable, receive extra grants beyond this. There is also an income tax adjustment for single parents. Welfare authorities give special attention to "weak" families—culturally or geographically isolated families, families with an alcoholic or mentally ill parent, families in which both parents are unemployed, and families with handicapped children. There is a means-tested "youth allowance" for children 16-17 years of age still in school, and orphans receive a full-scale income, two or three times the usual children's allowance. Also, of course, as mentioned before, there is a liberal maternity policy: 14 weeks of maternity leave at 90 percent of usual pay, guaranteed reemployment and health examinations, and complete medical care and midwifery services.[59]

Summary

Denmark has a comprehensive social policy for families and children, a comprehensive medical care insurance program that covers the entire population, and a child health program. The child health program is not spelled out in detail, does not involve a special child health service as in Holland or France, and relies heavily on the interest and actions of the general practitioner. There is heavy reliance on a special, pediatrically trained nurse, however, to work with the family and maintain close contact with the child. Legal and social concern for the child are officially observed and carried out by special groups whose major concern is the child's interest. The system seems to work well and to the satisfaction of all concerned. Infant mortality is low, all the children are immunized, handicaps are found and treated, and there is good nursing follow-up to ensure that these matters are dealt with properly.

SWEDEN

Sweden has a population of eight million people, and in 1972 the infant mortality rate was 11.1 per 1,000 live births. Health services are organized under the Ministry of Social Affairs and dealt with by the Directorate of Health and Social Welfare in that ministry, which has a medical administrator at its head. One of the directors is concerned with public health and social services for children. Administration of health services is hierarchic, delegated through a provincial medical officer to district medical officers at the commune level. In rural areas, the salaried district medical officers are permitted to make a small charge for medical services. Hospitals are the responsibility of provincial councils, and there is no charge to patients. There is a comprehensive health insurance scheme that covers virtually the whole of the population. A visit to a clinic costs twelve to fifteen crowns, a fixed charge reimbursed by the insurance fund. Seventy-five percent of specialists' fees are reimbursable by the insurance fund.

Immunizations against small pox, diphtheria and polio are compulsory. None of these diseases has occurred in Sweden for many years. BCG (tuberculosis immunization) is given to about 95 percent of newborns. The maternity welfare centers and infant welfare centers are under the control of the local communities and are the responsibility of the district medical officers.

School health is the responsibility of the Directorate of Education, which has a chief school medical officer who must consult with the Directorate of Health on policy. Local communities provide school health services. In 1972 there were 11,000 active physicians, 32,000 qualified nurses, and 2,000 midwives.[60]

Social Action

Sweden has a long tradition of social concern and provides extensive social benefits to its citizens. "Sweden [has held] a leading international position in paediatrics and child health services [since] the first half of the 19th century."[61] Improvement along broad socioeconomic lines generally has helped, and accompanying sociolegal developments have established Swedish social action as the most advanced in the world and the most beneficial to children, from the standpoint of any public health standard one chooses.

Maternity benefits in Sweden today include not only an 18-week maternity allowance, but also seven months at full pay and guaranteed re-employment. The father also may take time from work for child care, instead of the mother, with the same pay and right of return—"Equal parental pay." This is not simply to underline a basic definition of sexual equality, but actually to demonstrate to children the need for a father's presence and the balance required for a wholesome home.[62] In addition, the father receives ten days off with pay to look after the children during and immediately after the birth. There is paid parental leave for either parent to stay home from work to look after a sick child.[63]

There are, of course, children's allowances—the most generous in Europe (paid to the mother)—and a youth allowance, as in Denmark, for 16- and 17-year-olds still in school. There are other compensations: family allowances and rent subsidies for larger families, extra sums for single parents or widows, child minder allowance for the working mother if she chooses not to use or cannot find a suitable day care center, and a special nursing care allowance for families with a handicapped child. Furthermore, an absent parent is ordinarily required by law to make support payments. If the absent parent cannot be located or is found unable to make support payments, a child support advance is paid by the Child Welfare Board.[64] "Social wages" is what the Swedes call this system of adjusting family income to special needs—a basic amount, not means tested and not taxable.

The Swedes seek to avoid institutional care for children, according to their " 'at home' principle [which] signifies that a social worker or other suitable person lives with the family, sharing their own conditions for some time, thus functioning as a participating therapist."[65] This is done rather than separate the child from parents because of neglect or social difficulties.

The nature of illnesses and problems has changed as the result of social and economic progress. Physical, somatic, and nutritional problems have been replaced by psychosomatic and mental hygiene problems. There are no more slums in Sweden, no more nutritional deficiency diseases or frequent infections, but interpersonal conflict and environments with high sociomedical risks exist today. The role of the nurses from the child welfare clinic is to try to change this national situation.

Preventive Services

The counties support child welfare clinics, where the district medical officer, with nurses and midwives, provides child health and maternal health services. In 1972, 100 percent of births were in the hospital. Doctors and nurses with special training work in the outpatient maternity clinics. High-risk cases are cared for by doctors specializing in obstetrics. More than 90 percent of expectant mothers register at maternity clinics and make an average of twelve visits per pregnancy.

All newborn babies are reported to the local child welfare clinic. Information about the pregnancy and birth is included in the notification to alert the nurse to possible extra risks on the first visit, which must take place within 14 days of receipt of the notification. Nearly 100 percent of all babies are examined and immunized in these clinics in the first year of life. An active preventive service includes a visit a month to the clinic, three routine nursing calls at the home per year (or more if an appointment is missed), provision of medicines and vitamins, nutritional counseling, and a variety of educational child care activities. Hospital assessment clinics are provided for those with apparent handicaps discovered at the periodic screening.

Children are followed in this clinic until school age. Ten visits are made by the child the first year, three the second, and two per year thereafter until school. In addition, there is a special "target" examination of four-year-olds to document undiscovered illnesses or handicaps, or failures to obtain needed care. In 1970, a review of this four-year-old examination was undertaken. About 20 percent of the four-year-olds in Sweden, 25,000 children, were examined. Half were found to have at least one minor abnormality of some kind, but the important aspect of the findings was that practically no serious defect was previously unknown or untreated.[66]

School health services include periodic examinations, extensive health education programs, and treatment as well as diagnosis in the school clinics. When necessary, children are referred to pediatricians, but ordinarily the child will be referred back to the family doctor for care.

Summary

Sweden is an advanced society with a strong social conscience, from which families and children benefit tremendously. In addition to extensive child and family allowances, there is a well-organized, well-staffed, official health system with special services for children, a system that has a remarkable record of achievement in reaching high levels of child health. Although substantially comparable to the Dutch system, it differs in its success in meeting preventive and curative objectives. The nurse is the key element of the preventive services for children, but the service is essentially physician-controlled. The official clinic, and not the private doctor's office, is the site for provision of services, and the private sector plays practically no part in the organization or implementation of the system. It may be that the decentralized funding and control are sufficiently powerful factors so that parents and the public make up a cooperative partnership that accounts for the success of the program.

BRIEFER COMPARISONS

Olla Podrida

The European countries discussed in the previous sections share a common approach that makes their different efforts and different achievements comparable. They all focus on the child to accomplish specific goals: to reduce infant mortality, to reduce handicapping conditions or their effects on children, and, through social benefits, to protect the family and the child and attempt to give each child an equal footing in its start in life. These common efforts had a variety of expressions. A national health service or national health insurance program, variously funded or administered, made medical care available to children. In some, the preventive needs of the child were met by resorting to the medical care system alone; in others, a separate child health preventive system was organized. In some, the family doctor was the primary figure, or promoted as the primary figure, in the preventive as in the curative field. In others, a specially trained child nurse was given a principal role. Even in family doctor-oriented systems, often the child nurse had a key role in prevention. The presence or lack of follow-up procedures was also of great significance.

Too often lack of concern for maintaining records multiplied the difficulty of assessing the value or success of a system. In most instances, however, this lack of records reinforced the impression that some children, or specific groups of children, were overlooked, and that the critically necessary follow-up was not carried out. What does emerge clearly from the review, though, is the fact that there is a relationship between process and performance. Intention is fairly universal—"We all love our children," might be said honestly and sincerely in every country. But good intentions are not enough. As a measure of effectiveness, even expenditures are not terribly useful. Money, of itself, cannot do the trick. Process counts: a separate focus on prevention in childhood, social benefits to offset some of the struggle related to family size, and assigned and supervised responsibility for child health services. But there may be notable exceptions, both in success without these factors and failure with them. A superficial glimpse of child health services in a few other places confirms this impression.

Switzerland

In Switzerland, for example, the cantonal system, with its stubbornly individualized approach to political and social action, heavily influences the health and medical care service activities for the whole population, not only the children. The designated characteristics of a "good" process are not all present. The almost fanatical devotion to privacy that motivates the Swiss (cf. numbered bank accounts!) makes them resist reporting and casts grave doubt on the validity and utility of data on immunizations and handicaps in children. In addition, professional organizations, like the physicians' organizations, are quite powerful, have succeeded in resisting governmental control in health insurance legislation, and dominate the voluntary health insurance system. Also, as Robinson notes, "It is accepted by most Swiss that the family does have, and should have, more power and responsibility than the State in educating and caring for the child."[67] However, Switzerland is a wealthy country; agriculture, dairying, and tourism are protections against rural poverty, industry and banking against urban poverty. One does not see slums or even decaying housing. As a result, nearly 95 percent of the population is covered by the voluntary insurance.

The cantonal rivalry that takes the form of competing for the *least* expenditures needed to conform with national laws, and the lack of any effective child interest group make investment in child health minimal. Nevertheless, in a survey in Berne, 78 percent of handicaps in children were discovered before age three and 97 percent before school entry at age seven. The cantons tend to subcontract for prenatal and well-baby care to a private organization.[68]

The *Säugligsfürsorgeschwester* (infant care nurse) who works in the private agency is carefully trained—three years in an approved nursing school, two more years in a pediatric hospital, and six months of special training in infant care. In addition to educating the mother and family in child care and child needs, these nurses can and do participate in the diagnostic and therapeutic activities on behalf of handicapped children. All children with birth defects are entitled to care under federal (not cantonal) auspices, and the "WSK" nurses do a large share of the home treatment needed. There is no parents' organization of handicapped children, so the doctor and nurse estimate of need is final and prescriptive.[69]

The 22 cantons and 6 million inhabitants prefer to consult private physicians, and the communes within the cantons offer little in the way of public services, school doctors being the exception. Yet the children are immunized, and, apparently, the handicaps found and treated. Infant mortality in 1972 was roughly comparable to that of the Scandinavian and Dutch levels: 13.3 per 1,000 live births in 1972.[70]

West Germany

West Germany offers another example demurring from the pattern described. With over 62 million people, of the European countries it ranks next to Sweden and Switzerland in gross national product per capita and just below Sweden in health expenditures per capita.[71] It has more physicians per 10,000 population than any of the other countries discussed and a full scale social benefits program. Children's allowances after the first child, for example, are paid to the child's 18th year, not just to the 16th, as in most other European countries, and a student allowance is paid to the 25th year. There is a maternity benefit, maternity leave without loss of earnings, and guarantee of re-employment. Interest-free home building loans are made to families with large numbers of children, and there are means-tested rental allowances as well.

Medical care services are paid for through a national health insurance fund, in which 90 percent of the population are inscribed, most under the compulsory law and the rest, with higher incomes, voluntarily. The rest, the unemployed, pensioners or those in the civil service, are covered by government contributions.[72]

Preventive services are the responsibility of the Federal Ministry of Youth, Family Affairs, and Health. But the discharge of public health obligations, such as maternal and child health clinics, is left to the city and rural district health departments. Nursing outreach is limited. The patients are left to seek out the bulk of these services from their own physicians. In West Germany also, parental responsibility weighs more heavily than in Holland or Scandinavia. The looseness of the organization and the relative ineffectiveness of the system, despite heavy financial investment, is underlined in the relatively high infant mortality rate in West Germany (22.8 per 1,000 live births in 1972) and in the lack of data on the immunization status of children, although it appears that fewer than 75 percent of the population under three has been immunized against diphtheria and tetanus.[73]

Canada

Although Canada has advanced beyond the United States with a comprehensive national health insurance scheme, it has extremely limited social benefits related to welfare eligibility, more in line with U.S. standards, rather than full-scale child or family allowances (though there is a modest children's allowance). In discussions of child health and welfare, the concept of poverty and the burden of illness, handicap, and early death associated with poverty, particularly for children, is emphasized. Over 20 percent of Canadian children live in poverty, particularly the children in rural areas. Poverty as a concept in child care rarely enters into the discussion of child health and child welfare in European countries.

The Canadians also lack an effective national or even comprehensive provincial preventive service for mothers and children.[74] It appears that the situation with regard to child health and school health is no different and no better in Canada than it is in the United States. Certainly the infant mortality rates have been close and remain almost the same today: 17.1 to 18.9 per 1,000 live births in 1972.

New Zealand

Finally, as an example of what puzzling contradictions logic can lead us to, there is the case of New Zealand. New Zealand has had long-standing social benefits very like the British ones, a comprehensive medical care insurance system for almost 50 years, and a separate and distinct child health service, including maternity care provided principally by specially trained nurses who also serve in the schools under the School Health Service. The nurses are part of a private national group (the Plunkett Society), to which members pay dues. The organization not only trains and employs the nurses, who incidentally are also trained to do dental work in the schools, but operates maternity hospitals and child health centers as well. Government support to this private agency has supplanted public services, which are minimal.[75]

In any case, economic stress since the entry of Britain into the European Common Market—with resultant reduction of prices and income from New Zealand exports—has resulted in slow erosion and underfunding of these health services. A colleague who has spent several years there off and on, including the past year, writes that the rise in infant mortality is disturbing health authorities and that small outbreaks of diphtheria and tetanus indicate that immunization and school health services are increasingly a privilege of the well-to-do.[76] Most recent data from New Zealand gives the infant mortality rate as 16 per 1,000 live births in 1974, which, since it is for the white population only, is closer to the United States', than the Scandinavian countries'.[77]

SUMMARY

We have looked at some of the ways in which selected European countries deal with the social, health, and medical problems surrounding childbirth and child care so as to improve the opportunity of every child born to have a fair chance. In each case, society has made the decision that without regard to family income certain obligations have to be discharged to assure that fair chance. A working mother should be able to take time off from work, without loss of pay or job status; be physically fit for giving birth; be supervised by appropriate professionals during pregnancy to ensure that no condition threatening the health and safety of her or the child should go unnoted or untreated. In addition, the family should have sufficient added social and financial support to see to it that mother and child are properly fed and housed. When the child is born, every effort should be made to examine and find any handicapping condition that needs to be treated, and to see to it that it *is* treated.

Between the time of a child's birth and school entrance, other health measures should be taken. Some are economic, and the family is supplied with additional money to see to it that the child is properly fed or clothed. Other social steps are taken, such as providing housing subsidies, so that a family of four children is not at a disadvantage compared with single workers or couples who earn identical salaries. The child is given physical examinations, in many instances on a mandatory basis and when handicapping conditions are found, a child is treated, and glasses, hearing aids, physical exercises, special equipment, or nursing is provided. This procedure is followed through the child's school years as well.

The results are obvious. Lower infant mortality, fewer untreated handicapping conditions, fewer unimmunized children and less morbidity of those epidemic diseases to which children are subject. The premise behind such preventive services is that it will result in a healthy adult population which will be reflected in the increasing longevity of and lower mortality in the productive years of the adult.

OVERVIEW

There is a certain danger in making firm judgments on social policies and programs and proceeding to recommend national policies and programs based on those judgments. National factors change, in the countries reviewed and in the country for which the recommendations are intended. If I had not received the letter from Dr. Kronick in regard to New Zealand and then made further inquiries to obtain information from recent observers, my picture of the New Zealand situation would have been totally different. I would not have seen it as aberrant as it is, given the national program of social benefits, comprehensive insured medical care, and the private preventive service aimed at children. I might have used it as an example of what a beneficial role these factors play in improving child health. In the other direction, I would not have believed the Swiss system to be as effective as it is, given the almost nonexistent public activity on behalf of the health of mothers and children.

It may very well be, then, that changes in economic status, social conflict, or other factors may emerge to modify the quality and effectiveness of the programs for which I developed such admiration and respect as a result of my observations. "Pronounce no man fortunate until he is dead," cautions the proverb. One should hesitate to put an imprimatur on a national program of child health or an interdict on another. Nevertheless, there does appear to be a strain of common sense that runs through effective programs that cannot be gainsaid. While programs derived from the historical experience and social values of one country will not survive transplantation as such, the principles that inform these programs may.

Holland may be the victim of uncontrolled expenditures because of the chaotic complexity of its multidenominational, public/private, medical care/preventive service operations. Apparently, it is an expense they are willing to bear. Whatever the unwieldiness or diseconomics of the system, it serves the children well.

The director-general of health services for Holland and the director of child health for Amsterdam both emphasized the necessity for coordination and for elimination of duplicative or ineffectively small child health services. In Amsterdam the program is already underway. Cross societies may disappear in the future. But for us, the lesson of the potential of such mechanisms should not be lost. In the 100 years of Cross society operations, such a strong base for child health has been built that the framework cannot be dismantled. For the United States, without an effective national child health system, perhaps the idea of creating such a framework may have merit.

Finland, Denmark, the Netherlands, and Sweden give children rights, and back them up in ways we have not yet learned to accept in the United States. Perhaps we cannot give the child priority over the parent in court, or in social decision making. But the usefulness of this approach deserves wide debate and informed discussion. Our income redistribution policies are related to poverty, not to children's needs. The assumption is that parents have the right and the responsibility to look after their children's needs. Neglect with all the tragic consequences is only reluctantly perceived and timidly reproved or punished. Social benefits—maternity care and payments to mothers, child allowances as "equalizers," housing and rent subsidies to ensure a decent place for children to grow up—these are yet to be considered American values, American attitudes, American laws.

The corollary of this concept of children's rights is the superior right of the state, as *parens patriae*, over the rights of the child's parents, to ensure health, well-being, and social equality for all children. It means that privacy of information, at present so jealously maintained on behalf of the family, will have to be breached.

It should be clear that not all individuals, and sometimes not even the majority, accepted the imperious character of the state's demands meekly. It may be that the common sense of the populace rejects control that is too tight and intrusion that is too emphatic and that the fuss that then takes place results in modification of the rigidities of the law. In Denmark now, the state's right to decide whether parents are "fit" to look after a child is coming into question. A tremendous campaign is being waged on behalf of parents who kidnapped their daughter from a welfare home in which she had been placed by authorities because the mother was said to be retarded. It should be noted that sympathetic police have refused an order to arrest the mother.[78]

Social benefits that may flow to children from changes in American attitudes and legislation must not be viewed as the sole effective force in improving child health. In Europe the social benefits, medical care programs, *and* preventive services are all necessary parts of the child health care whole. What we have seen is that the elements vary in their emphasis, and the results seem to vary with the emphasis. Perhaps we will not be able to change America into a nation that orders increased state power over children and lessened parent power, or one that appropriates billions of dollars for child and family allowances and for extensive rent and housing subsidies. But does that mean that we cannot have a more effective child health program?

Not at all. A medical care system that works, that provides reasonably equal access to modern medical care is also necessary. Where the medical care system limps for one reason or another, the children suffer. And that medical care system need not be government controlled. It does not have to eliminate private practice, operate on a salary basis, or follow any of the authoritarian lines so feared by American doctors and many patients. None of the countries so respectfully described as "successful" operate in this manner. Holland has private practice, negotiated fee schedules and payments, and private agencies engaged in preventive care and does extremely well by governmental subsidy and supervision, but without government control. A "Special Correspondent" writes of the Danish medical care system in the *British Medical Journal*, "Here, then, is a system which provides a good standard of medical care ... and gives the doctors working in it satisfaction with their jobs, their incomes and their way of life ... the results are impressive—they have been achieved by consensus rather than confrontation, without much of a private sector, and without any financial barrier between doctor and patient."[79]

But neither is access to medical care alone enough in itself to make a difference in child health, because it is the need for extensive preventive services that marks the difference between children's health needs and adults' health needs. The existence of a separate preventive service for children, or at least a separately organized service within the medical care system, is a *sine qua non*. This preventive service *may* be physician controlled, but physician interest in preventive services is so low that it is more desirable to give this responsibility to trained child health nurses. In any case, specially trained child health nurses should play a major role in preventive services for children.

The Wynns argue convincingly that their studies in Finland, France, Sweden, and Britain have persuaded them that it is the pediatric community nurses, working in the child health centers and home visiting, who are responsible for the remarkable achievements in lowering infant mortality. In Finland the nurse makes an average of 3.5 home visits per infant in the first year of life, in Sweden 3.1, and in Britain 1.1. Of course, there are three times as many nurses (health visitors) in Finland available for this purpose as in Britain.[80]

The number of physicians, beyond a reasonable number, is of little consequence in assuring child health care. West Germany, with four times the pediatricians that Britain has, and an even greater proportion than Finland, had an infant mortality rate of 22.7 per 1,000 live births in 1973, nearly twice that of Finland. Finland is a poor country and West Germany is wealthy. Also, Finland spends far less money proportionately than West Germany on child health. The improved cost-effectiveness derives from the better organization, focus on prevention for children, and the more extensive use of pediatric community nurses.[81]

In short, European experiences, with minor variations, point up six essential ingredients of a successful child health service:

1. social support (nutrition, housing, welfare)
2. medical care (guarantee of care in case of illness)
3. special preventive service (immunizations, guidance and counseling, screening and assessment of handicaps, routine school health supervision)
4. special pediatric nursing (home visiting, with or without physician control)
5. midwifery (with or without physician control, in the hospital or at home)
6. private sector activity (this essentially involves an advocacy approach—local decentralized operations, at the least; private organizations for legal and welfare services as well as for preventive services; and parental involvement where possible.)

The Wynns, who make no bones about their passionate concern for children, note that Sweden has the best child health system in

Europe, and there the arrangements are entirely official—no private agencies to speak of to look after children's health needs. Even the advocacy arrangements are officially sponsored. Finland's system, they note, is nearly as good, and much less costly. Finland and Sweden are saturated with nurses, the doctors being a bit more visible in Sweden. But in both countries, there is local control (In Sweden funds to pay for the service is raised by local taxes.), and both focus on community nursing and visiting. Outreach is essential. In Finland, as in Holland, children not brought to the clinic for appointed visits are considered "at risk."[82]

It may be of interest to amplify a bit on the need for and value of careful early screening examinations of the preschool child. Kohler, a pediatrician, emphasizes the need in the context of the level of the society. Reporting on the special study of the four-year-olds done in Sweden in 1971 as part of a larger continuing study, he points out, "The second highest living standard in the world, reasonably well-distributed among different socio-economic groups, and a well-organized care of pregnant women, deliveries, neonates and infants must result in physically well-developed and healthy children."[83] Then why all the fuss about special examinations and systems? The system had made the four-year-old examination virtually unnecessary, or so it seemed, since so few new important illnesses were uncovered. "The justification for collecting all these [data on defects] . . . is that we believe that they are all in some way important for the child and we have the resources for detecting and taking care of them."[84] The reasoning may be a bit too logical: we owe the children this debt and we have the resources to carry it out, so we should do it in the most effective and cost-efficient way. It is a type of reasoning, as he notes himself, applicable only to a wealthy country with illnesses that reflect an advanced society, and not one in which life-threatening epidemics and severe nutritional deficiencies are the major social and health problems.

The influence and importance of the nurse in the preventive system is underlined by the dry reporting in Wagner's "Sweden's Health-Screening Program for Four-Year-Old Children." Nurses were instrumental in the case finding process and where comparison was made, the nurses did as well as doctors in case finding.[85]

Setting a health system in place is, of course, not enough to guarantee good health services to all children. Examinations must be followed by treatment. Outreach is essential. Dividing children into social or economic classifications of any kind is to obstruct the appropriate action of the system. All children must be considered the responsibility of the system, for while parental responsibility is desirable, it is no substitute for systematic care of children.

The care of the child is the care of the people.

Table 10-3   Some Selected Data on Selected European Countries*

Country	Population	GNP	Social Expend.	Health Expend.	MDs	Nurses	Tax Paid For Health	Out of Pocket	Social Security
							(% of cost of medical care)		
Belgium........	9.7	54.7	NA	2.3	17.3	NA			
Denmark......	5	30	NA	1.4	9	40.7			
France..........	52.5	266	4.7%	12	75.5	26.6	7	33	60
Finland.......	4.7	21.8		0.88	6.2	38			
Netherlands	13.5	69.5	3.1%	3.3	21	44.8	21.6	34.6	43.8
Sweden.........	8	55.5		3	13.2	40.7	34	7	9
Scotland......	5		1.7%	1	77	35.5	85	7	8
USA..............	220	1200		139	350		38.5	61.5	—

Population = millions
GNP = billions
Social expenditures = family benefits
Health expenditures = billions
MDs = thousands
Nurses = per 10,000 population

* Data obtained from   Ruth L. Sivard, "World Military and Social Expenditures," 1977, Leesburg, Va. Robert Maxwell, "Health Care: The Growing Dilemma," (2nd ed.) McKinsey & Co., N.Y., 1975

Table 10-4   Social Policy, Preventive Services and Infant Mortality*

Country	Infant Mortality	Percent Immunized	Degree Social Policy	Separate Prevent Service	Midwifery	Hospital Delivery	Strong Nursing Input	Public Agency Child
Sweden	1	1	1	1	2	1	1	1
Holland	2	1	1	1	1	3	1	3
Finland	3	1	1	1	1	1	1	2
Denmark	4	1	1	3	2	1	3	2
France	5	2	2	2	3	2	2	2
Belgium	6	2	3	2	2	2	2	2
Scotland	7	3	4	3	3	1	3	3

* Except for the ranking in infant mortality, the numbers "1, 2, 3" are used arbitrarily to indicate the standing of the countries noted in their reaction to the titled column. Under "percent immunized," for example, all the "1's" are better than 98% but "2" is not much below that. In "hospital deliveries," Netherlands has 50%, Finland 100%. Holland has almost all children registered in private dues paying preventive nursing services, ("Cross" organizations) agencies for historic reasons to accommodate to religious denominational requirements; but in the large cities, the government agency operates and controls the private agency. Under "separate preventive service," to a greater or lesser degree, each country permits (and some encourage) use of the private practitioner ("family doctor") instead of, or along with the official clinic. However, in Belgium, the clinic service is free and the client must pay the doctor.

REFERENCES

1. M. Wagner, *Sweden's Health Screening Program for Four Year Old Children* (Washington, D.C.: Government Printing Office, 1975), HEW pub. no. (ADM) 76-282.

2. Regional Office, World Health Organization, *Health Services in Europe* (Copenhagen: WHO, 1975).

3. Margaret Wynn and Arthur Wynn, *The Protection of Maternity and Infancy: The Study of the Services for Pregnant Women and Young Children in Finland* (London: Council for Children's Welfare, Spring 1974), p. 14.

4. Ibid., p. 17.

5. Ibid., p. 18.

6. Ibid., p. 17.

7. Ibid., p. 19.

8. Association for University Programs in Health Administration, "Health and Health Services in Finland," mimeographed, (Washington, D.C.: AUPHA, 1975), p. 20.

9. *Ibid.*, p. 23.

10. Ibid., p. 60.

11. Wynn and Wynn, *Maternity and Infancy*, p. 20.

12. AUPHA, "Health and Health Services in Finland."

13. Wynn and Wynn, *Maternity and Infancy*, p. 7.

14. AUPHA, "Health and Health Services in Finland."

15. Wynn and Wynn, *Maternity and Infancy*, pp. 25-26.

16. R. L. Sivard, *World Military and Social Expenditures 1977* (Leesburg, Virginia: WMSE Publications, 1977)

17. Wynn and Wynn, *Maternity and Infancy.*

18. J. Lindgren, "Family Policy in Finland" (Paper presented at the Arden House Conference of the International Working Party on Family Policy, Arden House, Harriman, N.Y., April 17-21, 1977, under the auspices of the Columbia University School of Social Work), mimeographed.

19. Barry Pless, Book Review of Wynn and Wynn, *Maternity and Infancy*, in *Developmental Medicine and Child Neurology* 17 (1975): 121-123.

20. Wynn and Wynn, *Maternity and Infancy*, p. 1. They also point out that the deprived minorities in Finland who do not receive regular attention comparable to that of the majority are a much smaller fraction of the minority group population than is true in Britain (p. 32). They make the point that while it is often said that immigrants are responsible for Britain's relatively poor showing in infant mortality, immigrant population perinatal mortality increases the perinatal mortality for that country by only 0.5 percent (p. 7).

21. Conversation with Dr. Leo Kaprio, director of the European Regional Office of WHO.

22. R. Boulin, *Pour Une Politique de la Santé*, Report for the Ministry of Health (Paris: La Documentation Française, 1971).

23. Margaret Wynn and Arthur Wynn, *Prevention of Handicap of Perinatal Origin. An Introduction to French Policy and Legislation* (London: Foundation for Education and Research in Childbearing, 1976), p. 9.

24. R. Mande, N. Masse, and M. Manciaux, *Pédiatrie Sociale* (Paris: Flammarion, 1976), Chap. 2, p. 13.

25. M. David and I. Lézine, *Early Child Care in France* (London: Gordon & Breach, 1975), p. 57. Also printed in the journal, *Early Child Development and Care*, vol 4, no 1 (1974).

26. N. Questiaux and J. Fournier, "Family Policy in France" (Paper presented at the Arden House Conference International Working Party on Family Policy, Arden House, Harriman, N.Y., April 17-21, 1977, under the auspices of the Columbia University School of Social Work), See also, S. B. Kamerman, *Child Care Programs in Nine Countries* (Washington, D. C.: Government Printing Office, 1976), Department of Health, Education and Welfare pub. no. (OCD) 30080.

27. David and Lézine, *Child Care in France*, p. 62.

28. See the Centre International de l'Enfance publication, "International colloquium on children of migrant workers in Europe" (1974) for a fuller discussion of the fate of migrant children. In 1973, over 6 percent of the population of France was composed of "guest" workers—migrants—about 1.7 million workers and 850,000 children under 16 years of age. Over 10 percent of all births in France were in migrant families. Studies showed a 20 percent higher infant mortality rate among these families than among the rest of the French population. Hazemann and Rossignol, "Aspects Socio-medicaux et Éducatifs de la Périnatalité Chez les Migrants," mimeographed and issued by the Service de la PMI in Paris in February 1975 make a number of telling points in this connection. They point out that migrants, with their special problems, require special preventive, educational, and social actions to compensate and need special family planning programs and activities to reduce prematurity and to look after children at risk. Since language and cultural barriers represent the greatest problem, special interpreters are provided at their centers, and special teams made up of midwife, puéricultrice and an assistant social are assigned to migrant groups.

29. M. Manciaux, *Abrégé de Pédiatrie Préventive et Sociale* (Paris: Flammarion, 1971).

30. The education of the special child nurses (puéricultrices) results in a state diploma. The candidates have to be nurses, midwives or social workers (assistant socials). They are trained on the pediatric service of hospitals as well as on the maternity service during the year's work. See the section on personnel by L. Lefèvre-Paul in Mande, Masse, and Manciaux, *Pédiatrie Sociale*, p. 612.

31. Pierre Pene, in *National Health Services*, ed. John Z. Bowers and Elizabeth Purcell (New York: Josiah Macy, Jr. Foundation, 1973) pp. 9-13; and the section on France in World Health Organization, *Health Services in Europe* (Copenhagen: WHO, 1975).

32. F. Cannone and B. Pissarro, in Mande, Masse, and Manciaux, *Pédiatrie Sociale*, p. 653.

33. Ibid., p. 653.

34. *Le Monde: Dossiers et Documents*, no. 36, December 1976. Translated by the author.

35. Wynn and Wynn, *Prevention of Handicap*.

36. Margaret Wynn and Arthur Wynn, "The Right of Every Child to Health Care," in *Occasional Papers on Child Welfare No. 2* (London: Council for Children's Welfare, 1974)

37. Mande, Masse, Manciaux, *Pédiatrie Sociale*, Chap. 29.

38. Personal Communication from Dr. Rossignol.

39. Personal interview with Professor Bernard Pissarro.

40. J. J. Hazemann, "Résultats des 20,000 Premiers Bilans de Santé de l'Enfant," mimeographed (Paris: Chaisse Primaire Centrale d'Assurance Maladie de La Region Parisienne, 1975).

41. Margaret Wynn and Arthur Wynn, "Pediatric Community Nursing" (Address presented at Moor Park College April 26-29, 1976), mimeographed.

42. Centre d'Études et de Récherches Marxistes, *La Petite Enfance* (Paris: CERM, 1976), Colloque du CERM, 13 decembre, 1975.

43. Shari Steiner, *The Female Factor* (New York: Putnam, 1977), p. 138.

44. Wynn and Wynn, "Pediatric Community Nursing."

45. European Region, World Health Organization, *Health Services in Europe* (Copenhagen: WHO, 1975).

46. European Institute for Social Security, *Evolution and Financing of the Cost of Medical Care* (Leuven: Aurelia Press, 1972).

47. Ruth Roemer and Milton Roemer, "Health Manpower Policies in the Belgian Health Care System," mimeographed. (Los Angeles: School of Public Health, University of California at Los Angeles, 1976).

48. European Region, WHO, *Health Services in Europe.*

49. Roemer and Roemer, "Health Manpower Policies."

50. Oeuvre Nationale de l'Enfance, "Oeuvre Nationale de l'Enfance" (Brussels: ONE, undated); also, 1972 statistical Report of ONE, dated 1974.

51. Roemer and Roemer, "Health Manpower Policies."

52. Ibid.; and European Region, WHO, *Health Services in Europe.*

53. Personal communication from Mme. Peerts-Niçoise, ONE official.

54. D. Gannik, E. Holst, and M. Wagner, *The National Health System in Denmark: A Descriptive Analysis* (Washington, D.C.: Government Printing Office, 1977), Department of Health, Education and Welfare pub. no. (NIH) 77-673.

55. Personal communication from school physician Dr. Marie-Louise Jensen and from Dr. Marsden Wagner at the Institute of Social Medicine.

56. Marsden Wagner and Mary Wagner, *The Danish National Child Care System* (Boulder: Westview Press, 1977), pp. 7 et seq. See also, Mary Wagner and Marsden Wagner, "Child Advocacy in Denmark: Seventy Years Experience with This New Idea," mimeographed, undated.

57. Ibid.

58. Personal communication, Nanna Jensen.

59. J. Vedel-Peterson and H. Friis, "Family Policy in Denmark" (Paper presented at the Arden House Conference, International Working Party on Family Policy, April 17-21, 1977, under the auspices of the Columbia University School of Social Work), mimeographed.

60. European Region, WHO, *Health Services in Europe.*

61. P. O. Petersson, "Child Health Services in Sweden," *Current Sweden,* no. 124 (June 1976).

62. Rita Liljestrom, "Strands of Swedish Public Policy Towards Families" (Paper presented at the Arden House Conference on the International Working Party on Family Policy, April 17-21, 1977, under the auspices of the Columbia University School of Social Work), mimeographed.

63. S. Kamerman, *Child Care Programs in Nine Countries* (Washington, D.C.: Government Printing Office, 1976), Department of Health, Education and Welfare pub. no. (OCD) 30080.

64. Ralph Husby and Eve Wetzel, "Public Assistance in Sweden and the United States," *Social Policy*, March-April 1977, pp. 29-31.

65. R. Berfenstam and I. William-Olson, *Early Child Care in Sweden* (London: Gordon & Breach, 1973).

66. Petersson, "Child Health Services in Sweden."

67. K. K. Lüscher, V. Ritter, and P. Gross, *Early Child Care in Switzerland* (London: Gordon & Breach, 1975), p. 17.

68. Personal communication from Professor J-C Vuille, Department of Pediatrics, University of Berne.

69. The entire issue of *Pro Juventute*, monthly publication of the Foundation, called "Stiftung Pro Juventute," July/August 1970 issue is devoted to this subject. Published in Zurich. (WSC is an acronym for a pediatric nurse.)

70. R. Maxwell, *Health Care: The Growing Dilemma*, 2nd ed. (New York: McKinsey and Co., 1975).

71. R. L. Sivard, *World Military and Social Expenditures 1977* (Virginia: WMSE Publications, 1977).

72. Ministry of Labor and Social Affairs, *Survey of Social Security in the Federal Republic of Germany* (Bonn: Ministry of Labor and Social Affairs, 1972).

73. European Region, WHO, *Health Services in Europe;* see also Maxwell, Health Care.

74. National Council on Welfare, *Poor Kids* (Ottawa: National Council on Welfare, March 1975).

75. New Zealand Institute of Public Administration, "Health Administration in New Zealand," mimeographed (Wellington: New Zealand Institute of Public Administration, 1969).

76. Communication from Professor Jane C. Kronick, Bryn Mawr College, School of Social Work.

77. Sivard, *World Military and Social Expenditures 1977*.

78. Bernard Weinraub, "In Denmark, Child Custody Case Stirs a Major Dispute," *New York Times*, 16 March 1976.

79. Special correspondent, "A British View of Danish Medicine," *British Medical Journal*, 18 October, 1975, pp. 154-156.

80. Margaret Wynn and Arthur Wynn, "Pediatric Community Nursing."

81. Ibid.

82. Personal communication from the Wynns.

83. L. Kohler, "Health of Preschool Children in Sweden," *Courrier* 24 (May-June 1974): 239-243.

84. Ibid.

85. M. Wagner, *Sweden's Health Screening Program for Four Year Old Children* (Washington, D.C.: Department of Health, Education and Welfare pub. no. (ADM) 76-282).

Part IV

An American Program of Child Health

Chapter 11

An American Program of Child Health

It should be clear from the presentations in the preceding chapters that I did not begin the writing of this book without some very definite ideas in mind on the shape and direction of an American child health program. The broad outlines of that program were presented in Part I. In this section I shall try to amplify those elements of the proposal merely enumerated before and defend the suggestions where they seem radical or unrealistic by calling upon historic precedent and analogy in defense of the proposals. The design of a "perfect" system, of anything, is not very difficult. What is difficult is to make it work, in the face of implementation by quite imperfect people. This is certainly true of a proposal for a child health service. So much of traditional values, attitudes toward children, social philosophy regarding family authority and government intervention, and opinions of what the "product" should be, not to mention professional issues of organization, specialism, and standards of child care, enter into a child health service, that an ideal model is out of the question. One might almost come to the conclusion that any suggestions for change of one national system, derived from the experiences of another, may be unrealistic, even impossible to put into effect.

It is for these reasons that in putting forth proposals for change, a cautious and defensive posture (paragraphs surrounded by references and citations to the past and present) is essential. Nevertheless, the problem of child health in the United States is so pressing, the evidence of the bankruptcy of the existing programs so evident, the necessity for a national social policy so clear, that I feel

229

that many of the facile objections and rejections of the past can be challenged with boldly different proposals for child health protection and promotion.

America may have paid relatively little attention to the matter of child health in the past, secure in the belief that this wealthy, child-centered culture was doing everything necessary and possible to protect and advance the health of its children. True, occasional messages were received—confused signals for the most part—that there were *some* children, the "disadvantaged," so defined because they were poor or belonged to minority groups, who were not so fortunate. But this, too, tended to be dismissed as exaggerated or inadequately statistically verifiable. This is no longer true. We now know, beyond doubt, that a large number of American children, and not just the disadvantaged, are brought into the world with handicaps that are not discovered early enough, then not dealt with appropriately. We also know that a large number of American children are neglected by the preventive services and go unexamined, unimmunized, and untreated. A large number of American families fail to receive the attention and education that would help them bring into the world, and raise, healthy and wholesome children.

The American child health care system, such as it is, is not working for many, too many, millions of American children. Today's children are tomorrow's adults. Handicapped children will mean handicapped adults. Our future is, in some measure, in jeopardy. Not only concern for our children—natural and moral concern, love and affection—but national need, the national health, is at issue as well. Reports flowing out of concerned bodies recognize the danger, the somber facts and the somber future.[1]

In Part II, the effort to isolate and identify a possible critical factor in the failure of the existing American child health system was described. Lack of funds was apparently not a crucial element, although there probably is not enough money available to do everything that might be required. But the failure exceeds this factor by a wide margin. Billions of dollars *are* being spent by the federal government, more by individuals and families themselves. These huge sums, however, are being diverted, because the channels of the system into which they are fed are not directed toward achieving the goal: child health services. The diversion is not the result of evil or corrupt misuse of funds. On the contrary, upstanding and well-intentioned principles are the cause of the diversion. The failure is then compounded by lack of sufficient information on the failure, so that those who are responsible for deciding on what is to be done and how much should be spent to do it, are veiled from knowledge of what is wrong and, certainly, why.

To some extent, one may blame the legislators and parents for not having asked specific questions, been more concerned, dissatisfied, and questioning. But on the whole, while one might argue that there is a suspicious lack of concern in this long period of treadmill operation of a failed system, the blame lies elsewhere. Legislators and parents have been assured that what can be done is being done and that more extensive effort requires more extensive investment. So, in an economy with so many demands on resources, especially in recent years, the social decision was to wait, investing more ever so slowly. In fact, the public was apparently justified in this cautious approach to more lavish investment, since more of the same, given the skewed direction of the effort in any case, could hardly be expected to have had the desired effect, even at a much higher price.

The difficulties uncovered (to which attention must be paid, if a truly effective child health program is to be developed) are of two kinds. On the one hand, there is the philosophical basis upon which child health expenditures are now being made out of the public treasury. We build health departments, structures which will supposedly provide the functions desired. Yet the nature of the building is such that the structure can never be finished and thus can never really start to fulfill its functions. Something on the order of an analog to the Malthusian Law appears to be at work here. Funds increase arithmetically, and staff specialty levels and, consequently, expenditures, increase geometrically! The second difficulty is more complex and might be covered by a blanket of "social" benefits. Much of child health promotion depends on adequate instruction, housing, and family stability that require kinds of social action other than purely health activities: income maintenance and/or family and child allowances; large-scale housing and/or rent subsidies; and effective home visiting for education, psychological guidance, and for uncovering and preventing child neglect and abuse.

Some of the subsidiary difficulties, such as legislative inaction at the state level, or lack of oversight by federal or state agencies, contribute to the deficiencies. Better controls would improve even present operations. But the overriding etiological factors that make these evident difficulties intractable derive from American social and professional philosophy. On the social side is the unsettled issue of "universal" versus "targeted" social activities. For the most part, the American people, and their lawmakers, insist on offering help, where necessary, only to those presumably unable to help themselves. The laws aim at the "poor," the "handicapped," "poor areas," "areas in which there is a high proportion of disadvantaged people (or children)." Further, the law will aim specifically at forbidding noneligibles to participate. The inclusion of the poor excludes the nonpoor. A means test is intended not only to bring in those needing help, but to keep others out. In theory, this is to foster independence and discourage sloth and, on the other hand, to reduce the taxes the unneedy must pay. Strict rules and regulations are formulated to this end. Some children whose parents are well enough off (by the eligibility standards) are deprived because their parents are neglectful or forgetful, or in such precarious economic, physical, or psychological state, as not to be able to provide immunizations or school lunches. The children are unhappy, unhealthy perhaps, eventually damaged in some way. Other children, clearly eligible by virtue of their parents' status, feel stigmatized by being singled out, called from the classroom or given a special card, for immunization or school lunch. They do or do not accept, because of the stigma. In any case, they too may be unhappy, unhealthy, eventually damaged.

Could we not and should we not devise a system that includes all children, selecting out none of them, marking none of them, stigmatizing none of them? Isn't there a way of offering the same to all children, using taxes, dues, and home visits by social agencies to collect money from those who can pay (by whatever financial level is established) so as not to burden children with social norms not of their making and possibly damaging to them? Universal rather than targeted health services for children would be a tremendous step forward in accomplishing the social objective of improving the health of *all* America's children. Targeting may seem more efficient to economists, but it doesn't work, socially or professionally or even economically. Steiner writes, "The obvious lesson is that providing health services to poor children is too complex, too expensive, and too consequential a matter to be legislated without a plan. Neither the federal carrot nor the federal stick accomplishes the federal objective. ...the fraction of the $1 billion per month Medicaid program targeted to children will command relatively little attention."[2]

The basic requirements of all children for an easily accessible, comprehensive program of preventive and therapeutic services is so clear that logic and reason dictate the wisdom of a universal *health* service for children. Furthermore, even conservative economic sense would prefer such a solution. On the basis of experience with the kind of costs involved in tailoring a series of compensatory programs and staffing them, a universally applicable system would inevitably be cheaper to provide and operate. Targeted programs, in addition to perpetuating a two-class system of care, also perpetuate the profusion of parallel, competing programs with the continuation of duplicating overhead and organizational rivalries.

We need to test whether America's fierce devotion to independence and family responsibility, expressed in opposition to universal health services for children, will stand up under public debate of the issue. I think not. I believe most parents would prefer a universal system, provided payments reflect family income. Medicare, bitterly contested on grounds that it was public service to those able to pay, did pass the Congress and seems to be thriving, albeit suffering common inflationary stresses.

Another philosophic issue that separates us from an appropriate perspective on child health derives from professional dogma. This, even more than the social philosophy wedded to targeting may be the major obstacle to reform of the child health system in America. Medicine in the United States cleaves to a philosophy of unity of preventive and curative services and unity of the provision of these through the physician. It hardly matters that physicians, despite herculean public and academic measures, have failed to exhibit any interest in or concern for, preventive medicine. No one dares challenge the dogma or announce the nakedness of the king. Professional role designations follow this obstructive concept. Effective performance of child health activity depends heavily on interested persons and on a preventive emphasis.

In short, major defects that have hampered delivery of child health services, defects such as concentration on roads to child health rather than on services themselves, and lack of adequate information have been fixed by the inability of society and the medical profession to transcend dogmas obstructing improvement—targeting and the preeminent role of the doctor. A modern child health program has to deal with the defects in performance and the inadequacies in philosophical approach, correcting both.

THE ELEMENTS OF A PROGRAM

In Part III, a number of European systems of child health care were examined and their details compared, for an explanation of their success or failure in achieving worthwhile child health goals, in comparison with American results. It turned out that no two systems were exactly comparable, but discrete elements were, and the results were evident.

Taking a long look at the variety of programs observed, one can only guess at the extent to which attitudes toward children were decisive in the program inclusiveness or effectiveness. No attempt was made to assess parental attitudes in the review, but that hardly seems important since it was evident that other matters were clearly closely related to success or failure. It was the *pattern* that was important, not individual elements, and it is the pattern that can help us on the way to an American program. If that is so, then it is necessary only to describe the pattern (or modifications) and a political strategy for achieving it.

If, on the other hand, the problem were attitudes, the case would be hopeless. Changing social attitudes is a monumental task requiring literally generations of effort. One has only to reflect on the difficulty with which revolutionary political action has been able to achieve the "new" citizen, in order to recognize the formidable task implied by such a notion.

Let us take for granted then, that Americans *do* cherish their children and are concerned for their health (witness the large scale investment of federal funds) but are unwilling to invest more because of their justifiable suspicion that more money is not the answer. However, they do want an answer. The successful European child health programs do *not* require greater investment of funds (they are cheaper on the whole) but *do* require a different form of organization, sponsorship, and operation. Further, much of the form of that different structure is well within American traditions, is congruent with the cultural value system, and is relatively easily put in place.

Europeans focus on the *child* and his or her needs. They provide family support (money) to ensure adequate feeding, clothing, and housing for the children. They provide supervised care through trained nurses who work in clinics, visit homes, and offer help, advice, and access to other social agency and legal assistance programs. They emphasize prevention and provide screening examinations and assessment, immunizations, treatment for handicapping conditions, and psychiatric guidance in clinics and in schools. This focus on the child includes prenatal care (with emphasis on the midwife and nonphysician supervision of pregnancy), family planning services, and postpartum supervision.

It may be worthwhile just to list the elements that make up this pattern under discussion and go on to see what America can do about it.

1. An umbrella of social protection for children, which includes,

   a. money, or the equivalent, to offset the added costs of child rearing and allow for decent housing, nutrition, and clothing

   b. special housing subsidy and nutritional programs for children, especially free school lunch

   c. special treatment for the pregnant woman—maternity leave if she works, home helps before and after childbirth

2. Health (preventive) services, including,

   a. prenatal care

   b. infancy and preschool supervision

   c. school health services

3. Comprehensive, prepaid medical care services for all children

4. Organizational innovations, including,

   a separate child health services in 2 above

   b. emphasis on nurses with pediatric training and on midwives

   c. local organizational control

   d. private sector involvement in public sector activities

5. Financing preventive services separately through family and local community contributions along with state and federal funds

6. Social and legal protection for the child against abuse and neglect by parents, schools, and society in general

7. A vigorous children's advocacy program, including 4 and 6 above—a separate, national program, publically funded

Come now, the puzzled reader may be muttering, whatever makes you think Americans—parents, public, or professionals—are going to do all that? Furthermore, where did you get the idea that these were appropriate actions based on fundamentally American attitudes?

It may be true that the social support measures described above are beyond consideration today. Yet, much of the discussion over the last ten years about "welfare reform" is in this territory, including as it does references to income maintenance plans, support for the working poor, and initiatives to modify the support of children in one-parent families. It may not be too much to hope that within the next decade a resolution of the critical antagonisms will allow for a new and vigorous social policy that is pro-family in this sense. At the moment, it is quite true that there is no point in trying to make social support in the European sense an issue or, at any rate, a mandatory basic issue, when discussing and designing an American program of child health. Housing subsidies are pitifully scant, but they exist and can be increased. Maternity leave is now a debated legal issue and a union bargaining effort, and it may very well come to be national social policy. So two of the three elements of the umbrella of social protection are not difficult-to-transplant "foreign" inventions, and the third is becoming "Americanized!"

However, notwithstanding the difficulties in obtaining a suitable range of social protective measures to institute an effective program of child health, there is every reason to believe that the institution of the other measures suggested may be important and valuable in improving child health services, and child health, in the United States. As a matter of fact, if a workable system of child health services is introduced, and it narrows the differences in access between rich and poor, black, brown, red and white, urban and rural, the social protection measures needed may rise to the surface as key issues for discussion and legislation. So it is not futile to attack the inadequate and ineffective existing child health system, at the same time endorsing a different and more effective one. Lack of the umbrella will hamper the maximum effectiveness of a child health program, but not preclude it. And improving the health system may promote the needed umbrella services.

This is said in reply to the expected criticism of the social reformers who place a low value on the health measures and a high value on the social ones as major contributors to child health.[3] Too many critics of the medical care system in the United States, disheartened by years of gradualism in which the fruits of struggle are bitter and possibly even less than what was aimed for, forget that the bitter fruits are not of gradualism itself, but of the nature of the compromises made. This is true of young radicals as well, who see no future in accommodation, considering the past record. Postponing social protection while enhancing other health measures cannot but be beneficial, particularly if the feedback from the improved health measures will hasten the arrival of the social benefits as well.

THE PREVENTIVE SERVICES

It would be difficult to discuss the preventive services that need to be made available without simultaneously discussing the organizational modifications and innovations that will be required. So it may be just as well to adjust the discussion in such a fashion as to alternate between requirements and process rather than marshal the arguments serially as in the outline above.

Prenatal Care

There are important social and personal consequences of infant mortality rates that may not ordinarily come to mind, but which must be considered over and above the sad and tragic fact of the infant deaths themselves. Failure to attend to even moderately high infant mortality rates is to invite totally unnecessary and avoidable personal tragedies and, consequently, families' and society's lifetime obligations to physically and mentally crippled children. As Margaret and Arthur Wynn, ardent proponents of active social policies on behalf of children, have written:

> Perinatal mortality gives a broad indication of the health of women of reproductive age and of the strength of antenatal and obstetric services in any community. Perinatal mortality rates are closely correlated with the extent of damage among infants who survive. One official governmental estimate assumes that two children survive so severely and permanently handicapped as to become a charge to the state for every one that dies, so that reducing the causes of death does on the average reduce the numbers of the handicapped in the same proportion. Mortality rates are indicators not only of infant loss but of infant damage.[4]

So the authors persuasively argue the value of careful prenatal care in helping to offset circumstances that might result in premature birth, the preeminent cause of both infant mortality and handicapping conditions in the newborn.[5]

This prenatal care requires 1) early registration, 2) careful identification of high-risk mothers and/or infants for special continuing attention, 3) home visitation to identify environmental or social factors that might make the childbirth unhealthy for mother or child, or both, 4) education in maternal and child care, and 5) supervision of the health of the pregnant woman to ensure early diagnosis and treatment of infections and other conditions that might weaken the mother and render her incapable of carrying the child to term.

Childbirth and After

Since pregnancy is a normal (as opposed to a medical) condition, a woman should have the privilege of bringing her child into the world with appropriate technical assistance (not necessarily a physician); without an overload of drugs to induce birth or heavy anesthesia or surgical procedures in childbirth, unless clearly indicated; and in a location of her choice (not necessarily a hospital), provided that location offers a clean, safe environment for childbirth. In the postpartum period, however soon a woman is sent home with her child—and it should not be too many days after childbirth—a trained home helper should be available to assist in household duties and simple child care procedures. Nursing visits for observation and education should follow promptly.

Under certain circumstances, of course, hospitalization, obstetrical care, induction, operation, anesthesia and the full panoply of modern medical technological procedures are appropriate and necessary. High-risk women—the very young and the very old, the woman who suffers associated physical or mental illness—all should be carefully labelled and handled as *medical* cases. They have special needs, and modern medicine can help bring about a happy conclusion to their pregnancies. Ninety to ninety-five percent of all pregnancies are, however, normal and do not involve risk.

Infancy Care

Monthly visits to a clinic, office, or infant care center should be made. Child nursing visits to the home after the first postpartum visit should be based on perceived need and will primarily involve psychological and nutritional advice. Sick children will be screened by telephone or by visits and referred to the pediatrician for medical care. Nurses need not visit healthy babies when mothers already have one or more children or where there is no extensive environmental or social problem, suspected congenital defect, or handicapping condition. Family planning information, if not provided in the childbirth period, can be handled in the clinic or at home, immunizations likewise. Every child should receive protection against diphtheria, tetanus, whooping cough, polio, and measles during this period. Physicians (pediatricians, preferably) should see the healthy infant at least twice in the year.

Suspected handicaps found in the child nurses' or pediatricians' screenings should be evaluated in regional assessment centers associated with hospitals with sufficient sophisticated personnel and equipment. The handicaps found should then be dealt with appropriately and promptly. Regional units for special care or follow-up of permanently damaged children will be needed.

Preschool Preventive Services

Not unlike infancy care, preschool preventive services could possibly be arranged in the same facilities. Children between one and five will be seen routinely three or four times a year the first two years and twice a year thereafter. Again, home visits should be made only for cause or if there is suspicion of mistreatment—not necessarily abuse or neglect, but, for example, failure to deal with nutrition or growth problems. Pediatricians should see the child no more than once a year, unless the child is sick. Immunization boosters will be given, as will a rescreening (after the first year) at two and four.

It should be clear by now that a system such as this requires attention to all children and that the organizational focus is the nurse. What kind of organization do we have in mind? How will we accomplish the full-scale rounding up, early prenatal registration, scheduled visiting, examinations, assessments, and so forth?

In Europe, the social payment measures offer the opportunity for reward and punishment to assure early prenatal registration. Don't register before the third month in France and you lose a sizeable allowance. Late birth registration generates a fine in Denmark. In the United States we will have to depend on a neighborhood network, nurse visiting, cajolery, and peer group pressure. Success will depend on the degree to which the system managers believe in it and the advocates pursue it.[6]

ORGANIZATION

Having described what is expected to be done, it is time for me to attend to the framework within which this could be accomplished. If we assume that every pregnant woman and every child will be eligible, 3.5 million or so women, the same number of infants, and a total of 14 million preschoolers will need care and follow-up. It goes without saying that some percentage of these will not appear for "system" care. Some simply will not appear anywhere, and others will prefer private care, whether or not this system involves payment on their part or not. In the best of circumstances, 95 percent will be looked after in the system; in the worst case, only the poor and near-poor, about 35 percent, will take advantage of the system.

A decentralized, locally organized and controlled mechanism will be proposed and, for personnel management reasons, would serve a minimum of 200 births a year and be responsible for up to 1,000 children. This would permit the employment of two midwives, one public health nurse, and four home helpers. This nucleus would be one child health center. For five such centers, a pediatric consultant and an obstetric consultant would be needed. In the early years, before midwives do most of the deliveries, only one midwife would be needed and perhaps even fewer obstetrical consultants. Before becoming established, the child health nurse might do well to have a nurse's aide—one specialized in child care, not the usual hospital nurse's aide—who could become a permanent fixture of the team.

Since in the United States today the birth rate is 15 per 1,000, 200 births a year would involve a population of roughly 15,000 people. A group this size would ordinarily come under the jurisdiction of a local health department, or at least a district of a municipal health department. However, to ensure community participation, it would be desirable for local community groups to organize themselves and request the health department to supply the services, for which the self-organized and administered group would pay a nominal sum. Where this does not happen, the local health unit will be expected to organize a management board to supervise and accept accountability for its services. The experiences of OEO should be invaluable in motivating community groups to create health services.[7]

Nor is this the only way in which collective action can be mobilized to organize child health services and child health units. A variety of groups with common interest, ethnic groups and trade union organizations already in existence; or ad hoc cooperatives, like the ones organized by the Rural Electrification Administration during the New Deal years; neighborhood and community groups, school boards, adult organizations aiming at helping children like the Boys' Clubs and Boy Scouts; religious organizations and other types of institutions could set themselves up as preventive service child health centers. Some paper work might be required to authenticate the group, establish its credibility and capability of performing the duties required, and assure the government agency that would be supplying the federal funding that the center would abide by the standards and agree to employ only trained and federally certificated child health nurses, midwives and other professional people. This approach, of independently sprung child health center organizations, is the master key to this kind of operation. It counters the bureaucratic lethargy and stubbornness, even hostility, that characterizes so many public welfare activities. The helplessness of bureaucracy is the centerpiece of Schultze's masterful analysis in "The Public Use of Private Interest," and as Maclaury says in the introduction to that book, "Government often seems to fail when it tackles a critical issue."[8]

More to the point is the intense modern interest in converting public activities into private or at least privately and cooperatively managed activity. Schultze believes that "social intervention" should work both ways, not only with government intervening to rectify antisocial action in the private sector, but with the private sector also intervening to protect the public against heedless bureaucracy in the public sector. Schultze sees "market analogues," efforts by government to introduce market-like programs to create competition, to keep bureaucracy on its toes, so to speak. He suggests letting the best government-designed system win, as the game is played out with various government-supported programs competing for popular support.[9]

The argument of Berger and Neuhaus in *To Empower People* is even stronger. They attack the "megastructures, the modern state, large economic conglomerates, big labor, bureaucracies like education and the organized professions."[10] They are "hard" and the private areas of people's lives are "soft." Between them is needed the "mediating structures," *"those institutions standing between the individual in his private life and the large institutions of public life."* And, they add, "Mediating structures are essential for a vital democratic society." So, *"Public policy should protect and foster mediating structures."* Most strongly they emphasize, *"Whenever possible, public policy should use mediating structures for the realization of social purposes."*[11] These "mediating structures" are the ones that should become the vehicles for child health center formation— "neighborhood, family, church and voluntary association." (all emphasis, the author's.)[12]

Richard Cooper, a distinguished economist, in reviewing another economist's book, notes "neither private enterprise nor public provision is likely to offer the best solution" to the problem of day care centers, a very similar issue.[13]

In theory, those who want to will form their own organization or join similar small ones, if they themselves are too small to establish a private health center of their own type and choice. Those who don't want to will have the public agency to provide the service.   In actuality, some dangers exist and damage may be done. Ethnic and racial groups should not be permitted to *exclude* others, even though their organizations are established to serve the special needs of the special groups. Also, in the case of professional workers, trade union membership must be protected. It may turn out that subcontracting of services might be used to disestablish unions and avoid accountability.[14]

National certification and transferability and portability of those credentials, along with national performance standards and supervision in the form of reporting, inspection, and accountability may serve to minimize the risks. National legislation plus state conforming legislation will be needed, as will national standards and a national body to ride herd on the performance. Nonetheless, national operation and control cannot do the trick. We have the example in European countries with centralized controls, where a local modification is impossible because anything done for one must be done for all. Local flexibility must be encouraged. Local control is essential to avoid the least common denominator approach of national decision making.

One other word needs to be said on the national organizational role. I was impressed with the separation of powers in Holland, with the director-general of health services planning, organizing, and supervising the health programs while an inspector-general of health services with decentralized administration of inspectors evaluated the programs and staff efforts. It would be useful to look to an inspector-general's office as a responsible force in keeping the states and independent child health centers efficiently operating at top standards.

THE STAFF

We must return now to the consideration of *who* will carry out these obligations and under what conditions. To be blunt, physicians should be relieved of their responsibilities for preventive services for children and those services turned over to preventive-service-minded people. This implies, as well, an independently run, independently funded service under the control of these preventive-service-minded people, with consultation and support from physicians, principally pediatricians and obstetricians, and perhaps a public health or managerial-type physician here and there for good measure.

There can be little doubt that doctors could not care less about prevention. Well people are boring; only complex and difficult cases are interesting. People don't like to pay high fees for simple services when they are quite healthy, or seem to themselves to be; very sick people do pay high fees. Even the doctors admit this, recognizing the unequal struggle between the desire to use highly trained skills and exciting procedures to save lives, on the one hand, and attending to pedestrian "housekeeping" measures on the other.

A distinguished physician and editor, Franz Ingelfinger, writes, "The curious idea is abroad that the doctor should be the factotum of health ... The doctor ... is supposed to provide treatment to families, not individuals, and 'treatment' is envisioned as an umbrella encompassing sexual problems, job dissatisfaction, scholastic ineptitude and personal incompatibilities. The doctor, moreover, is supposed to undertake preventive measures, not only to immunize and to avert such traditional concerns as excessive smoking and overeating, but also to keep Johnny from driving too fast while drunk, to make sure that Susie uses contraceptives, and that Daddy restrains his paternalistic tendencies.

... the doctor's basic responsibility is cure. Yes, CURE.

If the role of the doctor were clearly defined in this fashion, the services that he could offer would not arouse false expectations."[15] Another doctor writes, "the physician's unique contribution lies in the care of the sick," and he insists that in an important sense it cuts the doctor off from other roles.[16]

In a study of differences between American and British general practitioners, one thing was clear: there were differences in practice, use of laboratory services, and prescribing, but not in their avoidance of well-child and preventive services and their lack of association with social service agencies for nonmedical help for patients.[17]

Where economic interest is not attacked, the necessity for physician intervention can be minimized. A recent Swedish survey, revealed that nurses' examination results were as good as those of the general practitioners;[18] a British review of school health activities is much the same. "Much of the routine screening work could be carried out as effectively and more economically by school nurses," and if doctors are going to be used, "the school doctors . . . should be trained to such a level that they are regarded as Specialists in Educational Medicine," not for purely preventive service.[19]

On the other hand, there is a host of trained people with an interest in children and a concern for and professional stake in just these preventive services. Public health nurses, pediatric associates, pediatric nurse practitioners, pediatric nurse assistants, and others skilled in some or all of the areas of public health, pediatrics, and child care, are available. An evaluation group reports, ". . . NHPs (non-health practitioners) are more attuned to recognizing information from physicians than the other way around." The NHP is more related to nondrug therapy and follow-up, the doctor less so. "When a physician saw a patient following a previous visit to a nurse practitioner, there was a significant drop off in the follow-up rate of problems and therapies."[20] The quality and capability of these professional people is good, as attested to in evaluations by physicians and teachers in various parts of the country,[21] and we should make better use of this resource.

For the country as a whole, given the 15,000 center population base, about 20,000 child health nurses would be needed to carry out these responsibilities. Curriculum, national certification, negotiated salaries—all would require extensive arrangement. But this is not an unusually high number and is not beyond the capability of the educational system or the other U. S. health services.

FINANCING

Hard numbers, in a book written in one time, published in another, and read in a third, can be misleading and frustrating. Inflation eats away at us monthly, and as each year goes by, the cost of equipment and staff salaries will be different. A round sum, in the general area of cost, can, however, be arrived at, and it should be considered as just that—a round sum, applicable on the day of writing. From calculation of staff costs, nearly $2 billion would be required for the services designated. In addition, assessment would have to be paid for as part of the preventive services and the center facility overhead.

More important than the nearly $3 billion that this might come to is, where would it come *from?* I suggest that the Dutch solution might fit very neatly. If every registrant with a family income over the U.S. median income pays $50, this would come to $500 million. The states should pay 40 percent of the difference, and the federal government the other 60 percent, or $800 million from the states and $1.3 to $1.5 billion from the federal government. None of these sums is excessive in the present situation, costs of medical services being what they are. Accounting and exposition of the plan would be simplified by the fact that half the population would pay nothing, while the other half would pay nothing after registration, i.e., dues only. State/federal formulas for reimbursement of the centers could vary according to negotiated formulas, but each child health center conforming to proposed standards and employing designated staff would have a fixed and recognizable budget, easily reimbursable.

MEDICAL CARE

The cost of the preventive service for pregnant women, infants, and preschoolers isn't the total cost of medical services, by any means, as you can readily see. A very small percent of the children in this age group will be hospitalized during the year and that will have to be paid for; in-hospital maternity care (nearly 100 percent of deliveries at the moment) has to be paid for. Sick children will be treated by physicians outside the hospital, too. In the age group under five, visits to doctors for illness average about one visit per child per year.[22] The total of these costs can amount to as much as the preventive services, but will reduce as the system generates confidence, reducing hospitalization (for maternity care certainly) and demands on physicians for primary care.

In any case, there will be costs for medical care. Those costs should be met by a national insurance program. This sort of program, too, has been talked about for the past 75 years and should be approaching fruition soon. Without such an insurance scheme, there may be great confusion when a doctor charges for treating a sick child and the family supposes that their registration fee covers these costs. Without a full-scale insurance program introduced simultaneously, for mothers and children, at least, if not for the whole population, complications will ensue. Universal entitlement to preventive care will be interpreted as universal entitlement to medical care as well. In considering a program of preventive services for children, medical care insurance must be considered at the same time.[23]

At this point there will be those who will ask, reasonably enough, if a national health insurance scheme is needed to make the preventive service fully effective, why not just concentrate on a national health insurance scheme? Experiences of other countries, as described earlier, suggest that universal entitlement to medical care will not automatically provide preventive services to children. A national program aimed specifically at children, staffed by child specialists with a preventive orientation working in local centers particularly accessible to children, is absolutely necessary for child health care. National health insurance alone cannot be relied upon to guarantee child health care. Theodore Marmor, professor of political science at the University of Chicago, has submitted a proposal for consideration by Congress dealing basically with financing, but offering some unusual and interesting refinements. These refinements would make it possible to introduce prevention and medical care services at the same time.[24]

SCHOOL HEALTH SERVICES

A simple outline should suffice to describe school health functions, staff, and cost. If the child has obtained the necessary preventive services and supervision in the first five years of life, school health services need involve only extensive school health nurse supervision and little, if any, doctor involvement. School health preventive services will involve, in large part, attention to nutritional needs (school breakfasts and lunches), health education, sex education, family life education, and psychological guidance. In addition, schools should be aware of the special environmental responsibilities, such as safety measures, sanitation, and sports. But little of this is the doctor's role. Nurses trained and educated in school health needs, with strong organizational support from the departments of health and education, in-service training programs to maintain morale, and a bit of medical (physician) consultation, can probably manage school health programs. Planners can figure on one specially trained nurse and a part-time secretary for about 2,500 students. One physician consultant may be needed for no fewer than 10,000 students. Screening examinations and referrals most certainly can be carried out by the nurse. Either the school or the putative medical care insurance should pay for treatment and prostheses such as glasses and hearing aids. Nurse-teacher conferences can reveal "risk" cases and establish home visiting priorities. Home visits for follow-up and for child abuse prevention and treatment can be arranged through these conferences.

The school has been a neglected resource in prevention and medical care for children. In part, it may be the reluctance of both departments of education and of health either to accept or allocate the responsibility. Schools represent an immense potential for reaching families for health purposes and should be visualized as a leading public health tool.[25]

Schools can be the center for a child health program, since almost every child attends school and even those below school age can be involved through older siblings or can be brought there by parents. Schools represent a potential resource for all preventive and referral services for children, if not for total care. However, since local school boards are required by many states' laws to do so little, and since custom has separated responsibility for health and education in local communities, where the state again, by tradition, has only an advisory role, not much is done.

Existing legislation (Title I of the Elementary and Secondary Education Act) does provide added funds to school districts for experimenting with school health services, but this resource, too, has not been sufficiently tapped.[26] Aggressive attention to prevention, through specially trained school health nurses, can change the situation radically and make the school health service the linchpin of a preventive service for children.

LEGAL CONSIDERATIONS

European governments are taking children's rights much more seriously than we do, and radical changes in the law regarding the child's relation to the family and to the state are under way. We have accumulated insufficient experience to be altogether definite in making recommendations, but the issue is rising to attention here and ought to be considered. Rodham writes, "legal policy is ambivalent about the limitation of parental control and the assertion of state control over children ... the state generally fails to evaluate a child's independent interests ...[27]

Judge Polier is even more bitter in her denunciation of the court actions that ignore the simple human needs of abused and neglected children and force judges to make social work decisions—decisions on custody, adoption, and whether children should remain in the home. Judges "judge." She feels, however, that they need better administrative and community leadership attitudes and less "justice." She describes the myths in the wide discrepancy between conventional beliefs and the harsh realities for children in need of protective or rehabilitative services. "Of major concern is raw denial of basic and equal services still omnipresent in America's treatment of its children and youth."[28]

If there is to be effective health service, it will have to be backed up by an effective legal service focused on children. The state of the law and the child should receive national review.

In that same connection, it might be well to explore as well the role of the judiciary in fostering or improving child health services. Rulings from the courts on equity have had profound effects on medical institutions. Litigation from consumer groups seems to be driving the judicial branch into a much more important and powerful role in lawmaking, on a footing with the legislative and executive branches, particularly in issues such as welfare, EPSDT, and Medicaid. It is not only the law in regard to the child that might be reexamined, but the laws that bear on matters of health and their implication for children.

ADVOCACY

A whole new range of activities on behalf of children ought to be generated if there is to be effective political action. The American way of politics is to allow for "creative tension." There have to be adversary groups presenting opposing viewpoints, and then compromise that results is the law of the land. Only a child-centered interest group can offset the pressures of professional interest groups like those of the doctors, hospitals, or pharmaceutical manufacturers, the coalition that has hampered national health service organization and financing programs over the years. The comparative strength of the adversaries also enters into the ensuing degree with which the law is carried out, supervised, and enforced. Children need representation. All the helpless in society do—the aged, the handicapped,

the poor, and minorities in general. Society should be made politically aware of the needs, and of the magnitude of discriminatory acts
against all of these. It is desirable and necessary to have a vocal and
powerful children's interest group. Child needs must be kept at a
high level of visibility: every year should be Year of the Child, every
month Child Health Month, every week Children's Week.[29]

It is so generally recognized that the lack of a national group
representing children's interests is a basic deterrent to needed
legislative action, that it hardly needs repeating here. However, I
would undertake to support the thesis with a different style of plan,
beginning at the bottom rather than the top. First of all, local
communities and municipalities should involve themselves in child
care activities by creating official child health review committees as
part of the town council or board of alderman or selectmen. This
committee, chaired by an elected official, should be local ombudsman
for children, receiving complaints and holding hearings on child
abuse and neglect. Representatives from these bodies, along with
representatives from the child health boards responsible for the child
health centers, would be candidates for election to a national child
care council. This national council would review problems and make
suggestions and proposals to the Congress and the executive branch.
This council would nominate, and the secretary of HEW appoint, for a
fixed term, a national ombudsman who would receive complaints and
redress grievances—administrative, pertaining to the bureaucracy;
professional, referring to staff; and political, pertaining to inadequate or misdirected legislation.

The need for advocacy and for a powerful national voice for
children cannot be overemphasized. None of the suggested approaches—generating large scale health services via the schools, for
example—can be accomplished without changing social attitudes
about parental responsibilities for, and control over, their children.
The massive investments needed in social programs dedicated to
children cannot be obtained without great public willingness and
stimulation. A national organization formed as described may do
this. As Arden Miller has said, "Government administers well those
programs for which we have a strong commitment."[30]

Planning agencies can be stimulated to pay attention to child
health in community health planning, a rare occurrence otherwise.
Advocacy groups can agitate for child-care-oriented people to be
placed on local planning boards and employed on planning staffs and
for child health problems to become a planning policies concern of the

newly created health systems agencies. Such action will make a useful contribution and help turn around health priorities and even social policy.

A strong national advocacy program can make children a higher national priority and result in better plans and more funds for child health services. The local base for this national program can make it even more influential. Slater writes, "It is at the level of local politically defined jurisdictions that the arrangements determining access and quality of service encounters are ultimately implemented and where the mix of private and public, and professional and voluntary endeavors must be melded."[31]

FIELD TRIAL OF THE PROGRAM

We have become accustomed to the use of field trials in various areas of the health field: medications, therapeutic procedures, and immunizations. It is time to give thought to the feasibility of field trials for larger health and social medicine experiments. We have not been too kind to this idea, using instead the "pilot" model, and not terribly successfully. In the latter form, without any consensus, an individual or group decides some program or other is a good idea, writes research grant proposals, and tries it. Even if the results of the pilot program are good, there doesn't seem to be comparability enough to try it elsewhere. The report sits on the shelf, and the money spent is all but wasted. A field trial is somewhat different. In this case there is general agreement on the need to find out if a process will work or not, what the hazards and uncalculated ill effects may be. If found to be safe and effective, the procedure under trial will be put to use.

Alice Rivlin, Director of the Congressional Budget Office, has suggested that such field trials be undertaken before important, expensive national legislation is passed.[32] The OEO neighborhood health centers, while they partook somewhat of the nature of "pilot" programs, were much more on the order of field trials.[33] My own feeling is that there is something of the subconscious folk wisdom in this idea. People generally will be reluctant to make sharp social change without having had a good look at what the change might do. In all probability, we have not had a national health insurance (or health service) law because we have never had a state model. What shall we say, then, to a proposal for child health services that contains a number of quite sharply different elements in it? True, these elements are not too far off the American road, but they are different from what is being done now. Can we try a state program as a field trial of the feasibility, desirability, and success of such a proposal?

I think we can. Justice Brandeis is said to have called the states the "cradle of experiment." There are reasons for my confidence in the possibility and also in the eventual success of such an effort. First of all, some states have been undertaking studies and have suggested program developments along similar lines.[34] Then there is a long history of federal involvement with states in just such enterprises through the Department of Agriculture and the State Extension Service. It has been very successful. Another, perhaps less persuasive reason is that physicians will not oppose such a trial as violently as they would an immediate national effort. As a matter of fact, some physicians are arguing for immediate action by their state societies to get state health insurance programs into place in order to forestall any rigidly uniform national program.[35]

Finally, existing legislation and the associated appropriations permit the secretary of HEW, on request from the governor of a state, to provide waivers that would allow the governor to set up a child health program like the one proposed here. Title V and Title XIX funds, along with Community Health Service, and National Center for Health Services Research funds could all be put to this use without any additional legislative action—as an experiment, of course, and for a limited time period.

The question that needs to be answered, however, is whether states are capable of undertaking and carrying through such an innovative and different approach to child health services. The arguments among political scientists, officials in Washington and state capitals, and among the general public all reflect the federal government's previous lack of commitment to state governments. Laws are federal laws and states have been treated as federal agents, but negligently. Here the state would be fully responsible, not as a federal agent, but as a principal. Without delegation of authority, there cannot be acceptance and recognition of responsibility. Accountability for federal programs is adrift somewhere between the agencies of the executive branch, the regional offices, state agencies, and the field people who are carrying out the directives. There needs to be a localization of responsibility and direct accountability. The federal government is too large a bureaucracy, and the 220 million of us too large a crowd to be handled from one office for anything. Even sending out checks centrally from the Social Security Administration, hardly a complex maneuver, ran afoul of a sizeable new program. SSA, whose accuracy had been the pride of the federal government, broke down in the effort to include a few hundred thousand new eligibles from state lists under the supplemental income program and mysteriously lost hundreds of millions of dollars by virtue of a stubborn computer error and perhaps just the perversity of animate things. We need to deal with human and service problems in our society with smaller and more manageable units. Regions are smaller, but without political boundaries and therefore dangerously unaccountable on that score. States are our natural subfederal units. Lufkin, in his staunch defense of the states in his book *Many Sovereign States*, makes good points. "If the states had not existed before the nation, they would inevitably have been invented."[36] Elsewhere, Lufkin makes a valid point that enriches this concept when he writes:

> For most of our history the states, not the federal government, have been the primary agents both for social improvement and for the preservation of local customs and mores which the people have wished to retain. Until Franklin Roosevelt, when the balance of power began shifting dramatically to Washington, individual states operated as major change agents, with the federal government either following along tardily or, through the Supreme Court, declaring such state action unconstitutional. Without experimentation on the part of the states, most of the legislation protecting the economic rights of [the common men] would have been long delayed.[37]

Martha Derthick added, in a similar vein, "The real question is not, 'Why doesn't the federal government achieve a particular object?' but 'How on earth does anything get done at all?' "[38] Maybe the question should be not Can we trust the state? but How soon can we delegate authority to the state? Under the circumstances, a state trial of a child health program on the model notes is possible, feasible, and desirable.

AN INTERIM PROPOSAL

This happy time—when laws will pass and child health centers will be formed and tested in a number of states, when we are secure in the knowledge that this *is* the way of the future—may be a long way off. Even under the best of circumstances, this may take years. In the interval, it will be most useful, and instructive, if the system that remains in operation can be made more efficient, more effective, and of greater service to the children it is intended to look after. To this end, the following recommendations are made, recommendations that can be put into operation *at once*, without waiting for added federal legislation and appropriations, and that assuredly will have a beneficial effect on the status quo.

At the Federal Level

- A much better system of data collection, one simplified and focused on specific outcome measures, should be instituted for uniform reporting by all states and other jurisdictions. (How many children, at what ages, are in need of this specific service? Detail locations. How many of these can be served by your program? How many were served?)

- Improved regional office supervision is needed. This should include closer and more frequent review by the central office of regional child health service data.

These two elements by themselves can do wonders. Wallace Sayre, very wise in the ways of local public administration, characterized federalism in the health field as composed of a "lengthy, loosely articulated but stubbornly omnipresent chain of command ... [a] mix of expediting and obstructing links in the chain. ... If we could discern the expediting links in the chain, then we might be able to strengthen or even increase them. And if we could discern the obstructing links, we might be able to do something about them."[39]

Strengthening the regional offices has been suggested so many times that it is something of a joke. Washington officials cannot maintain their identity or political strength if power is delegated to the field. Yet oversight, orientation, persuasion, and unification of standards cannot be achieved without delegation of authority to the regional offices. It cannot be done from Washington. This will be particularly true if funding of child health centers includes state participation. It may be that regional supervision will become unnecessary after states develop their capability. Until then, more power to the regions.

- Congressional oversight must be more than routine. Careful attention should be paid to the legal requirements regarding fulfillment of state obligations; congressional committee hearings must be supplied with detailed, useful, evaluative information. It might be pointed out that federal officials do not necessarily see as their responsibility the conversion of states to obedience to federal programs. In regard to EPSDT, Howard Newman, former commissioner of the Medical Services Administration, in charge of Medicaid and their EPSDT, said at a National Health Forum meeting in March 1974, "A 1967 Amendment to the Social Security Act, introduced by Senator Abraham Ribicoff, required all states with Medicaid programs to provide early and periodic screening, diagnosis and treatment of physical and mental defects for all Medicaid eligibles under 21. *To maintain the state initiative ...*" (emphasis added)[40]

In the Congress itself, since several congressional committees have jurisdiction in areas that overlap or parallel one another, it is vital that a joint committee on child health meet formally or informally for exchange of policy information. The needs of children deserve a special committee designation by both houses—like the Joint Economic Committee—for consideration of policy, evaluation of programs, and budgetary recommendations. Program details should be available to all members of the constituent committee. Executive agency representatives may be asked to appear and participate in decision making. Something of this sort is already in existence, but it should be formalized and empowered.

At the State Level

- State legislative health committees need to establish strong national liaison among themselves and with congressional committees. More interaction of this kind could stimulate better oversight at the state level, better lawmaking at the state level, and more concern for children at the state level.

- Better data collection at the federal level means better data preparation at the state and local level. Weaknesses in regional supervision have encouraged state agencies to continue confused and confusing accounting procedures.

Fiscal information is particularly difficult to trace since the information is there, though obscured and tucked away in unexpected places. Operating data—who needs what and who gets what—do not really exist. The two different kinds of information have to be made available in clear, consistent form.

Kaufman has expressed only limited faith in information return as a useful tool for improving bureaucratic performance. He writes, "We are impressed with how many assumptions about the functioning of our governmental system rest in the last analysis of untested faith in feedback as crucial component of that system. Just suppose that faith is misplaced."[41]

Nevertheless, there must be better feedback of critical information. It can be hoped that it will be acted upon. We are getting poor results from *no* information. Lack of information plays into the hands of the bureaucrats, who in this way can make decisions—social policy decisions, not just operational judgments—because other layers of government simply do not know what is going on. In a brilliant analysis of another public policy issue, Graham Allison has called this "bureaucratic decision making."[42] The present mechanism of combining block grants, categorical funding, and revenue sharing is a useful masking device whereby the actual responsibility is obscured and the responsible individuals hidden. No one actually knows what tax dollars buy; no one ever knows who actually decides what is bought.

- Pressure needs to be put on state planning agencies to seek out and publicize data on child health needs and child health services under the Planning Act (PL 93-641). This is, in a way, an extension of the point made earlier on the need for wider dissemination of information.

- Health departments' focus on child health services must be sharpened into a major departmental concern. It may be possible, without additional legislation, by gubernatorial order, for example, for a state to order a separate child health service.

CONCLUSION

Be that as it may, reassessment of child health services, at the state and local level, and the federal policies now being pursued, cannot but be helpful. It is obvious that much of what is wrong comes from ignorance and inability to find the right information that might redirect our energies. Child health services are worse than they need to be, even under the existing system of child health services.

But for the future, the whole package should be delivered. We can and must reduce infant mortality, untreated handicapping conditions, and child abuse and neglect. We can do the whole of it with some changes, a bit of reorganization, new types of financing. But we can do it.

On December 9, 1970, on the occasion of the decennial White House Conference on Children, Vice President (then Senator) Walter F. Mondale delivered a moving indictment of our national neglect of children, along with direct and precise recommendations for change and improvement in our national child care services. In that address he pointed out our tragic infant mortality rates, the differential between rich and poor, and the gaps in resources, in insurance coverage, and in programs. Among other things he said:

> I wonder why we do not try to find out and report upon how many children are born with or succumb to severe and crippling illness, injuries to their bodies and brains, diseases that affect their growth and development—and then go on to get thoroughly inadequate treatment for such affliction.
>
> Perhaps if we knew how many children need pediatricians, and surgeons, need physical therapists, need child psychiatrists, need one or another kind of machine, or instrument or mode of therapy—and do not get what they need, then we would be in a position to weigh our priorities, so that when generals and admirals, already in control of enough military hardware to destroy the entire planet, tell us they have needs, they want another kind of plane or ship or gun, we can say to them: Yes, we want to protect this country, and protect it not only from outside enemies but from diseases that every single day unnecessarily kill and maim and stunt and cause pain and suffering to American children.[43]

Mr. Mondale urged that a child advocacy center be created to help achieve the child health services needed, and he concluded his address, fittingly titled "Justice for Children," "let this be the first White House Conference ever to focus on creating a legislative strategy for implementing its findings."[44]

I was moved by that address to attempt to find that legislative strategy. And this is where I have arrived.

the young, young children . . . weeping in the playtime
of the others
in the country of the free

Elizabeth Barrett Browning, "The Cry of Children"

REFERENCES

1. National Research Council, *Toward a National Policy for Children and Families* (Washington, D.C.: National Academy of Sciences, 1976); Children's Defense Fund, *Doctors and Dollars Are Not Enough* (Washington, D.C.: Washington Research Project, 1976); and Trude W. Lash and Heidi Sigal, *State of the Child: New York City* (New York: Foundation for Child Development, 1976).

2. Gilbert Y. Steiner, *The Children's Cause* (Washington, D.C.: Brookings Institution, 1976), 230-231.

3. Rene Dubos, *Mirage of Health* (New York: Anchor, Doubleday, 1959); Thomas McKeown, *Role of Medicine: Dream, Mirage or Nemesis?* (London: Nuffield Provincial Hospitals Trust, 1976); and J.B. McKinlay and S.M. McKinlay, "Questionable Contribution of Medical Measures to the Decline of Mortality in the U.S. in the Twentieth Century," *Milbank Memorial Fund Quarterly/Health and Society* 55 (Summer 1977): 405-428.

4. Margaret Wynn and Arthur Wynn, *The Protection of Maternity and Infancy: the Study of the Services for Pregnant Women and Young Children in Finland* (London: Council for Children's Welfare, 1974).

5. Margaret Wynn and Arthur Wynn, *The Prevention of Preterm Birth* (London: Foundation for Education and Research in Childbearing, 1977).

6. At this point, it may be useful to suggest, tentatively, a modest expenditure to parallel the European example. It need not be very expensive. A $100 bonus for early registration, for example, would cost $375 million, at current birth rates, if *every* pregnant woman registered early, an unlikely eventuality. More than half of this would be recaptured if the allowance were included as income and taxed.

7. Daniel I. Zwick, "Some Accomplishments and Findings of Neighborhood Health Centers", *Milbank Memorial Fund Quarterly* 50 (October 1972): 387-420.

8. Charles L. Schultze, *The Public Use of Private Interest* (Washington, D.C.: Brookings Institution, 1977), p. vii.

9. Ibid., p. 13.

10. Peter L. Berger and Richard J. Neuhaus, *To Empower People* (Washington, D.C.: American Enterprise Institute, 1977), p. 2.

11. Ibid., pp. 3-6.

12. Ibid.

13. Richard N. Cooper, Review of *The Moon and the Ghetto*, by R.R. Nelson, in *American Scientist* 66 (January-February 1978): 82.

14. D. Mopey, "Subcontracting Imperils Public Workers," *In These Times, Feb. 1-7, 1978.*

15. Franz J. Ingelfinger, "The Physician's Contribution to the Health System," (*New England Journal of Medicine* 295 (September 2, 1976)): 565-566.

16. H.M. Schoolman, "The Role of the Physician as a Patient Advocate," (*New England Journal of Medicine* 296 (January 13, 1977)): 103-105.

17. G.N. Marsh, R.B. Wallace, and J. Whewell, "Anglo-American Contrasts in General Practice," British Medical Journal, May 29, 1976 pp. 1,321-1,325.

18. Marsden Wagner, *Sweden's Health Screening Program for Four Year Old Children* (Washington, D.C.: Government Printing Office, 1975), HEW pub. no. (ADM) 76-282.

19. J.B. Morris and M.D. Hird, "Employment of Local General Practitioners in the School Health Service," *Health Bulletin* 35 (May 1977): 119-127.

20. D.W. Simborg, B.H. Starfield and S.D. Horn, "Physicians and Non-physician Health Practitioners: The Characteristics of Their Practices and Relationships," *AJPH* 68 (January 1978) 44-98.

21. H. B. Perry III, "An Analysis of the Professional Performance of Physicians' Assistants," *Journal of Medical Education* 52 (August 1977): 639-647. Also, C. I. Dungy and D. L. Sander, "Evaluation of a Child Health Associate Program," *J Med Educ*, 52 (May 1977): 413-415; L. L. Fine and H. K. Silver, "Comparative Diagnostic Abilities of Child Health Associate and Practicing Pediatricians," *Journal of Pediatrics* 83 (1973): 332-335; and J. W. Runyan, Jr., "The Memphis Chronic Disease Program," *JAMA* 231 (January 20, 1975): 264-267.

22. National Center for Health Statistics, "Ambulatory Medical Care Rendered in Pediatricians' Offices During 1975," *Advancedata*, October 13, 1977.

23. Preventive service costs have been estimated high deliberately. Much more careful economic analysis will be required to fix the costs accurately. According to latest data (R. M. Gibson, M. S. Mueller, and C. R. Fisher, "Age Differences in Health Care Spending, Fiscal Year 1976," *Social Security Bulletin*, August 1977, pp. 3-14.), total health care expenditure per child under 19 is *$167 per year!* My estimate doubles that partly because it includes cost of care of women in pregnancy, of which hospital costs alone would reach nearly $2 billion. If we had out-of-hospital childbirth arrangements...

24. An unusually detailed approximation of what an insurance program for children would look like has been offered by Theodore Marmor, in "Rethinking National Health Insurance," *Public Interest* 46 (Winter 1977): 73-95. My own inclination is to avoid tying child health to the national health insurance kite, even as an entering wedge. My own impression is that it would be easier to introduce a salaried service with child health nurses and pediatric associates working in community centers if child health were independently legislated.

25. See L. Edwards and E. C. Kelley, "Three Level School Health Program—A Shared Responsibility of Education and Public Health," mimeographed (Dupage County, Wheaton, Ill., undated). And also, D. N. Broadbent, L. Carpentier, and M. Webber, "Effectiveness of Differing Nursing Patterns in Ten Elementary Schools," presented at the annual meeting of the American Public Health Association, October 19, 1976. mimeographed. (Monroe County, Rochester, N. Y., undated).

26. S. R. Guarnieri, R. Kohn, and J. Alfred, "Comprehensive School Health Program: ESEA Title I Schools in Baltimore City, Maryland" (Paper presented at the 104th American Public Health Association meeting, Miami Beach, Florida, October, 1976.)

27. H. Rodham, "Children Under the Law," *Harvard Educational Review*, Reprint Series #9, 1974, pp. 487-513.

28. J. W. Polier, "Juvenile Justice and the Rights of Children," *Harvard Educational Review*, Reprint Series #9, 1974, pp. 108-111.

29. A. J. Kahn, S. B. Kamerman, and B. G. McGowan, *Child Advocacy* (Washington, D.C.: Government Printing Office), Department of Health, Education and Welfare pub. no. (OCD) 73-18.

30. C. A. Miller, "Health Care of Children and Youth in America," *American Journal of Public Health* 65 (April 1975): 353-358.

31. R. J. Slater, "Advocacy: Organizational Issues in Child Health and Child Development Practice," *Ross Laboratories Reports*, in press.

32. Alice Rivlin, *Systematic Thinking for Social Action* (Washington, D.C.: Brookings Institution, 1971).

33. Zwick, "Neighborhood Health Centers."

34. W. M. Schmidt and H. Goldmeier, "Pediatric Care Services in Massachusetts," mimeographed (Massachusetts Chapter of the Academy of Pediatrics, 1975).

35. J. H. Lavin, "How Would You Fare Under State Health Insurance?" *Medical Economics*, September 6, 1976, pp. 77-81. ". . .experimentation in one state can serve as a good or bad example to program administrators in another—without saddling a whole network with a trial project that later proves unfeasible."

36. D. W. Lufkin, *Many Sovereign States* (New York: David McKay, 1975), p. 17.

37. Ibid., p. 179.

38. Martha Derthick, *Uncontrollable Spending for Social Service Grants* (Washington, D.C.: Brookings Institution, 1975) p. 106.

39. Wallace Sayre, "Organization and Administration for Health Affairs," *Inquiry* 10 (March 1973): 74-77.

40. National Health Council, *Proceedings of the National Health Forum 1974* (New York: National Health Council, 1974).

41. Herbert Kaufman, *Administrative Feedback* (Washington, D.C.: Brookings Institution, 1973), pp. 79-80.

42. Graham T. Allison, *Essence of Decision* (Boston: Little, Brown, 1971). Also, G. T. Allison and M. Halperin, *Bureaucratic Politics* (Washington, D.C.: Brookings Institution, 1972).

43. Walter F. Mondale, "Justice for Children," *Congressional Record*. Senate, December 9, 1970, pp. 40505-40518.

44. Ibid.

Index

Housing and housing subsidy, 11, 13, 42, 149, 189, 206, 208, 218, 235

I

Immunization, 2, 7, 8, 14-15, 30, 33, 65, 79, 86, 87, 117, 119, 138, 156, 162, 163, 164, 176, 180, 187, 191, 195, 196, 198, 202, 203, 207, 209, 211, 212, 213, 218, 220, 235, 239
Indian Health Service, 20
Indians, 66
Indirect services, 19
Indonesians (in Holland), 156, 170
Infant care, 18-19, 28-29, 186-187, 238-239
Infant mortality, 7, 62-63, 66, 76, 116, 119, 120, 138, 181-182, 184, 186-187, 190, 194, 198, 199, 202, 211-212, 213, 214, 218, 220, 237, 238-239
Inflation, 19, 35, 81, 244-245
Influenza, 66
Institute National d'Assistance Maladie-Invalidité, 199
Institute of Child Therapy, 163
Insurance. See Health insurance
Intensive care units, 191
Interest groups, 90-91, 107-108
See also Private and professional organizations

L

Labor unions, 168-169
Lead poisoning, 8, 62, 66
Legal considerations, 12, 33, 247-248
See also Court and court systems
Local government, 34, 39, 44, 51-55, 112-116, 154-155, 160, 164, 180, 182, 185, 188, 203, 204, 205, 211, 212, 233, 238, 249-250, 251-252, 253
Long-term care, 153, 154, 161

M

Mannerheim League, 182
Maternity allowances and leave, 11, 28, 33, 37, 51, 118, 150, 176, 188-189, 191, 192, 206-208, 234
Maternity and prenatal care, 8, 18-19, 28, 33, 37, 51, 67, 116, 118, 156-158, 161, 180,

182, 183-185, 186, 191-192, 194, 195, 200, 202-203, 207-208, 209, 212, 214, 235, 237-238
Belgium, 200
Denmark, 202-203
Finland, 182, 183-185, 186, 190
France, 191-192, 194, 195
Great Britain, 214
Holland, 154-156
Sweden, 207-208, 209
West Germany, 212
Maternity aids, 156
Malnutrition, 65
See also Nutrition and nutritional programs
Maturation, 63
See also Child, growth
Measels, 65, 87, 195
Medicaid, 17-20, 43, 58, 67, 73, 74, 87, 89, 91-92, 232
See also Social security
Medical education, 44, 54-55, 132, 159-160, 174, 182-183, 246
See also Training
Medical insurance. See Health insurance
Medical research, 6
Medical services. See Curative services
Mental disabilities, 66, 153, 163
See also Psychological factors and services
Middle ear infections, 66
Midwives, 28, 33, 37, 44, 52, 156, 157, 176, 182, 184, 185-186, 198, 202, 203, 235
Migrant workers, 41, 66, 110, 156, 193
Minority groups, 8, 16, 62, 65, 67, 170-171, 236
Mondale, Walter F., 61-62, 256
Mortality rates, 2, 62, 181
See also Infant mortality
Moluccans, 170

N

National Center for Health Services Research, 251
National child health program, 51-55, 229-257
National Children's Bureau, 31
National health insurance, 55, 72, 78-79, 108-109, 212, 213, 245-246

Rent subsidy, 28, 33, 37, 42, 150-151
See also Housing and housing subsidy
Reporting, data, and information collection, 20, 35, 75, 76-77, 87-88, 153, 187, 199, 211-212, 219, 242, 253, 254-255
Representative democracy, 107-110
Revenue Sharing Act, 72
Roosevelt, Theodore, 73
Rubella, 191, 195
Rural Electrification Administration, 53, 241

S

School health services, 14-15, 28-29, 34, 38, 44, 61-64, 87, 121, 151, 155, 163-165, 194, 204-205, 207, 209, 213, 246-248
School lunches, 33, 37, 65
Scotland, 28-31, 110-140, 220
  administrative considerations, 29-31, 113-120, 134-138
  Area Health Authorities, 29, 112
  Area Health Boards, 115-116
  childbirth, 116
  Community Medicine Specialist, 29-30
  cost of health care, 117
  deficiencies in health care services, 29-31, 118-135
  environmental factors, 111-112
  financial considerations, 31, 115, 122-124, 220
  GNP, 220
  Health Planning Council, 29, 114
  historical perspective, 111-112
  local government, 29, 112-116
  National Health Service, 112-115, 120
  poverty, 123
  preventive services, 28-29, 30, 116-117, 128, 131, 133
  social services, 117-118
  unemployment, 125
Scottish Model Health Center, 132
Scottish National Health Service, 112-115
Screening examinations, 38, 88, 120, 194, 196-197, 219, 235, 239, 247
Sex education, 14
Smoking, 2
Social benefits, 33, 37, 42-43, 150-152, 217
  Belgium, 201
  Canada, 213

Denmark, 188
France, 191-193, 197-198
Holland, 33, 150-152
Scotland, 28, 117-118
Sweden, 188, 202-208
Social considerations, 187-189, 207-209
Social responsibilities, 17, 185
Social security (abroad), 38-39, 173, 220
Social Security (U.S.A.), 18-19, 58, 74-75, 78, 89, 91-92, 192, 117-118
  See also Medicaid
Social workers, 13, 42, 160, 171, 208
Socialized medicine, 159, 161
Speech impediments, 69, 70
Society Against Cruelty to Children, 175
Society for Family Guardianship, 175
State government, 58, 75-78, 84-89, 231-232, 247, 251-252, 254-255
  deficiencies in health care, 17, 84-89
  health departments, 80, 86
  planning agencies, 255
  relationship with federal government, 71-73, 254
State Extension Service, 251
Sudden infant death syndrome, 124
Suicides, 7, 63
Sweden, 22, 37, 38, 39, 121, 151, 180, 181, 216, 218, 220, 207-210
  administrative considerations, 180, 207
  financial considerations, 121, 180, 220
  GNP, 220
  local government, 180
  maternal care, 207-208, 209
  outreach programs, 39
  preventive services, 208-209
  social benefits, 188, 202-208
Switzerland, 211-212

T

Targeting, 232
Trade unions, 30, 154, 239
Training programs, 44, 54-55, 74, 155, 182-188

U

Unemployment, 31, 111, 125
United Nations, 123

About the Author

After graduating from Jefferson Medical College, Dr. Silver began his career interning in a small community hospital. For three years, prior to World War II, he had a general practice. During the War, he served as a medical officer with a field hospital in various countries. When he returned from the War, Dr. Silver began working with the Migrant Labor Program as Regional Medical Officer. Dr. Silver then earned a master's degree in Public Health from Johns Hopkins University. He then worked as a local health officer in a rural county in Maryland, later to become a district health officer in Baltimore, during which time he taught at Johns Hopkins University. In 1951, Dr. Silver became the Chief of Social Medicine at Montefiore Hospital in New York, where he built the prepaid group practice, home care program, and Family Health Maintenance Demonstration, which were its component parts. At the same time he taught Administrative Medicine at Columbia University School of Public Health. After that he became Professor of Social Medicine at the newly organized Albert Einstein College of Medicine. In 1965, Dr. Silver moved to Washington, D. C. to become the Deputy Assistant Secretary for Health in the Department of Health, Education and Welfare. In 1968, he left to join the former Secretary of HEW, John Gardner, to head up the health program of Urban Coalition. He stayed there until he took his present job in 1971 as Professor of Public Health and International Health at Yale University School of Medicine. Currently, he is also a consultant to WHO for medical care organization.

Dr. Silver has authored two books on the Family Health Maintenance Demonstration, both called *Family Medical Care*. Appearing ten years apart, the most recent was published in 1974. In 1976 he authored *A Spy in the House of Medicine*, published by Aspen Systems Corporation. He has also published works on medical care problems both here and abroad in professional journals, and in *The Nation*, and as chapters in books.